HANS-GEORG GADAMER
ON EDUCATION, POETRY, AND HISTORY

SUNY Series in Contemporary Continental Philosophy
Dennis J. Schmidt, Editor

Hans-Georg Gadamer on Education, Poetry, and History

Applied Hermeneutics

Edited by
Dieter Misgeld and Graeme Nicholson

Translated by
Lawrence Schmidt and Monica Reuss

State University of New York Press

Published by
State University of New York Press, Albany

© 1992   State University of New York

For information, address State University of New York
Press, State University Plaza, Albany, N.Y. 12246

Production by Bernadine Dawes
Marketing by Fran Keneston

Library of Congress Cataloging-in-Publication Data

Gadamer, Hans-Georg , 1900–.
    [Essays. English. Selections]
    Hans-Georg Gadamer on education, poetry, and history : applied
hermeneutics / edited by Dieter Misgeld and Graeme Nicholson :
translated by Lawrence Schmidt and Monica Reuss.
       p.   cm. — (SUNY series in contemporary continental
philosophy)
    Translated from German
    Includes bibliographical references.
    ISBN 0–7914–0919–8 (alk. paper) : $54.50. — ISBN 0–7914–0920–1
(pbk. : alk. paper) : $17.95
    1. Gadamer, Hans-Georg, 1900–   . 2. Philosophy.
3. Hermeneutics. 4. Philosophy and civilization. 5. Education,
Higher. 6. Philosophers—Germany—Interviews. I. Misgeld, Dieter.
II. Nicholson, Graeme. III. Title. IV. Series.
B3248.G32E5   1992
193—dc20
                                      91–15119
                                        CIP

10 9 8 7 6 5 4 3 2 1

CONTENTS

EDITORS' INTRODUCTION

The essays of Hans-Georg Gadamer that are collected in this book present his thought as an applied hermeneutics. But Gadamer's is not the sort of theory that becomes constituted all by itself in the first place, then to find application in some sphere. Gadamer's hermeneutics incorporates the aspect of application right from the beginning. The essays gathered here are not an application of hermeneutics that came after he wrote the theory down in *Truth and Method*: they highlight the moment of application that accompanied every step of his thinking. So our title is using the word "application" in the sense which Gadamer himself sought to define in *Truth and Method*.

Only an age of engineering would suppose that the application of a science or a theory would take the results of a theory erected in its own domain, and then impose it somewhere, hoping to produce results useful to human life. Such an understanding also shows up in contemporary discourse about social science and practical politics, on the one hand, or psychology and practical education, on the other hand. By this account, the original science or theory is supposed to be erected without any thought for human welfare. But this is a late and derivative concept, whereas Gadamer himself always understood *applicatio* in an earlier sense that was first generated in antiquity, and which then produced a series of further meanings, articulated well prior to the modern experience of engineering.

In the usage of the ancients, notably in rhetoric, *applicatio* was the joining or attaching of oneself to a thing—it might have been the attachment of a lesser being to a ruler, or an attachment to a city or to some principle or to a rule of life. In the rhetoricians, *applicatio* could then take on the movement in the opposite direction: the application of a rule or a principle to oneself and one's mode of life. In the Protestant hermeneutics of the seventeenth century, it was this movement of *applicatio* that was made central to the undertaking of interpreting the Scripture: the understanding or interpretation of the Word was accomplished not only by understanding (*intelligentia*), and not only by exegesis or exposition (*explicatio*), but also by applying the Word to one's own life (*applicatio*). Gadamer himself is the one who set this out in Part Two of *Truth and Method*, while showing the import of this theological idea for *every* experience of interpretation.[1] In the same text he showed the analogy between interpretation and the Aristotelian account of practical wisdom, a virtue whose principle could only be discerned through the effort of trying to live by it. This meaning of *applicatio* is addressed in our collection by way of a discussion of themes and issues from contemporary historical experience. Attention is given to problems of university education and the university as an institution in contemporary society (Part 1), to poetry and its relation to modern culture and society (Part 2), to the humanities, philosophy, and their relation to the changing context of history in the modern world (Part 3). In each and every case the central question is one of *paideia*, of the education needed for contemporary human beings to be in an adequate relation to their times, to be able to "apply" themselves to it, to its promises as well as frustrations. The interviews, which were undertaken by the editors during the summer of 1986 in Heidelberg,[2] all address these themes as well, especially because they have the philosopher's and scholar's relation to his times in Germany between the 1920s and the present as their focus and center. When the interviews are read in conjunction with Gadamer's essays here, it becomes clear how central an adequate relation to the times and events of the twentieth century is for Gadamer. He began his career as a scholar in a small German university town, but in response to the worldwide recognition of his work, he now reaches beyond his original attachment to a global one. His work culminates in inquiring into a world civilization that only now begins to emerge. The application of hermeneutical thought to the times seeks out experiences through which new and more encompassing cultural and social attachments and identities can be formed. It foreshadows the creation of a new *paideia*, or *Bildung*, one which moves from its European origins toward the worldwide communication of cultures.

Thus a further meaning of *applicatio* comes to the fore: Both in the original Latin and in later formations in various European languages, *applicare*, apply, also had the meaning of steering a boat, a meaning akin to that of our English root word "ply" and one sense of the Latin original *plicare*. To direct our ship, we ply its course, we ply the waves and the wind, or, as we also say, the ship will ply the waves and the wind. The application of the ship to its element may bring storm and stress, but the ship will not consent, ultimately, to be driven off course, even though it bends to the waves and the wind. This sense is also a relevant one for Gadamer's applied hermeneutics. It is present not only in the opening of the mind to the realities of the academic institution or of the society and culture in which it lives. More dramatically, it informs hermeneutics when it is applied to modern poetry. Because reading is an application in this sense, it is open to the storm, and can never be certain of the pathway or even of the destination. It would be wrong to think that the hermeneutical intelligence that sets sail upon the waves and the wind of poetry has defined in advance any particular destination. One who is prepared to set sail in this spirit is embarking on an adventure. With this, we have introduced another of the fundamental themes of Gadamer's hermeneutics, for this is the actual sense of the hermeneutical concept of *experience* that is likewise set out in Part Two of *Truth and Method*.[3] Here, Gadamer builds upon the sense of experience, *Erfahrung*, that Hegel[4] expressed in his *Phenomenology* and that Heidegger[5] singled out in his commentaries on Hegel. An *Erfahrung* is the sequence of things that befall you when you undertake to travel, *Fahren*. The journey in the eminent sense is one that is made for the very first time. Although there is a destination, it is at the start nothing but an unreal sketch for guiding the traveler. Although there is a route set up in advance, most of it is utterly unknown ahead of time, and the beings and the experiences that will make their appearance along the route cannot be anticipated. It cannot be known in advance whether experiences to be had enroute may outweigh the journey's end in their eventual importance and impressiveness. Nor can one know in advance whether the journey may change one utterly, in body or in mind. In this particular sense, it is clear that life itself is an adventure. This is the concept of experience that guides not only Hegel's *Phenomenology*, and all the concurrent philosophies of *Bildung*, but also the account of reading and interpretation in Gadamer. It is utterly different from empiricist concepts of experience, and those of most philosophers of science, just as the Humboldtian ideal of education is different from the behaviorism of Pavlov and Skinner. At its core there lies the concept of self-consciousness, basis of the possibility of self-formation (*Bildung*). In the modern variant of the idea that we find in Heidegger and Gadamer, self-consciousness needs an adventure, an experience—it needs *applicatio*. It cannot constitute itself in advance of its application upon another; it constitutes itself only through application. Our modern English-language empiricism and behaviorism, on the other hand, have processed *Erfahrung*, or experience, through a preconstituted atomistic grid. Thereby, of course, they have remained oblivious of the very adventure of travel on which they themselves have been embarked since the scientific revolution of the seventeenth century. The adventure that is the very essence of modern science must be relived, rethought, and its very character as adventure brought to the fore, just as the *Odyssey* relived in words the wanderings of Odysseus.

In these relationships, of hermeneutics and the sciences, of hermeneutics and poetry, of hermeneutics, the humanities, and modern society, it is notable that hermeneutics has donned the robes, actually, of philosophy itself. And just as the university has formed the essential, irreplaceable environment, in the contemporary age, for philosophy itself, so the university is the condition of the possibility for scholarly interpretation and for the hermeneutical reflection upon interpretation. The university that the hermeneutical philosopher studies is of course his own irreplaceable matrix and environment. There is a circularity in this practice. And in an age like ours, caught in the conflict between education in the humanities and scientific forms of planning, every reflection on this conflict is itself caught in the conflict, making a response to the history which produced it. And there is a similar circularity, though at a deeper level, the level of the very existence of language, between the poems, on the one hand, and the scholarly, philosophical interpreter of them, on the other hand. The hermeneutical philosopher, as a philosophical interpreter, thinks and speaks with an impressive endowment of self-consciousness. And yet the experience is one of listening for the poem, for the poet, or for the voices of history and those of many cultures. As such it is open for *more* experience.

I.

Hermeneutics is the opposite of management or of social engineering as a method for the steering of human behavior. Adaptation and adaptability are not the human qualities it favors. Therefore hermeneutics also is a *critique* of the present. Whether Gadamer reflects on the university and contemporary education, on poetry in relation to the mass media, or on the encounter between modern science and the culture-forming force of the humanities, the present age is always in question; for it is too deeply defined by a concern with social engineering. It is shot through with the consequences of the belief that social forecasting, rational planning and scientifically informed administration can make a profound difference, and lead to improvements. For Gadamer such expectations are illusory, frequently troublesome, and often dangerous. They make it impossible for members of contemporary societies, especially in Europe and North America, to appreciate properly the history of which they themselves are a part, to respond fully and openly to the claims of other cultures and to situate themselves in relation to the problems and possibilities of the present.

In every essay published in this collection, the question is raised whether the modern ideal of method which arose with the development of the natural sciences in Europe may be allowed to define and circumscribe one's entire view of the world. Were we to accept this ideal without reservation, we would lose the capacity for understanding that we require to overcome the tightening of our world picture. Modern science and its ideal of method, ultimately rooted in Greek philosophy, have led to the planetary expansion of technology and a confidence in the manageability of everything, from sequences of events in nature to the organization of human relations and of the relation between states and economies. Therefore Gadamer points to experiences and forms of learning and acculturation which do not fit the model of action defined and determined to have a foreseen and foreseeable effect.

First, there is the place of humanistic learning in the universities—institutions which in Germany as much as elsewhere have mushroomed into oversized organizations processing large numbers of students and making the experience of scholarship impossible. Gadamer claims that scholarship can only be experienced if students are confronted with scholarship as a way of life, exemplified in the experienced scholar's commitment. University education is not merely training to become an expert. For someone like Gadamer the classical German university of the Humboldtian type still remains alive, insofar as it at least suggested education as a form of life, a form of cultivation of the person which required a persistently maintained encounter with a subject matter, an encounter which would demand personal growth as much as the development of cognition and understanding, thus linking one with the other. Ours may no longer be the way of "solitude and freedom," of the Humboldtian university,[6] to which philosophy appeared to be integral, as Gadamer shows. But we still need a form of education—*Bildung*—which does not separate learning from its application to oneself (as happens in the case of technical or administrative knowledge and managerial action) but encourages a person's development through knowledge, learning as a form of self-encounter and encounter with what is other and different. This kind of learning still requires a presence, face to face and in dialogue, the teacher exemplifying to the student his or her presence to a subject-matter, as if he or she belonged to it, rather than its being in the teacher's possession.

Gadamer's essays on education, with special attention to university education and the structure of the university institution particularly in Germany, are not proposals for the reform of universities that might bring them into line with the ideas of Hans-Georg Gadamer. Instead they are the application of the hermeneutically attuned mind to the reality of the university. What claims attention, first and foremost, when Gadamer applies his learned and questioning mode of thought to this institution, is the character of the claims that are made in Western societies for the ideal of science. In particular, there is the question of the place of the scientific research ethos in the life of the professions. For mainly it is the practitioners of a certain group of professions that receive university training. Why is it that academies of science are also the schools that train lawyers, doctors, engineers, architects, and so on? Are these professions defined as applied science? Gadamer proposes several answers that go much deeper than that proposal. For one, the emergence of universities shows us the central role of the very ideal of science in generating all civilizations that we call modern and Western. And he also sketches at two or three places a clear-cut conception of the essence of universities, an interpretation of the Humboldtian idea embodied in the foundation of the University of Berlin. It is the mark of a profession that the education of its practitioners incorporate a prolonged and intense exposure to the life of science or scholarship as it is undertaken at the highest, most advanced level of research (today we call it "the cutting edge"). The professional life of the doctor or lawyer would receive the imprint of science at the outset. For this idea, it matters *not at all* whether that science be relevant *in its content* to the professional's later practical duties. The formative mark of science qualifies the professional and the citizen at once—the professional is therefore for the rest of his life a kind of scientist or scholar. This idea embodies a more subtle concept of *applicatio* than does the usual idea of "applied science." And yet Gadamer's essays raise the hard question whether the Humboldtian idea of the university could possibly apply in modern conditions.

We might also ask, however, whether service to an ideal of scholarship, which is the ultimate authority in a university teacher's activities, is still possible under conditions which undermine the independence of the university from society. Gadamer's idea of university education, exemplified in one version in his 1947 response to the Soviet government of East Germany,[7] and most recently in his reflections on university education and research in the present,[8] always points to the opposite from being trained in one's profession or acquiring the pertinent skills. The primary achievement of education is to have learned to apply oneself to the possibility of experiences which awaken our questions. The hermeneutical account of education (*Bildung*) is one of the formation of *persons* through an encounter with the subject-matter. Therefore the scholar must not merely strive to be an outstanding scholar, but also to be an exemplary teacher. He or she has to stimulate the need and desire for *more* education.

This is the idea of research operative here, one inseparable from the belief that research itself is formative, educational, but only as long as we do not treat it as a means for subjecting the materials researched to pre-given interests and needs. And in order to become fully aware of the educational force of the idea of research defended by Gadamer, one merely needs to consult Gadamer's critique of German scholarship during the Nazi period (in Chapter 2), in order to see that he advocates the uncompromising pursuit of truth as the route of *paideia* through scholarship.

One also might usefully compare this essay, as well as the two most recent essays (Part 1, Chapters 4 and 5), with Heidegger's rectoral address of 1933. Gadamer comments on it in the interview introducing Part 1 of the book. Clearly, Gadamer never harbored Heidegger's misplaced expectations. In fact, it seems, Heidegger's rectoral address was something like a negative turning point for him. Therefore the issue for him became that of reflecting on failure, the failure to resist. But for our times, other hopes and dangers are central. Among them are how to keep alive a consciousness of cultural traditions and modes of communication, ways of reading and saying—which neither can be made part of nor replaced by the major organizing forces of modern societies, forces associated with the engineering of perceptions and understanding carried forward by the electronic media or the practices of administrative coordination.

II.

The probing of these dimensions of modern life and of its openness or resistance to education is the theme of the two other sections of our book. Underlying the most subtle and supremely respectful interpretations of poems by Paul Celan or Stefan George, Hölderlin or Benn, there is always the disquieting question whether the poets and poetry might not fall silent, whether they might not voluntarily retreat from a world defined by the loudness of electronically magnified voices. For Gadamer makes it clear that poetry and the poets educate only insofar as they bring a disconcertedness to our lives: a distrust of all too facile reconciliations, an incredulity, (*Glaubensunwilligkeit*), as he puts it in another one of his Celan interpretations.[9] And as we read on, and consider the essays on Europe and the humanities (including the role of Jewish philosophers in it), on planning and expertise, a constellation of attitudes appears constitutive of the meaning of *paideia*, of being educated, which indicates more than an individual's capacity to survive with integrity. It is the very solidity of cultural traditions and of their conviction-forming force, noticeable for example in the universal presence of burial rites in human societies,[10] which for Gadamer outlasts and has outlasted the brutality of twentieth-century history and especially the cold frenzy of bureaucratically organized mass-murder in Germany.

In a constant reactivation of historical consciousness reaching across the entire range of Western-European cultures, Gadamer attempts to educate us about the strengths of European culture, even while its underpinnings in the former European nation-states are disappearing and it is driven on into a more encompassing civilization. We learn to ask whether a philosophy formed in the encounter with literature and poetry, the humanities and classical studies, can help us perceive a new challenge: to grow beyond the limits of history as it has been and slowly to become ready to enter into a set of global relations.

Gadamer's sense of and respect for non-European civilizations is deeply formed by romanticism. It replicates, for example, Herder's appreciation of the varieties of histories and peoples. There is a richness of experience and expression to be found on a world scale which can become our own, as we learn to recognize what is specific to us in comparison to other cultures and civilizations. Europe in its intellectual history has produced a system of differentiations—between art and science, philosophy and religion, religion and art—which Gadamer shows was not found in Asian societies and cultures.[11] But noting this should not have us adopt the "Eurocentric" standpoint that truly developed societies everywhere must accept such a system of differentiations. Gadamer's is not a theory of universal patterns of development.[12] Rather the learning which can take place, is to see the otherness of other societies as something complementary to one's own. One reflects on this otherness because of respect for it and lets oneself be called to account by it.[13] The drama of a worldwide conversation of cultures is situated here. *Paideia, Bildung*, always expresses a concern with what human beings can *become*, over against what they already are.

In the case of poetry and the poets, poets of the German tongue in the instance of our selections, there are the voices of Benn and Celan, for example: They reach us from the depths of hopelessness and destruction caused by Nazism and the Second World War. As such they express a loss of metaphysical and transcendent hope. They call into question much that has guided the West. They find words for experiences largely hidden from public view and, in ways which move and unsettle, call the hardened and hurried citizens of an achievement-oriented world into a slower pacing and rhythm of existence, one that fosters listening. Without listening there can be no becoming. It is for these reasons, for reasons of the need for cultivation—and education—by way of a most intimately speaking (therefore never to be silenced) voice, that poetry and the poets are singled out from among the genres of literature and writing. A poem must be read, as if by at least silently moving one's lips, by *not* simply letting oneself be driven along in the pursuit of mastery, one could gain an understanding of the whole of existence. This is a perspective which usually eludes us.

One of the most beautiful statements about Gadamer's life-long interest and love of poetry occurs in an essay which has modernist poetry as its theme. In "Are the Poets Falling Silent?" (Chapter 7), two poems are cited, one by Paul Celan and one by a less-known poet of the German language, Johannes Bobrowski. For both poets destruction and human destructiveness are a cental theme. It informs their view of the entirety of our being. And the fate of Germany as well as the murderous terror unleashed by Germans in 1933, a terror which then rebounded on Germans themselves with the Second World War, provides a perspective on the whole, as it does for Gadamer himself. This perspective has a latent presence in his work and is frequently addressed in our interviews with him.

Contrary to what is often believed, Gadamer does know of the limits of classical and traditional learning, and his sincere and lasting dedication to the poetry of Paul Celan has to do with this sense of limits. It also has to do with the question, what future, what space there is for the human voice, human speech, under conditions in which this voice may be amplified so to overwhelm and overpower millions and more than millions, as with the radio broadcasts of Hitler's raving speeches, or, as now, with the soft sell of the insistent commercial propaganda that mobilizes all conceivable wantings among human beings toward a "need" for consumption.

Therefore the serious and moving question: Are the poets falling silent? That amounts to asking: Can there be speech, from human to human, across the abysses of terror and the grim and brutal perversion of all that binds us? In his own way, Gadamer endorses what Paul Celan says about Osip Mandelstam, the Russian Jewish poet (who appears to have died as a consequence of Stalin's purges in Siberia): Mandelstam's poems are 'poems of one who notices and is attentive, one who is turned toward what shows itself, who questions it and addresses it. They are *dialogue*. In the space of this dialogue, that which is addressed constitutes itself, becomes present, assembles itself around the I who addresses and names. But the addressed brings its otherness and alienness to this presence. In being named it has become a You. It lets its remoteness speak even in the here and now of the poem, in its immediacy and nearness. It preserves what is most its own, its time.'[14] These are reflections on being, time, and poetry,[15] as are Gadamer's. And it is no coincidence that in another one of his essays addressing the poetry of recent times, and its relation to these times, he interprets the much quoted poem by Paul Celan, *Todtnauberg*, which was written after Celan's visit with Heidegger in the Black Forest.[16]

The poets, we might say, have not fallen silent. They merely have become quieter. Their "messages" are uttered discreetly.[17] This is the side of Hans-Georg Gadamer, the philosopher of language, of human speech, and communication who has learned so much from the quietly insistent words of modernist poets in the symbolist tradition, and who has also, working against the grain of the times, persistently remained absorbed in the classics of the European tradition, while never yielding to the temptation of either treating them as if they had given the final word or wanting to overcome and correct them (and with them the course of European history as Heidegger at times appears to intend).

Gadamer knows of the limits of the philosopher, and sincerely seeks the voices of those who are not. He draws attention to the poet's presence, and therefore the presence of culture *in* the society, even in a society such as German society was after Hitler, saddled—directly or indirectly, willingly or unwillingly—with responsibility for the genocidal policies of the Nazi regime.

There is present, then, in Gadamer's thought, an awareness of the problem of culture in the late twentieth century, and of the unwillingness of modern European societies, and also of North American societies—as our interviews show—to fully respond to those voices which most profoundly call them into question. This is why his essays on poetry and the poets are so important.[18]

III.

Gadamer's essays on poetry matter not merely because they say much that is valuable and highly perceptive regarding particular poets or poems, or regarding poetry as a genre of writing, but also because they provide a contrast to his more tradition-bound reflections on the university and education, or on planning in the new "world-order" of the decades after the Second World War. They also provide a contrast to his belief that the tradition of the *Geisteswissenschaften* representing for him the cultural and intellectual spirit of Europe, can survive the various pressures of modern society, pressures for which he uses terms such as mass society, the anonymity of a society of order (*Ordnungsgesellschaft*), technological mass civilization, etc. It can hardly be doubted that in Gadamer's reflections on our times—the theme of our collection—a vocabulary occurs which reminds one of forms of cultural criticism having their origins in an aristocratic culture of the intellect and in an exclusive order of communication between scholars only at home in the universities (especially the "unpolitical" German university of the past, an origin to which Gadamer openly admits[19]). But it is also apparent, that there is a more radical sensibility at work, a willingness to step beyond the limits of the continuity of tradition and the integrity of an intellectual culture dating back to the Greeks. The selection of essays which we present to the reader thus displays a dimension of this urbane philosopher which is not usually noticed. Gadamer, a citizen of the former Federal

Republic of Germany, who was born in Wilhelminian Germany and also has his intellectual roots in it (as, e.g., with Neo-Kantian philosophy), who then experienced his most formative years during the Weimar Republic, does indeed strongly respond to the loss of social and cultural bearings which we must regard as the legacy of two world wars and a total regrouping of cultures and societies since then. He does not live or work in isolation from the times. The new historical constellations which have become visible since then therefore become the central object of reflection in the last section of this book. It contains two recently published large essays on Europe and the *Geisteswissenschaften*, accompanied by a third considering similar themes.[20]

An extensive interview covers the period between the two wars and its consequences. Much ground is covered in it with occasionally startling frankness. The essays on the limits of planning and expertise display the hermeneutic philosopher's ability to move into the very terrain of applied scientific thinking. These essays, as well as the interview, present us with the cautious open-mindedness characteristic of the hermeneutical philosopher's attitude to modernity. And while all these texts were written prior to the dissolution of Eastern-European and Soviet Communism and the completely unexpected reunification of Germany, they reveal a concern for Europe and its future which might be even more to the point after the occurrence of these epochal and still unfathomable changes.

For these essays, especially the two essays addressing "The European Humanities" (Part 3, Chapter 16) and "The Diversity of Europe" (Part 3, 18) raise the question of the legitimacy of Europe in the face of the slow evolution of new global linkages. The legitimacy of Europe is situated beyond the exercise of economic and political power. Here Gadamer definitely overcomes the legacy of the German 1920s (and before), of Benn and of Jünger, of Spengler and even of his teacher Heidegger, who saw Europe hovering on an abyss and losing its cultural force, as it could no longer muster the political will for the formation of empires and nation- states. Here he draws closer to a perspective recently put forward, albeit on very different grounds, by Jürgen Habermas.[21] Both Habermas and Gadamer situate Europe and its possible world role outside of and beyond the pursuit of power. They side with European intellectual traditions fostering capacities for conversation and having a conviction forming force. The *paideia*, the *Bildung*, envisaged here is one tied to the recognition of difference and the need for, and worthwhileness of, open and nonmanipulative communication. As such the *Geisteswissenschaften*, in the hermeneutic philosopher's idealizing[22] interpretation of their history, are located beyond the amassment of cultural capital required for a global struggle for power.

Thus hermeneutics applies itself to itself: It draws its sustenance from traditions to which hermeneutical reflection itself has given form. A prudent and frequently shrewd observer of the times such as Hans-Georg Gadamer knows, of course, that this is an idealizing projection: The *Geisteswissenschaften* certainly have been—and sometimes still are—part of the struggle for power among nation-states and large economic or political blocs. But they cannot be consistently harnessed to these competitive endeavours. They suggest to the educated members of the middle classes in late twentieth-century societies, that there are voices to be listened to and claims to be accepted which are not backed up by coercive force or pragmatic calculation. Those who can listen to these voices and respond to these claims show themselves to be educated, to have entered on the path of *paideia:* They can relinquish their claims to superiority and free themselves of the need for guarded and reserved self-possession, thus foresaking the preoccupation with control characteristic of managerial thinking and the mentality of social engineering. They can risk to take the step out into the open, to ply the intellectual seas, thus making good on the full meaning of *applicare*. They can find new attachments, as Gadamer suggests to Europeans, in our final interview with him (Part 3, Chapter 12): 'And if we then have to become part of a new world civilization, if this is our task, then we shall need a philosophy which is similar to my hermeneutics, a philosophy which teaches us to see the justification for the other's point of view and which thus makes us doubt our own.'

IV.

The reader may wonder, then, what made the editors undertake to question Hans-Georg Gadamer through the course of long and elaborate interviews. For the interview as a form does not usually allow for the interviewer's views to come into question. But our experience was different. Because of our knowledge and familiarity with Hans-Georg Gadamer's work and because Hans-Georg Gadamer did *not* practice the studied and calculated reserve of a well-known public "figure," the interviews became vigorously pursued conversations, which, however, had as their focus "Hans-Georg Gadamer and his times." As these times came into view and the philosopher with them, the interviewers—representing another generation—found themselves driven toward the future, the future of their own and of coming generations.

A very strong sense of the *openness* of the future and of history emerged for them, as it had for Hans-Georg Gadamer through the events and reflections of a life filled to the limit with unexpected change and events for which there was no model and for which no one could therefore be prepared. These events had to be responded to in their immediacy. It is this sense of immediacy which the interviews convey. In their entire recorded length in German (about fifteen hours) they would constitute a smallish book by themselves. So our procedure has been to condense the material considerably at the very same time as we translated it into English and turned it into a written text. Our English text was made directly from the tape-recorded voices. We have not preserved every question and every answer from the tapes, but on the other hand there is nothing printed here that is not in the tapes.[23]

Thus we have treated the interviews as *texts* which require a form of their own. We have transformed them into texts to be read in *conjunction* with the essays, rather than to be studied as separate documents. The interviews do contain some startling observations and revelations; but primarily they are not news. Thus there is the example (in the interview [Chapter 1] introducing Part 1) of Gadamer describing how shocked he was when Heidegger concluded a letter written to him with 'Mit deutschem Gruss.' This phrase was taken to be equivalent to 'Heil Hitler' at the time. And Gadamer used this example quite deliberately in his conversation with us. But he also makes clear that Heidegger withdrew from Nazism over time, thus making it possible for Gadamer to reestablish contact with him. But no such detail should detract from the primary point of the interviews: To illustrate the relation of Hans-Georg Gadamer the *philosopher* to his and our times. Thus the interviews convey the lively presence of a most influential philosopher who is deeply involved in the events of the times with all their shocking unexpectedness, but never lost in them. His is the response of a receptive, but also most active intelligence. Gadamer's capacity to exist in the midst of things—and his willingness to put his classical scholarship to the test of the times should move us.

Notes

1. *Truth and Method*, Second, Revised Edition. New York, 1990 Crossroad (translation revised by Joel Weinsheimer and Donald G. Marshall), 307–62. Hans-Georg Gadamer, Gesammelte Werke, Band 1. Tübingen, Germany. J. C. B. Mohr (Paul Siebeck).

2. All in all, the editors completed six separate interviews with Hans-Georg Gadamer, over a period of four days. Five interviews were conducted in German, and one in English. Dates and locations for the interviews are given at the end of the interviews included in the collection. We are indeed grateful for Professor Gadamer's generosity on all these occasions.

3. *Truth and Method*, as quoted, 346–62.

4. G. W. F. Hegel, "Introduction." *The Phenomenology of Spirit*, translated by A. V. Miller, Oxford: Oxford University Press, 1978.

5. M. Heidegger. *Hegel's Concept of Experience*. New York: Harper and Row, 1970

6. See Helmuth Schelsky, *Einsamkeit und Freiheit*. Hamburg: Rowohlt Verlag, 1963. See also: Karl Jaspers, *Die Idee der Universität*. Heidelberg, Berlin: Springer Verlag, 1923 and 1946. Revised edition 1961 (with K. Rossmann). Max Scheler, *Bildung und Wissen*, Frankfurt, 1947. Jürgen Habermas, "The Idea of the University: Learning Processes." In J. Habermas: *The New Conservatism*, translated by S. Weber Nicholsen, Cambridge: The MIT Press, 1989, and "Vom sozialen Wandel akademischer Bildung" (1963), in: J. Habermas, *Kleine Politische Schriften* I–IV, Frankfurt: Sukrkamp, 1981, 101–19. All these authors build on the writings on the university and academic study by the classical philosophers of German idealism, such as Fichte, Schleiermacher, Schelling, and, of course, Humboldt.

7. See Hans-Georg Gadamer "On The Primordiality of Science," Chapter 2, Part 1, in this collection. But obviously, these ideas are cast in a more classical form in essays 3 and 4, essays which offer significant insights into Gadamer's relation to the historical emergence of major universities in Germany and the ideological and social factors which contributed to it.

8. See Hans-Georg Gadamer: "The Idea of the University—Yesterday, Today, Tomorrow." Chapter 5 of Part 1 of this collection. This essay is based on a lecture delivered by Gadamer as part of a series organized by the Municipal Theater of the University of Heidelberg, in celebration of the 600th anniversary of the founding of the University. Four other prominent German scholars (including Jürgen Habermas) participated in the lecture series as well. See publication references at the end of this book. Gadamer's lecture on the University of Heidelberg (essay 4 of Part 1 in this collection) was held as the opening lecture for the festivities surrounding the 600th anniversary of the university.

9. See Hans-Georg Gadamer: "Celans Schlussgedicht." In: A. D. Colin (ed.), *Argumentum e Silentio: International Paul Celan Symposium*. Berlin and New York: Walter de Gruyter Verlag, 1987, p.71. The relevant sentence reads in German as follows: 'Zwar ist in allen Gestalten von Kunst immer etwas von Zeugenschaft für eine heile Welt, aber doch auch etwas wie Misstrauen gegen zu leichte Versöhnungen, eine Art Glaubensunwilligkeit. Das scheint mir der eigentliche Hintergrund in Celans poetischem Schaffen....' The poem referred to in this essay is the same poem by Celan as the one interpreted in Part 2, Chapter 10, of this collection: "Under the Shadow of Nihilism."

10. See "The Future of the European Humanities" (Part 3, Chapter 16, p. 207).

11. See Hans-Georg Gadamer, "The Future of the European Humanities" as quoted.

12. Despite the absence of such a theory, Gadamer does not share the antimodernist disposition of some German social philosophers of his time, such as Arnold Gehlen, Hans Freyer, or Helmuth Schelsky. He has usually retained considerable distance from them, as from younger "neo-conservative" philosophers in Germany, such as Hermann Lübbe. Gadamer clearly indicates, however, that he agrees with the diagnosis, given in German social thought since Max Weber and Georg Simmel, that modernization processes imply the dominance of objective and objectifying methods of social organization, and that the movement from a culture rooted in personal/communal relations (*Personalkultur*) to one based on objective exigencies of administration (*Sachkultur*) is typical of processes of rationalization which are fundamental to life in our times. This theme is present in most of our essays. See also the interview "The 1920s, the 1930s, and the Present—National Socialism, German History, and German Culture."

13. See the interview "Writing and the Living Voice" (Part 2) and the interview introducing Part 3 of this collection, especially its final pages and the discussions in Chapters 15 and 17 of Part 3 in this collection.

14. See Paul Celan "Die Dichtung Osip Mandelstams" in R. Dutli (ed.): *Osip Mandelstam. Im Luftgrab. Ein Lesebuch.* Zürich, Switzerland: Amman Verlag, 1988, 69–83. The passage which we have summarized can be found on p. 72.

15. Clearly, there is an affinity to be found in the passage quoted above to the later Heidegger's thinking about philosophy, poetry, and being. Celan mentions that Mandelstam had studied philosophy in Germany, in Heidelberg. But in Celan's view, elements of Latin and Greek thought are present in Mandelstam's poetry, beside the primary presence of Russian and Jewish traditions. One may therefore wonder whether this does not hold for Celan as well, thus making it possible for Gadamer to regard Celan as the poet who marks something like a watershed in German language poetry. Celan represents post-World War Two and post-Holocaust poetry, as Stefan George represents an earlier phase responding to and identifying the decline of liberal Wilhelminian culture in the late nineteenth and early twentieth centuries.

16. See the essay "Under the Shadow of Nihilism" (Chapter 10, Part

2). Further pertinent interpretations of Celan are contained in Gadamer's widely read book *Wer bin Ich und wer bist Du?* Frankfurt: Suhrkamp Verlag, 1986. It is a commentary to the series of poems entitled *Atemkristall.* See also references to Gadamer's interpretations in V. M. Fóti "Paul Celan's Challenges to Heidegger's Poetics" in K. Wright (ed.), *Festivals of Interpretation,* 184–208. Fóti mentions that Celan was "an assiduous reader of Heidegger's writings" (p. 185). Despite his respect for Heidegger which—as Fóti shows—clearly was reciprocated, Celan expected a 'coming word' (see the poem "Todtnauberg," written on the occasion of a visit with Heidegger at his Black Forest hut) of atonement, as Fóti says. This word had not been forthcoming from Heidegger, a matter on which Gadamer comments with great frankness in our interview introducing Part 1 of this collection entitled: "The German University and German Politics: The Case of Heidegger."

17. See Hans-Georg Gadamer: "Are the Poets Falling Silent?." Chapter 7 of Part 2 of this collection.

18. See Dieter Misgeld: "Poetry, Dialogue, and Negotiation: Liberal Culture and Conservative Politics in Hans-Georg Gadamer's Thought," 161–83 in K. Wright (ed.), *Festivals of Interpretation. Essays on Hans-Georg Gadamer's Work.*

19. See the interview introducing Part 1 of this book.

20. See Chapter 16 of Part 3 in this book. It has the relation between the human and natural sciences as its theme.

21. See Jürgen Habermas, *The Philosophical Discourse of Modernity.* Cambridge: The MIT Press, 1987.

22. There is a tendency, on Gadamer's part, to remove the discussion of the *Geisteswissenschaften* from the imperial history of Europe and the formation of nation-states in this history. But one may raise the interesting question—not to be answered in this introduction—whether Gadamer's critique of German historicism and Romanticism to be found in *Truth and Method* may not be extended to a critique of aspirations to power, domination and cultural hegemony in the Europe of the past. For this critique is itself implicit in his recent writings. But it is rarely turned against the *Geisteswissenschaften* and the traditions of European humanism, despite Gadamer's general openness to non-European cultures and civilizations. See the interview: "The 1920s, the 1930s, and the Present: National Socialism, German History, and German Culture." It introduces Part 3 of our collection.

23. The English text of the interviews included in this collection was made available to Professor Gadamer and approved after perusal by our editor, Professor Dennis Schmidt, whose generous and unfailing support for this project we wish to acknowledge.

TRANSLATORS' APPROACH

This translation has been guided by the intention of preserving Gadamer's unique philosophical style which is more cautious and caring than assertive and argumentative. He often allows the subject matter to speak in the passive voice and not the subject in the active voice. In as far as possible we have reflected in English Gadamer's choice of words so that what is said may to some extent echo what is not said. Therefore, we often have translated in the direction of being more literal and somewhat less flowing rather than attempting to rewrite what is said in another, more readable form. We attempted thereby to preserve the possibilities of interpretation. We also chose to preserve the original paragraphs. This should facilitate a careful investigation of Gadamer's thought within these essays.

Some particulars may be noted to exemplify our purpose. *Wissenschaft* has been translated as `science' although the German meaning includes any organized body of knowledge and not just one dependent upon the method of the empirical sciences: in this sense the humanities are also sciences. One should note Gadamer's discussion of the *Geisteswissenschaften*, that is the moral sciences or humanities, in the beginning of the essay, "The Future of the European Humanities" (Chapter 16). Where *Naturwissenschaft* has been used we have translated this as 'natural science.' Toward the end of "Citizens of Two Worlds" (Chapter 17) Gadamer uses the expression *die Wissenschaft vom Menschen* which we have translated literally as 'the science of humans' in order to indicate that Gadamer has not used the word *Geisteswissenschaft* which is usually translated as "the human sciences" or "the humanities." Although somewhat unusual in English we have felt it important to make this distinction in the translation, because the interpretation of this phrase would leave open, as it does in German, whether just a few or actually all forms of study of human beings were intended.

In "The Idea of the University" (Chapter 5) Gadamer discusses the relationship of the university to the society in which it exists and identifies the fundamental problem to be the special sense in which the university must remain separate from, while also involved in, the social-political context. To express this situation he uses the word *Abseits* which may mean standing alongside something, being at the fringes, or being apart from something. It can mean to stand aside allowing another to pass or it may indicate a region far away or remote. So the problem is to preserve the sense in which the academic world is separated from but also, to some degree, dependent upon political and economic concerns. To indicate this sense of separation and freedom we have chosen 'independence' as opposed to 'apartness,' 'externality,' or 'separateness' although, as a consequence, the quality of dependence does not become explicit.

In "Hölderlin and George" (Chapter 9) Gadamer introduces the term *Fügung* to translate Dionysius of Halicarnassus' characterization of Pindar's poetic style. *Fügung* as a noun is currently used to indicate an act of providence or fate, whereas Gadamer is here thinking of the verb *fügen* which means that one thing fits well with, is well attached to, or follows upon another closely, in the sense in which the parts of a well-crafted wooden chair would fit snugly together. Reflexively, as *'sich fügen'* it also has the sense of submitting to, obeying, or accommodating another. So in the context of Pindar's poetic style we have translated it as 'conjoining' in the sense in which the elements of a poem are carefully welded together to form a solid whole. However, an echo of the connotation that the poet is complying to the subject matter of the poem is lost. Gadamer discusses the related term *feinfügig*, and other variations of *fügen* as they are used in Celan's poems, in "Under the Shadow of Nihilism" (Chapter 10) where he indicates these different senses of the word. Here we felt it was appropriate to translate *feinfügig* as 'finely enjoined' to heighten the sense of accommodation.

Although we have retranslated all the poems and passages which Gadamer has quoted, we would like to thank those translators whom we have consulted: For Plato's *Charmides*, W. R. M. Lamb; for Goethe, John Oxenford; and for Hölderlin and Celan, Michael Hamburger, and for George, Olga Marx and Ernst Morwitz. We also owe a great debt to the editors, Dieter Misgeld and Graeme Nicholson, for their careful reading and many suggestions which have improved and refined our translations.

Monika Reuss and Lawrence K. Schmidt

PART 1

The Philosopher in the University

Chapter 1

INTERVIEW:
THE GERMAN UNIVERSITY
AND GERMAN POLITICS.
THE CASE OF HEIDEGGER

This Interview with Hans-Georg Gadamer took place in Heidelberg, July 1st, 1986. Translated by the editors.

QUESTION. As you know, Professor Gadamer, it used to be common for philosophers in earlier times and even in the 1920s and 1930s and the postwar period, to philosophize about the nature of the university. We think of Heidegger's inaugural address, and Jaspers, Schelsky, and others. And yet, although this is a topic on which you might have taken a stand, we don't think you have ever actually addressed it.

GADAMER. Throughout most of my life I avoided speaking about topics lying outside my own field of specialized work. Perhaps I was somewhat too reticent in this way. But in recent years, in fact, in recent weeks, I have given addresses on the topic of the university.

QUESTION. Do you believe that philosophy in our day has been marginalized? That its theories may be no longer so central to the life of the university?

GADAMER. But when was it so central, after all?

QUESTION. Perhaps not in reality, but at least there was the idea of philosophy as central to the university.

GADAMER. Yes, this idea remained strong during the period of German Idealism and in the period of Wilhelm von Humboldt. But with the death of Hegel and the countermovement of empirical science, this idea was abandoned.

QUESTION. Yet certainly in more recent years, people such as Schelsky and—in earlier times—Max Scheler contributed ideas for the reform of universities. Sometimes they were leading in the direction of the professionalization of the university, sometimes leading more in the direction of a traditional theoretical idea of the university. Certainly Habermas has also written on this. Are we right in thinking that you have not directly contributed to this debate? And we are wondering what view you would take of these different models that have been proposed to us for university reform.

3

GADAMER. I fear that if we look at our own contemporary situation we would not find anywhere a person who could really answer that question. I do not know how starting from the Humboldtian idea of the university, one could then develop it into the sort of mass institution that we see before us, of thirty thousand students. I heard a biologist say that trying to reform a university for 3000 students into a university for 30,000 students would be absurd and paradoxical. In biology, he said, I know of no case in which a mosquito has developed into an elephant, or an elephant reduced to the size of a mosquito.

QUESTION. Your illustration expresses, it seems to us, a terrific degree of distance. Distance from the kind of university in which you yourself began to study or even began to teach. Are we right in saying that you see very little continuity between the universities of today and those of the twenties or even those which you experienced when you began to teach or when you came to West Germany in 1948?

GADAMER. Actually, what I meant to express with that image is that we today have tried to hold much too closely to the older idea of the university. The upheavals of the 1960s derived in part from the belief that we could still hold on to the old Humboldtian idea in which it was the research of the faculty that continued to inspire their teaching activity.

QUESTION. Do you mean that you would have wished to separate research from teaching?

GADAMER. No.

QUESTION. What then did you have in mind?

GADAMER. I would have preferred the model followed in England—to found far more universities and thereby to bring about a healthy relationship of the numbers of teachers and students.

QUESTION. Do you also have in mind different kinds of universities?

GADAMER. Yes indeed, but most of all, far more institutions. We have founded more universities in Germany, and yet they are all still enrolling twenty to thirty thousand students. In my faculty in Heidelberg, we have today exactly one more chair in philosophy than existed in 1923. That is preposterous. The relation between the numbers of students and the number of professors remains absolutely unhealthy.

QUESTION. Just a word about the older system that you yourself experienced in your studies. We are not going to ask you to give a general evaluation of the older university—that would be too naive a question—but it would be worthwhile for us to hear what this meant to you in your experience. What would be at the heart of the undertaking of the older German university?

GADAMER. At the heart of it was a tremendous immediacy in contact between professor and student, and this immediacy, this intimacy, is what suffers with growth in enrollments. The teachers who attract students get burdened with enrollments in the hundreds, even in the thousands, and in this circumstance it proves to be no help at all to employ teaching assistants. The students find ways of bypassing those intermediate figures, the teaching assistants, seeking to achieve close, personal, intensive contact with the professors. Then those professors who are obliged also to hold qualifying examinations (the "Staatsexamen") are even more burdened. Professor Volkmann-Schluck in Köln, Professor Walter Schulz in Tübingen had hundreds and, indeed, thousands, in their lecture halls. And although people sought ways of assuring contact between senior faculty and the students, the bureaucratic means they employed led to very questionable results. In Heidelberg my colleagues sought at times to institute compulsory seminars that would be taught by senior faculty. And yet that very compulsory character led to very unsatisfactory results.

QUESTION. You have visited the United States and seen a much more regulated and quantitative system. We would like to know what observations you have made about the management of the curriculum there.

GADAMER. Yes indeed, I have observed bureaucratization much more strongly in the United States. Once I was teaching in Boston College and a student came to me and said, "Oh, Professor Gadamer, I see that you are teaching Plato this semester! What a pity, because I have already done Plato!"

QUESTION. You were saying that when bureaucratic measures are introduced, the students find a way of bypassing them, so it does not solve the problem of education.

GADAMER. Yes, I can certainly recall the personal contact in the classrooms of the university in which I studied, the style of lecture which I associate with phenomenology. Actually, the character of academic teaching was changed fundamentally by Husserl and Heidegger. I saw the contrast, the very evident contrast, by comparing a figure like Nicolai Hartmann who, after all, had also taught in Marburg, with the teaching style of Heidegger. Later on, on one occasion, I met him in Berlin when we were both professors, he in Berlin and I in Leipzig. He greeted me by my first name: "Hans Georg" (most unusual in those days) and he said: "What are your four courses?" And I said: "my four courses? What are you talking about?" And I realized that Hartmann was a person who devoted the full force of his interest to his publications and saw teaching as a secondary form of activity. Now with Heidegger, it was the exact opposite. In fact, we can see today that after *Being and Time* he didn't even write any more books actually. Those were all more or less university lectures or seminars—the Nietzsche lectures and so on. And even with Husserl that was also the case.

QUESTION. Is it true, perhaps, that you are different from them in the intensive activity you devote to seminars rather than lectures?

GADAMER. Well, that was true of them, too. It was remarkable: the personal attention to and awareness of the student which we saw particularly in Heidegger. Anyone who believes that he already possesses the truth is going to become dogmatic, isn't that true? And by contrast with that, Heidegger, during his early years prior to *Being and Time,* the years of the growth of his thought, was truly amazing, even fantastic, in his interaction with students. It was amazing how he took hold of every question that was asked and saw something in it that was positive. I watched him teach and thought to myself, "I want to try to do that," but I rarely succeeded to that degree. Rarely have I ever seen it done like this. An elementary student, a first year student would not be made to think that he knew nothing: his question was transformed by the teacher and at the end the student would say: "So, that is what I meant to say." Yes, that was truly remarkable. Perhaps I have a dialogical gift that may exceed that of Husserl and of Heidegger. You know, of course, that great story about Husserl at his seminar. Do you know the story?

QUESTION. Well, what is the story?

GADAMER. Once I came as a young Ph.D. to Freiburg, came into Husserl's seminar, and you know he always came in accompanied by Heidegger, Oscar Becker, and a whole gang of teaching assistants. When he sat down he posed a question to the seminar, and so I stood up and answered the question. Thereupon, Husserl got hold of my answer and he began to speak, and he spoke for two hours unbroken, and then the class was over. Then he got up and went out with Heidegger, and he turned to Heidegger and said, "Well, that was really a lively discussion we had here today." Yes, perhaps I have a little bit more of a gift for dialogue than Husserl did.

QUESTION. Yes, Professor Gadamer, but it is a well known fact that you have not really conducted small seminars during recent decades. You have been giving lectures in the Great Hall in the University of Heidelberg: 800 students at a time, students drawn from every discipline of the university: scientists, theologians, philologists, medical students, and so on. So it seems that you yourself incorporate in your teaching activity the very ideas of the older German university, shaped, as it was, by idealism. Is there not a contrast between the presence which you yourself have embodied in the university and your claim that the days of idealism and of the hegemony of philosophy are gone?

GADAMER. I must add one thing: It seems that not many philosophers are attending these lectures of mine. Those who are now drawn to analytic philosophy speak of my lectures as being vague.

QUESTION. Yes, we know you have heard that before.

GADAMER. Naturally, that is also the reproach that I see in critical reviews of my written work—that I am so vague in my expression. Yet the people who write that do not realize how flattered I feel. It is not so terribly easy to speak in such a way that many ideas are awakened in a person without his being hammered on the head.

QUESTION. Do you mean that to express one's self clearly and distinctly is not necessarily the right way?

GADAMER. Exactly. It may be a cultivated thing to eat with a knife and fork, but that is not the right approach in philosophy.

QUESTION. But if we may ask again about this collapse of idealism that you have spoken about so insistently since the years of the war. Was there not some sort of idealistic foundation for the rebuilding of the University of Heidelberg in which you took part, and for the rebuilding of the other universities of the Federal Republic? What guided you in taking up tasks related to the reconstruction of the German academic world especially after you came here in 1948?

GADAMER. When I came to West Germany, I had learned a great deal, of course, from my experience in the GDR and, also, of course, a great deal through the years of the Nazis, and I knew that to begin again directly where we had left off in 1933 was an illusion. Some people thought that they could start again in that spirit, but I knew that that was not possible. As a matter of fact, it was abundantly clear to me, even before the Nazi period probably, that it was not possible to expect a German student or teacher to attain the level of learning and scholarship that had been represented by a figure such as Dilthey or Wilamowitz or Harnack. Even to this day I am sometimes introduced to audiences as a great scholar, but that expression really makes me tremble because it is an expression that can no longer be used. There cannot be such a thing any more. Dilthey was a great scholar. But a figure like Dilthey is not possible in our period.

QUESTION. How then would you describe yourself?

GADAMER. It is not for any individual to dictate the terms on which he should be praised, but I suppose I would describe myself, if I had to, as a thinker who does not despise the scholarly life. But to possess the encyclopedic grasp that a Dilthey did, is well beyond my capability or that of anyone in our present generation.

QUESTION. You know, it is funny, today a lot of young people are telling us that they have discovered something amazing. They say that Dilthey knew a whole lot about the science, the natural science of his day. They believe that they are telling us something new.

GADAMER. Of course Dilthey had this encyclopedic grasp of natural science as well as historical or human science, at a level that can never recur again. In this way he was still in a continuing tradition that we see in a figure like Hegel or Schelling. It is well known that Hegel and Schelling, in their *Naturphilosophie*, had of course completely mastered the state of science in their time. No, ours is not the age of the great scholar or the encyclopedic philosopher. This is the age of the specialist—the great specialist.

QUESTION. To return again to the matter of the social responsibility of the university, we believe you have addressed that to some extent in your lecture given here at the celebration of the 600th anniversary of Heidelberg University in 1986.

GADAMER. Yes, there is a section in my speech in which I dwell particularly on the need for the university to preserve its autonomy relative to all the interest groups, the social pressures, and the requirements of publicity that exist in society at large. This, in fact, is the educational mission of the German university, that through even a distant and remote contact with the spirit of genuine research, every student exposed to university instruction would acquire the sense of what real research involves, and, therefore, be, to some degree, immune to the opinions that are so widely disseminated in the mass media.

QUESTION. You mean that a contact with the spirit of front-line research is important in the formation of lawyers and school teachers and all professions?

GADAMER. Exactly that is the point.

QUESTION. Yes, some recent literature in pedagogy is saying that the characteristic of the German school teacher is that he or she inculcates respect for the university in the students in the Gymnasium and in the other schools. Students are so educated as to acquire respect for the work of the university. We remember that you used to say in your introductory seminars, "I am not a school teacher."

GADAMER. That is right. That is what I said, but I said it with a view that those to whom I said it would become school teachers. I certainly did not wish merely to educate future assistant professors. Respect for the university and respect for research is, in my opinion, the formative element not only of the school teacher but of all of the professions, the learned professions. This is the idea of the Humboldtian university, in fact: that every practitioner of the professions would have been exposed to serious academic research and would preserve the research consciousness in the daily exercise of the profession. And there is a point that I should add (which is not always readily believed outside Germany, but is true)—that even in the Nazi period the teachers of the Gymnasium preserved this consciousness of objectivity and research. The Gymnasiums themselves were able to protect their teachers from politicisation. I was able to observe this first hand in the years when I lived in Saxony.

QUESTION. Now, Professor Gadamer, we would like to ask you some things about the year 1933, and in particular, about Heidegger. And I suppose, we might begin by mentioning the Rectoral Address of May 1933. Some recent scholars have begun treating this quite seriously as a philosophical document.

GADAMER. Yes, and it was already read, very seriously, too, by a philosopher like Karl Jaspers. You know that he wrote a fine letter to Heidegger in which he was enthusiastic about the Rectoral Address.

QUESTION. Well, we would certainly like to see that.

GADAMER. I am afraid it is not accessible. Yes, enthusiastic. Jaspers saw the speech as a kind of summa of Heidegger's thought up to that point, expressing the whole content of his philosophy in very immediate form, very living form. He did not, of course, hear the address. He reacted to it when it was published. He sent Heidegger this letter in 1933. In this way, Jaspers was actually reestablishing the broken contact with Heidegger, and, you realise, you must look at this in terms of the actual situation of Jaspers himself at this time. He himself was endangered. One did not know whether university teachers married to Jews would be able to continue under the Nazis. None of us knew how far the anti-Semitism of Hitler went, how seriously to take it, and to what extent it was just a selling point, an instrument towards the seizure of power rather than the real policy of the Nazis. My Jewish friends almost entirely took the view that it was not serious. They could not believe that it was seriously meant. And I, for my part, did not know that it was. We all believed it couldn't be serious. Nobody would be crazy enough to alienate international opinion to that degree. Now, as for Heidegger's speech itself, although Jaspers was excited by it, I reacted rather differently. I was impressed in a certain way by the speech, and yet I read it with an eye to the realities as I saw them, and at that time I had no expectation that anything good could come out of this national uprising. I have to say that I was only completely certain on that point after June 30, 1934,—that was the decisive turning point of the whole story. At that point, Hitler turned against his own people and formed his alliance with the German army. In that moment Hitler had acquired an invincible power. The whole world outside Germany is hypocritical or deceitful when they reproach us for having accepted Hitler. That is nonsense. It is the power of weapons that decides. Look at Russia today. Look at Czechoslovakia. Look at what is going on in Poland. Two plus two are four after all. It is pure hypocrisy when the people outside Germany say to us: "Well, why did you put up with Hitler"? Now what I am saying has a certain logical implication—that the preponderance of guilt over this matter must be assigned to the generals of the German army. At least, a certain part of them who sought to use this movement in order to resurrect the army and German militarism, and who, therefore, made a compromise with Hitler and identified their institution with the Nazis. There were, of course, many in the army and outside the army, in politics, who thought, "Well, this fellow Hitler, we will put up with him for six months or a year, and then, when he is finished, we'll come to power." That was an illusion that Hitler and Goering knew how to use. Hitler and Goering reckoned with that political illusion and thus were able to get rid of a figure like Schleicher on June 30 in 1934.

QUESTION. Now, if we could go back to Heidegger?

GADAMER. Yes, the speech. You know, Heidegger sent me a copy of it with a dedication "Mit deutschem Gruss" [that would be equivalent to saying "Heil Hitler"]. I thought to myself, "He has gone crazy." Earlier he used to write me "With cordial greetings" and now he wrote "Mit deutschem Gruss." From that moment on I gave him up. I was able to acknowledge the value or, at least, the power of that rectoral address. But it was certainly a most painful experience when suddenly a personal relationship should become politicized in such a way that he would write me "Mit deutschem Gruss." Certainly I answered him, but cautiously and rather ambiguously, because I did not want to hurt him. But this was the time that I first experienced that something false came into our relationship. Yes, and, of course, we know a lot about the whole story now. I still continue to fight with people today who have busied themselves on this matter. And now we have, of course, Heidegger's defense document that has been reprinted with the address. Do you know the one I mean? *Das Rektorat: Tatsachen und Gedanken.* Yes, and now all sorts of scholars are attacking this document, and nevertheless, the thing that I must make very plain to them is that you must understand what a brief for the defense is. It is even in our code of law that no accused is obliged to present evidence against himself.

QUESTION. Are you perhaps referring to a matter that has been discussed—that one might have hoped to hear something from Heidegger after the war in 1945? It is often said that he ought to have issued some type of statement and also that Carl Schmitt ought to have said something, or others who were implicated.

GADAMER. On this you are entirely right. This, to my mind, is the point that tells most seriously against Heidegger. Ernst Jünger, for example, had something to say in 1945 and even before. Of course you know that he has an enormous following in France. You know the French really find it quite strange that we Germans do not honour this "great man" more highly. Anyway, Carl Schmitt's case is very different. He was far more deeply involved in the machinery of the Nazi period than either of the other two, even though it was with a tremendous inner distance from the machine. Carl Schmitt was a very clever man, and he certainly knew about a lot that had happened during those years, but he was also much too realistic to think that he could resume a public life after 1945. He himself devoted himself to purely academic work in that period. And yet, of course you know that Schmitt had an enormous influence. Such people as Forsthoff and Kosellek and the first editors of the *Frankfurter Allgemeine Zeitung*, the prominent newspaper, and lots and lots of others were directly inspired by Schmitt; some of them took part in the construction of the Federal Republic of Germany and, in fact, in writing its constitution. Now, Heidegger came to play a certain role in public life after 1945, but certainly standing against the prevailing opinion, as Schmitt also did. And as you very well know, of course, Habermas did not become involved in the whole issue of Heidegger until Heidegger published in 1953 these notorious words from the 1930s about the "inner greatness" of the movement of National Socialism. I, myself, found the intervention of Habermas entirely convincing when he demanded an explanation.

QUESTION. Yes, we remember your praise of Habermas on this point.

GADAMER. Yes, Habermas was speaking for a new generation, a younger generation, that said to Heidegger that you owe an explanation to us of what you were doing.

QUESTION. And why is it you think that Heidegger would not provide any explanation after 1945 of what he had done? This appears to be a difficult and problematic question.

GADAMER. Yes, it has its problematic aspects. But my principal conviction on this point is that Heidegger still remained sufficiently a Nazi after the war that he was convinced that world opinion was totally dominated by Jews, and hence that anything he said would be turned against him. In fact that is what he always said to me and to others when we urged him to publish a statement in order to clarify what his goals had been during the 1930s. He always replied, "You know this would be turned against me." You know, it is a very sad business, and I would add that I have a biographical and psychological explanation for Heidegger's stubborn unwillingness to issue any such statement. The truth is that as a little boy Heidegger was all too much admired and adored at home. He never learned how to lose. A person who, in the first three years of life as a child, never learns how to lose will never learn that his whole life long. That is my opinion on this point.

QUESTION. So that is how we are to understand this stubbornness of Heidegger?

GADAMER. Yes, he did not want to take advice, although the truth is that he welcomed the help that I was able to give him. I introduced him to the Heidelberg Academy, for example, and that was not so simple. But now that everybody is researching Heidegger's activities in 1933, there is a point that has never been properly established, namely how Heidegger actually did become rector, and as it happens I know how that took place.

QUESTION. Well, how then?

GADAMER. It had to do with his friend, the classics scholar Schadewaldt, whom he was steadily protecting in all these intervening years. It is because of that that there were these gaps in Heidegger's account of the matter. It is never quite clear in Heidegger's account of his rectoral period that it was Schadewaldt who went to him and told him: "Now it is time for you to step in. You are the one with the international authority, you are the one who can have the political support of the party and the academic support of every scholar."

QUESTION. Heidegger said nothing about Schadewaldt in his memoirs.

GADAMER. No, that is absolutely conscious, and I happen to know this from Schadewaldt himself, who told it to me. He was a Nazi, yes, he really was a Nazi; although in that rather ludicrous form in which professors were Nazis. It is not that he was an opportunist: but the truth is he talked nothing but nonsense from beginning to end. It is an illustration of a specific form of the political incapacity of the German system of education. Schadewaldt is the perfect example of a very, very gifted academic who, however, was very, very spoiled by his early success. A very, very spoiled young professor who was simply infected with Nazism. And he stuck with it and continued; and during the war he was no better than earlier. And yet I know in fact that Schadewaldt was one of those who worked to bring me to Leipzig. He was not a Nazi in the rigorous sense of those whose goal in every act was to maximize the influence of the party. He was one of those cultivated or fancy Nazis whose nature I could perhaps best summarize in their constantly recurring phrase: "But the Führer does not know that." Have I ever told you the story of somebody showing his friend the map of the world, and saying, "Well, over here you see is Russia, and this blue here, that is the United States, and this red part, well, that is the British Empire." The friend asks: "So where is *Grossdeutschland* actually?" "Well, you see over here, that tiny yellow spot?" Then the other one says, "I wonder if the Führer knows that." This is the constant excuse, the alibi of those who, at the beginning, believed in Hitler and would not admit to what was actually going on: "Oh, but the Führer does not know it."

QUESTION. Yes, probably there were many who stuck with that to the very end. And perhaps especially soldiers at the front?

GADAMER. Yes, exactly, and perhaps they most of all. I saw that myself. My student Walter Schulz came on leave in 1944 and I tried to tell him about the political situation. He came from the Russian front, and yet he interrupted his leave to go back to the front because he did not want to hear anything further from me. He did not want to know about the actual political situation here at home. You know, the First World War had ended with a great mass of soldiers who had refused to return to the front, a kind of flood of deserters. In the Second World War the soldiers reacted in the exact opposite way. It is not because they were in favor of Hitler; rather what you have to try to understand is the horrifying schizophrenia that day by day in the front one has to risk one's life and yet in the full knowledge that there is nothing but a crazy man at home and a system that is fallen into absolute criminality. It is true that in 1944 I did not know about the Holocaust. One really did not know that it had been in its course for about a year and half at that time. But apart from that, this horrifying contradiction for those who were not in favor of the regime and yet were obliged to be at the front. You know, there is another bit of black humor in Germany that we used to hear: "Who is a pessimist? A pessimist is someone who thinks we will lose the war, but keep the party."

QUESTION. When you tell us these things, we see that it must have been terribly difficult for you.

GADAMER. It was for these young people who had to go to the field, to the front, they were the ones who had to bear this burden.

QUESTION. But for you with your wider vision, your great stock of information—and, of course, you had a relationship to the resistance. This must have been terrible for you.

GADAMER. Well, all I can say is that I was a grown man and able to answer for myself.

QUESTION. It must have been painful for you that you could not discuss these matters with younger people, with people like Schulz.

GADAMER. But I did talk quite freely with him. And, in fact, that is exactly why he went away.

QUESTION. That must have been very painful for you.

GADAMER. Not at all. I fully understood his situation. These young men in the armed forces were able to continue day after day on the front because they constituted a small group of comrades thrown together in the trenches in which everyone depended on everyone else. Common dangers glued them together. That is how it is with troops. Schulz was not an officer. I think he may have been a private or a corporal. No, it was not painful for me. But what was clear to me from the moment in which the war broke out, was that something horrifying was going to take place. I gave a talk to a group of my students about it in which I stressed the radical division between those who had to go to war and those who stayed at home. I did not say that this was a division between those who identified with the regime and those who did not—obviously, I could not say that. But the students understood that. And now, as for Heidegger, I must stress that what we must make plain to the world again and again is that at this time, in 1933, almost none of the subsequent events could possibly have been foreseen.

Chapter 2

ON THE PRIMORDIALITY OF SCIENCE: A RECTORAL ADDRESS*

We are all satisfied that this time for renewing the work of our university is one of the most decisive moments in its history. We have gathered to celebrate this hour and are aware that the form of our *alma mater Lipsiensis* is about to experience one of the major changes in its long and venerable history. After twelve years of oppressing and deforming rule by megalomaniacal and anti-intellectual tendencies, against which the University of Leipzig fought a particularly tenacious although often unsuccessful defensive battle, and after a war full of absurdity and crime, which materially and intellectually devastated the university in the most dreadful manner, the University of Leipzig, as well as our whole nation, has become aware that the time to prove its worth has arrived at a point more difficult and more fateful than ever before. It is evident to all of us, that, in the midst of the tremendous changes in our social life which we are experiencing today, the task can no longer be to cling to the old and what has been sanctified through a venerable tradition, with the aim of protecting it from the storm winds of world history. The university can wish this as little as the nation as a whole. What constitutes the dreadful position of our people is exactly that the good and noble tradition of culture and humanity, whose finest blossoms were the universities of our land, has now become questionable itself, apparent in its impotence and uncertain of its right to exist. How would it have otherwise been possible for the chaos of National Socialism to appear in our people? How would it have otherwise been possible for the places of free scientific research and instruction to have been taken over by the ravings of these uncontrolled evil spirits of our people? Have we not ourselves asked—we who were swept away by the horrible whirlpool of events—as well as the friends and admirers of our people in the whole world: how was this perversion of what they loved about the German soul into such chaos at all possible? We cannot conceal from ourselves that this question aims at more than the history of the last decade or decades, that with this question the whole manner of our people as developed in its long history is being put to the test, and that the whole impression of our German history, which we have

*Address delivered at the University of Leipzig, 1947.

15

received, will be violently shaken by this question. How could it not be the case that one also questions the essence of the German university and the image which we cherished of it!

When we recognize this, we know at the same time that we are facing a completely new task: to establish anew the reason for the university's existence. And we know that this is not just an internal academic concern—the solution can arise only when it comes from the fertile depths of our totality as social beings. Therefore we strongly desired to hold this celebration of our new beginning among the people and to allow the participation of all levels of workers, especially those whose hard manual labor serves the whole. I am deeply gratified that in fact the most various segments of our city and nation—from the highest officials to the representatives of the political parties, labor unions and factories—have followed our appeal and have united with us to celebrate this hour. Only someone who participated in the German university celebrations of the Third Reich will be able to assess the depth and extent of our satisfaction and gratitude. Because who turned up at that time as the high representatives of nation and party, what was said there and how we were pushed around, this all was insult and ignominy. It was a continual intensification of the pressure placed upon us. It was a continual reawakening of shame that we tolerated this. Now, however, we are allowed to hope that the true order of things will be established, since the dignity of science will no longer be defended only by us, but will resound in everyone with a new authentic tone of respect and expectation. That especially the workers advance this maxim in their political rejuvenation, is a joy and responsibility for us.

It is a responsibility, because we could only too well understand it when especially the men and women of our people working in the industrial process would withhold their interest and participation in science. Science—different from all other essential occupations—is quiet and secret in its work and incomparably confronted by misunderstanding, since its effects and successes are often invisible and always come to light long after and distanced from the creative activity. The professor in the laboratory, or even at his desk, is not by himself a communicative image of the intellectual working life. In fact, he cannot even want to solicit such an understanding—so strict and almost unapproachable is the law under which he works. All the greater is our appreciation since we, nevertheless, have been allowed to encounter so much attested and active understanding for our activity from all of you. Allow me to return our gratitude by saying that in the future we will accept with particular zeal and care those of you who, because of your talent and inclination, have been chosen to join our ranks—outside the usual manner of preparation through the secondary schools—i.e., the working-class students. Today however, allow me to choose another form in which to express my thanks, namely, by discussing with you in abbreviated form something about the activity of the man of science. Allow me to speak about the primordiality of science.

We are all in agreement that science is the essential foundation for our modern culture. Clearly modern machine technology, and so all of modern industry, is based upon the scientific discoveries and inventions of the last centuries. Never before has the mastery of nature by man been as successful as in our time. And it is an imperative demand for humanity, which it must accept in order to guarantee its bare existence, that this mastery over nature will never in the future be employed for destruction and annihilation nor in the service of particular interests—whether by capital, by the military, or in serving the thirst for power and self-deification of an individual person or entire nations. Rather it must alone be employed for social advancement, for increasing the general standard of human welfare, and for the prospects of peace. That just this mastery over nature could have had such horrible consequences for human nature, may lead to the questioning of the value of science for humanity and make these consequences appear as the fault of science. No one, however, can doubt that the guilt lies not with science and technology when they are used for destruction, but rather with the people who used them for this. The powerful means of the modern mastery over nature are the logical consequences of modern scientific thought. They have their roots in the new beginning which the science of the seventeenth century represents within human development. The philosophical expression of this occurs in the new methodological idea which Descartes developed and metaphysically justified. With this methodological idea, which has its exemplary fulfillment in the application of mathematical means to the understanding of nature, modern science won its law of development, and consequently a path of incessant expansion and specialization which has led to the highly differentiated and specialized state of the investigation of nature today. But the unavoidable reverse side of this splendid development appears to be that the application of this science and so also the purposes and goals of its use have outgrown more and more the men of research. Their work follows an immanent necessity of science and occurs with the complete consciousness of the freedom of research without being able to preserve the original relationship between this tremendous human means of power, which modern science presents, and the highest goals of humanity, the goals of human advancement. The increasing dependency of research on an expensive apparatus and the repercussions of its results on industrial production have created forms of unconscious dependency for science which are opposed to its original essence—up to the extreme of its orientation toward military-scientific and military-economic applications, as were outrageously forced upon German science and so humanity for Hitler's insane war.

What has been observed to be the case for natural science, which determines the image and method of science in modernity, applies to even a greater extent to the sciences of state and society, the humanities. Since Hegel we have known that they—and among them especially philosophy—are children of their time, but nevertheless the consciousness of the freedom of research has inspired their representatives. It is not the opinions and interests of a dominant society which should be cultivated nor justified by science, but rather the truth should be stated and taught no matter how it reveals itself. Nevertheless, in this domain too scientific investigation has been ruled by dependencies upon the *Zeitgeist*. Even the ethos of free scientific investigation itself has finally become tarnished—in the infamous accommodation to the delusions and false teachings of the last twelve years, to which even able researchers have allowed themselves to be misled.

In the light of this experience it is truly time to recall the primordiality of science in order to inform the sons of our people, whose hard work is to create and preserve the external conditions for the existence of science, what science really is and must again become, as well as what they are sustaining and actively supporting: science.

We will most easily discover the primordiality of science if we seek out its origin and that occurs with the Greeks, the creators and forefathers of Western culture. It was the Greeks—in their fateful confrontation with the spirit of the Near East—who first created the form of European science. Just as the defeat of the assault by the great power of Persia in Marathon and Salamis can be said to be the salvation of the Greeks' own independence and at the same time must be called the birth of Europe, in the same way the assimilation and further development of Egyptian and Babylonian mathematics and understanding of nature by the genius of the Greeks can be said to be the birth of European science and therefore today's world culture. The uniqueness of our fate in the history of humanity rests in this foundation of science which the Greeks established for world culture. Other great world powers and cultures have discovered the expression of their essence solely in religious and cultural creations—but only the Greeks turned the primitive impulse to know into the objective form of science and thereby changed the course of humanity.

What is this science? We find it exemplified in Greek mathematics, which is still the mathematics taught in our schools: a systematically derived structure of knowledge concerning figures and numbers developed in a particularly clear process using definitions and theorems, which were obtained from presuppositions, propositions, and proof. We know from modern science what sort of applicative success can be achieved utilizing this Greek creation for the mastery of nature. In its beginning, however, this Greek creation was not related to any application, but arose as an independent realization of human being. What is its essence? We can be most easily taught this by the Greek word for science, *episteme*. It is derived from a Greek verb originally meaning to oversee [*Vorstehen*] a subject matter [*Sache*] or project, to be able to do something. So originally it has a practical meaning. Also the word for science, *episteme*, just like the Latin *scientia*, is at first used only to refer to practical arts, especially the art of war, until it finally entered into the meaning of science with the Attic philosophers, i.e., exactly where Greek mathematics and cognition of the world reached its proud height. Consequently, in the essence of Greek science there is, as this etymology teaches, both the genesis from practical activity and the development to what we call, using another Greek expression, theory. This is very instructive. Theoretical knowledge is originally not opposed to practical activity but its highest intensification and perfection. Just as the true master of a craft, who has eliminated all pranks of chance by means of previous planning and a free control of the subject matter, is one who oversees the whole process of work with true sovereignty, so too the true man of science is the one who in the same way stands above [*darüberstehen*] the pure cognition of reality. An example may elucidate this. For one who understands mathematics it is not surprising that the length of a side of a rectangle, however small a rectangle is chosen, can never be equated to the diagonal of the same rectangle without remainder. It is not surprising to him, i.e., he knows this with complete certainty before any testing. To use our language: he knows that the square root of two is an irrational number. Intellectually he stands above the amazement of the novice, who may continually try again, unsuccessfully, to reckon this number to its end. Since he understands something of mathematics, he therefore stands above the subject matter. This standing above is what constitutes the position of science. But what is one actually standing above? Certainly not, as in the activity of working, above the whims and pranks of the tool and materials. What kind of chance or accident can be eliminated where it concerns only cognition of what is? Well, the accident of cognition is called a mistake. The mistake is what is eliminated and all that can lead to mistakes, therefore, all mere opinion.

Thereby we have encountered the original, human, and fundamental meaning of science. It is that place where opinions do not count but only reasons. What an enormous demand on the weakness of humans, all of whom so very much love their own opinions and being right in discussions. That science began with the Greeks is only too understandable, considering the power that speech and confrontation had over this fiery people. But the prejudice of public opinion rules us as well, and we are bribed by the appearance of truth and the gleam of effectivity. Science, however, occupies a solid position opposing all changing and glittering opinions; it stands above because it considers carefully the subject matter [*Sache selbst*] and its true foundations.

That is the original idea of science. This needs to be remembered, and we need to return to it from the manifold distance of the modern scientific enterprise. It is not as if we wished to deny that our possibilities of cognition are also continually influenced and limited by preconceptions and interests. But in us science changes the power of preconceptions over us into a noisy impotence. In the silence of our investigating work, we are alone with our selves and our doubts. In the silence of this solitude, the real which no human mind has seen before discloses itself to the investigator. This original power of science constitutes our assignment given by the society in which we live. It creates the strength to act according to one's own independent decisions and to master life. That is why universities are dedicated to science; why the unique forms of our life and work, which are so difficult to explain, are based upon it; why we wish to find understanding for science, especially in the ranks of all workers.

Allow me to attempt to illustrate to you what the man of science must be like in whom science is a true power. I will choose to discuss three traits which appear essential to me.

First, he must be able to be absent-minded in a specific manner, which can only happen to one who faces final questions of truth. An anecdote from antiquity tells of the first philosopher of the Greeks, Thales of Miletus. One day while observing the stars he apparently fell into a well—a maid helped him out. Even today there are innumerable anecdotes of absent-minded professors. What is important to understand is that being oblivious and absent-minded is the other side of the coin for the deepest concentration and absorption in the subject matter. These may be weaknesses and we do not wish to glorify them. Where they appear to lead to a real ignorance of the world, they are certainly reprehensible. However, every profession as every person suffers the weight of their virtues. The virtue that one has to recognize here is unconditional involvement in the subject matter, thereby forgetting every consideration due others and even oneself, God, and the world. Had the strength of this objectivity been strong enough in all men of German science, the meek accommodation to the National Socialists' regime would never have become a temptation for them.

Second, the man of science lives through doubting himself in the course of his work and this could grow into despair. It is so difficult to do justice to the inner demands of truth and cognition instead of to one's environment. What he has to say are truths which will first receive general recognition in the future. That is the tragedy of scholarship. Although he is a child of his times and world, he is also always already beyond it in a new and burdensome solitude. But he brings back from there what is the greatest strength of his character: his own judgment and unqualified determination for what has been cognized. Had the strength of this determination been strong enough in all men of German science, the meek accommodation to the National Socialists' regime would never have become a temptation for them.

Third: The man of science must have true humility. The vexation which he experiences in his work forcibly teaches him the boundaries of his ability and the overwhelming size of his task. It belongs to him to broadly acknowledge the judgments of others and to divest himself of all arrogance concerning his own position. Respect for all honestly done work, whatever type it may be, must naturally belong to him. So he possesses an inner freedom from the prejudices of his social extraction and is the natural colleague of all progressive forces in society. Had the strength of this humility been strong enough in all men of German science, the meek accommodation to the National Socialists' regime would never have become a temptation for them.

Honored guests! I have attempted to paint for you with a few brush strokes what science originally is and the way of life belonging to it. What I painted is the picture of a task. It is a responsibility for the teacher as well as the student of science. And it should be so, even if it is not always so. In light of this demand it is no longer necessary to present what contribution the university has to offer for the democratic renewal of our people. We know that in the area of science and scientific education we stand before the same tasks as our people as a whole stand. The only place where there can be a difference of opinion concerns where the strength will come from to accomplish this task. Some of us here believe it would finally come from the disbelief in humanity and the belief in God. Others, however, place their trust in the belief in humanity. This opposition will accompany us into the future of humanity, but it will not endanger the solidarity of all who strive for a peaceful development of our people and a peaceful future for humanity. For we are all united by the awareness of the enormity of our task. It is important to recognize to what extent patriotism among Germans has been ruined and laid waste. He who has recognized this will commit all his living strength to its renewal. May our university serve this task and may German science, supported by the trust of all progressive forces in our nation, lead the way to a humane culture and purify and restore the German name.

Chapter 3

THE UNIVERSITY OF LEIPZIG, 1409–1959: A FORMER RECTOR COMMEMORATES THE 550TH ANNIVERSARY OF ITS FOUNDING*

When one has been active at a German university for an important decade of one's life, it is difficult, during this moment of commemoration to resist the temptation merely to express one's thankful affection for the time one spent there and the community in which one participated.

There is something unusual about these German universities: the remarkably freest, the dangerously freest form of instruction which exists in the world. Dangerous for the common, average students; incomparably promising and beautiful for the most gifted students—and for us, the teachers, the very enviable possibility of being able to unite at the same time the lives of a researcher and a teacher. It is remarkable how much this form of the German university enters into the sentiments of those individual personalities who have participated, and to such an extent, that an extraordinary effort is required in this time of remembrance not to be satisfied with speeches of praise and celebration. However, it is important to heed the very different task of our time.

When I began to recall the history of the University of Leipzig, the first thing that fell into my hands was the jubilee address which Wilhelm Wundt gave for the 500th anniversary of the University of Leipzig. What a transformation from the self-assurance and confidence mirrored in that important address to our situation! What a change from the collective celebration of all German universities—and extending far beyond Germany to all universities of the world—in the anniversary year of 1909, to this anniversary year of 1959, whose celebration does not even unite all German-speaking universities, but gathers us here in remembrance, and our colleagues and fellow students over there in the East! In Wilhelm Wundt's address we hear a strong and manly confidence. We hear the proud conviction that the research and teaching institutes of Leipzig, which had attained high recognition in the whole world, would be able to victoriously solve on their own those new problems which were imposed upon this university by the development of the bourgeois

---

*Address delivered in Heidelberg, 1959.

state and the educational forms it brought at the beginning of the twentieth century. Today, after two world wars and the loss of the political unity of the nation, we see a tension-filled coexistence. On the one side, we see a university engaged in a planned reconstruction according to the principles of Marxism and Leninism. On the other side, we see the continuation of the inherited form of the university influenced by Humboldt. And its demand for a unity of research and teaching in an ever-changing world, piles one problem after another upon us, which demand all of our attention for their solution. Reason enough to recall how quickly the times of self-assured prosperity can change in life and science and how much the life of the universities is interwoven with the great fortunes of nations and humanity. But also reason enough to remind ourselves of what is shared, and to become certain that the universities are supported by the shared essential form of science, which is their task. Between us and our colleagues in the East, between our students and their students, there exists a far more common task than the individual can be aware of, considering the present confrontation of political goals and the structure of social life. Reason enough to undertake this recalling as a historical reflection. For what is historical reflection other than the continual self-correction of the present consciousness? Since it is preoccupied with its plans and interests and because of the pressing nature of the task to find a balance between opposing interests and conflicting world views, this present consciousness cannot know what it alone must know: the future and the truly correct, which would be able to serve it.

What is historical reflection, other than a confrontation with the experience that all planning and thinking by the presently living will be discovered to be biased, where each present becomes past? Such a historical reflection reveals the illusions which the presently living use, at any given time, to pursue their goals. But such a historical reflection also reveals to us the true results of these pursuits, i.e., what has happened and can never be undone. If the philosopher is able to contribute something from his own specific problematic to what must be characterized in this manner as the universal task of self-reflection, then it is the willingness, which follows from the above insight, to stand back from the near and the nearest and to recall what is shared by all of us, since it is our shared past. The shared past belongs incontestably to us as no present and no future can. It guarantees our future will surpass our imprisonment in the present.

We, who are gathered here today commemorating the University of Leipzig, are united in the desire to know what is, even though the East and West dispute the design of the German university just as much as the design of the whole state structure. For what is, are not only the goals which the state leaders, who support the universities as educational institutions for their academic leaders, pursue here and over there. What is, are not only the sentiments and convictions of the individuals, the learners and the teachers. What is, is also and especially the uniting force of science, which all of us in teaching and learning serve, and whose changes throughout the centuries, the nations, and the zones, obeys a developmental law of its own, which is not limited by any conditions which the aims of the state, church or society wish to place upon it. In thinking about these things one must realize the superiority of endurance. Whoever has felt something of what science is or has sought to experience it, that person will have a historically justified assurance of our strong ties to the University of Leipzig, which we are expressing today.

Leipzig to a lesser extent than any other of the old German universities was founded by a prince. It is not without reason that it has no accompanying name—neither one from a ruling prince, as Heidelberg, Marburg, Göttingen, or Berlin universities do, nor one of the names of a famous intellectual. It was founded by scholars and doctors themselves—though certainly needing the permission, recognition, and help of sovereign and church.

In 1409, the influence of the German nation—at that time that was the name given to the corporations whose union represented the *universitas*—was reduced at the University of Prague in relation to the Czech nation. So the German nation unanimously seceded and chose Leipzig as its new city. The festive inauguration of the university took place on December 2, 1409, in the refectory of Leipzig's Thomas Monastery. And although the princes, Margrave Friedrich the Valiant and his brother Wilhelm, were present at this ceremony, the university statutes, which were enacted then, were nevertheless expressly legitimated by the assent of the teachers. So the University of Leipzig was defined right from its foundation by the autonomy of its faculty. And it maintained its autonomy in a singular and outstanding fashion against the growing sovereign power as well as against the modern state and its interests. This defining characteristic of the University of Leipzig was made possible not only by the significant endowment left to it during its first centuries by the actions of its sovereigns. Its uniqueness also derived from its intellectual independence, which has continued into modern times and which was based upon its close connection with the city and bourgeoisie—that is, its situation in the middle of a center of power, which was represented by printing, publishing and theatrical and musical culture, on one side, and on the other, by the existence of higher and the highest judicial courts. The University of Leipzig had its role to play in this center of power. Until recent years, until our own times, this position permitted it to preserve its intellectual freedom even under oppressive circumstances.

The task of recalling the history of the University of Leipzig forces one to limit oneself to just what the story may teach. So I will refer to just one more condition from the time of its founding. This university's constitution was a so-called constitution of "nations," i.e., the university at the time of its founding was not built upon the principle of faculties, as most other universities were and as especially those to soon be founded were, but was built upon the principle of "nations," although the division of teaching institutions was also here based upon faculties. There were four "nations" which were founded at that time: the Meissian, which approximately corresponds to the present-day states of Saxony and Thuringia; the Saxon, which encompassed all of North Germany including Scandinavia; the Bavarian Nation—this actually included everyone who was a scholar from France, Italy, Austria, the Rhineland, Palatinate, and wherever they came from—; and finally the Polish Nation, i.e., the whole of the German-speaking East. These four corporations, these four "nations" were the decisive associations entitled to vote on all decisions of self-government, such as the choice of rector, appointments, distribution of scholarships and everything of that nature. The astounding thing is that this nation-constitution lasted until 1830. This medieval form of constitution was replaced by the common form of constitution only at the time when the predominance of state funding over the income of the "nations" fundamentally changed the structure of the university. And so the university developed into a modern German university under state administration. It is instructive that this most easterly university of the German Middle Ages represented to us for the longest time the universalist principle of the medieval university. And even if its initial formation experienced a major change with the strengthening of the territorial states, still the weight of the developing tradition, which had begun already in the fifteenth century, gave Leipzig its lasting character through good and bad times. The confrontation of this free corporation and the great institutions of church and state—this major theme of the modern history of nations—was also the continual task facing the University of Leipzig. It enacted this confrontation in itself by representing both sides in all their strengths.

Of course, one must be clear that the founding of a university in 1409 meant that the golden age of the scholastic university was over. It was the time of the decline and deterioration of scholastic science itself. Therefore, the history of the University of Leipzig from its first century is a history of its reform—a history in which the struggle between innovation and preservation allowed, whether in agreement or resistance, new powers to be formed producing long lasting effects.

It was the humanistic movement which already in the fifteenth century knocked on the doors of this *universitas scholastica* (this was the name of the University of Leipzig until 1830). It knocked at the gates of the city of Leipzig and its university, and then, at the turn of the century, won increasingly more influence in the university. Well known are names such as Conrad Celtis, the great humanist, or Mosellanus, who was especially then in the time of the Reformation a pioneer of humanism in Leipzig. The opposition of the teaching masters of scholastic persuasion was not less strong and attracted, as is well known, a whole flood of ridicule, which was poured over them by the circle of humanists in Erfurt in the famous *epistulae obscurorum virorum*.

But very soon after this, a new wave broke on the walls of Leipzig, in addition to the wave of humanism. It was the Reformation. In 1539, it led, after some hesitation, to the introduction of the Reformation into the city and the University of Leipzig. Under the rectorate of the mathematician Casper Borner—the older Leipzigers remember that modest-sleek and earnest building from the middle of the nineteenth century in the university square of Leipzig which is named the *Bornerianum*—new construction was initiated which, at that time, was supported by the donation in 1543 of the Pauline monastery, where the center of the University of Leipzig is still located, and by the donation of other very valuable property.

This restructuring of the University of Leipzig was determined by the influence of Melanchthon and Luther. In 1545 Luther held a celebratory sermon in the Pauline church.

At that time Leipzig was able to attract one of the most famous philologists, a man whose name is still known today to students of classical philology because his conjectures concerning the classical authors must still be seriously considered: Joachim Camerarius, "a shining light for all Germany, the most stable column of our school" as was said in a funeral oration. At the end of the war as we began again after the burning of the University of Leipzig and when I became rector of Leipzig, I hung his picture in the rector's office. Ever since, the strict, critical spirit of this man has touched every visitor of Leipzig's rector with his penetrating gaze.

This person was much more than just an important teacher at the University of Leipzig. He is no less important for the whole design of German education than, for example, Wilhelm von Humboldt was in later centuries. Joachim Camerarius was the student of Melanchthon. And it is due to his influence and his activity that the Saxon educational system acquired that foundation upon which the entire system of higher education in Germany, the so-called scholars' schools [*Gelehrtenschulen*], were established in the following centuries. Beginning at that time and through the successful efforts of Joachim Camerarius, not only was an exceptional school tradition created in Saxony, which we still admire today when we think of the Thomas or Nicolas Schools in Leipzig, or the Kreuz High School in Dresden, or the great schools of Schulpforta, Grimma, and Meissen. But also at that time, the profile of the German university was determined, fundamentally and for the future, by the initiation of this splendid educational tradition, to the extent that in the future the university was able to accept into its walls only a youth already prepared for science. The major factor which the alliance of the Reformation with the Humanist movement created is that since then the German university builds upon a school system which has already provided the general foundation for science, so that university instruction could dedicate itself exclusively to science proper and therefore was able to provide room for modern research especially in the last centuries.

But also a second period of the University of Leipzig, to which I will now turn, has exerted a continuing effect until today. It is clear that the development of the Humanist-Protestant university in the sixteenth century suffered due to the great event of the religious wars, the Thirty Years War. It is just as clear that the most decisive research developments and the intellectual profile of the times, approaching the seventeenth century, were not in the least influenced by the universities. The new natural sciences developed outside the European universities. Here we see—and in Leipzig perhaps more clearly than elsewhere—the other side of a great and proud awareness of tradition: the suppression of exceptional natures, who go beyond what is represented in the well-established average. Therefore, in the long list of famous Leipzigers, which we always proudly recite when celebrating the history of the University of Leipzig, we have to also name those who just received their first education here but did not continue here. The philosopher Leibniz belongs especially to this list, since he is Leipzig's greatest son, who completed his first studies in his home city and then left Leipzig already in 1666, because his precocious genius did not find its home here. Many other audacious innovators also belong to this list.

Of the many one could name I have chosen Christian Thomasius, since he already presaged in a certain manner the face of the University of Leipzig for the seventeenth and eighteenth centuries. In 1687 Christian Thomasius, who went to Halle soon after his first years as a professor at Leipzig, posted on the notice-board for the first time as a German professor the announcement of his lecture to be held in the German language, thereby challenging the irate opposition of the Leipzig university dignitaries. This was no mere superficiality. For the subject matter of the announcement was Gracian's fundamental rules: to live reasonably, intelligently, and courteously. Gracian's importance for the history of Western education can hardly be overestimated. He achieved an unexpected and far-reaching influence in Germany during the early Enlightenment in Leipzig. In the absolutist Spain of his time, Gracian was the first to formulate and to project into the future, a new ideal for education, the "hombre en su punto," the man who masters every situation in a proper manner, because he had the right sense of proportion, the correct tact, and the correct gusto—an ideal, which helped form a new society, a society which was no longer characterized by noble birth and the landed, privileged courtier, but by the powers of education.

What occurred then was like a prelude to the great history of the eighteenth century, which is well known to us. It was a prelude to the ascendency of the University of Leipzig during the eighteenth century to the head of German bourgeois culture. This was not so much due to the important scholars who worked there, as it was due to the great cultural image which was presented by the whole city, including its university. The conversion of the Saxon royalty to Catholicism in 1697 was also important for this development. The confessional difference required the king to be especially cautious in all cultural-political questions. This strengthened the civil autonomy of the university, but also its tendency towards inbreeding.

The first and most representative figure of the University of Leipzig in the eighteenth century was Gottsched, whose efforts in promoting a culture based on the German language are universally known. He exerted considerable influence on the University of Leipzig, to which he belonged for many decades and for several as its rector. Of course, he lives in our memory more through the portrait which Goethe drew in *Dichtung und Wahrheit* from a time when new powers overtook the old dignitaries. Gottsched's dignity (even when he had lost his wig), which Goethe portrayed, is an unforgettable image for us. Before Gottsched, Christian Wolff had taught there for a short time. In addition to him, there were many important people who established the atmosphere of the city and university. Among them, the most famous was Gellert, who was not a great person and yet whose lectures were the most important intellectual events in the city during the time Goethe studied in Leipzig. Hundreds of young people sat at his feet, attracted by the fine reasonableness and moral sincerity of this modest man. And he remained modest even when he rode through the streets on the white stallion presented to him by his king.

This image of one of its most celebrated and beloved teachers agreed with the image which the learners, the students, offered of the University of Leipzig. At this point we should recall Goethe's famous description in *Dichtung und Wahrheit* depicting his life in Leipzig:

"Everyone, who perceives here the decided influence which educated men and women, scholars and other persons who enjoy fine society exercise upon a young student, would be immediately convinced, even if it were not explicitly stated, that we found ourselves in Leipzig. Each of the German universities has a particular character: since no general educational system can pervade our country, each place holds to its own type and style and exaggerates its characteristic particularities to the utmost.

This is also true of the universities. In Jena and Halle coarseness achieved the zenith; physical strength, fencing agility, the wildest self-defense were the order of the day there. And such a situation can only be maintained and continued by means of the most vulgar riotous life. The relationship between the students and the inhabitants of those cities, as different as they might be, was nevertheless similar in this: the wild stranger had no respect for the citizen and saw himself as a privileged being permitted all freedoms and insolences. In Leipzig, on the contrary, a student could hardly be other than gallant as soon as he wished to have any relation with the rich, well-mannered and ethically correct citizens."

Referring to the fagging system which still continued into the late eighteenth century, Goethe is here contrasting the cultivation of the Leipzig students. We understand that this flattering picture does not depict all elements and circles of the Leipzig student body at that time, but rather, and especially, its social elite. And yet we know that a university is a whole, which, although it is formed and governed by all of its forces in general, is in the most part determined by its best forces and the standard of its elite.

In order to say just a few words concerning the research achievements of the eighteenth century which related to this humanizing achievement, I wish to limit myself to two names, because they, as well, have also had a long-lasting influence. One is Ernesti, who was for a long time the principal of one of the larger public schools in Leipzig and who became a professor of theology and professor of philology. He was an important researcher who contributed decisively to the development of historical Bible criticism. As a result of the historical Bible criticism, Leipzig acquired the character of an important philological research institution, which especially promoted with loving care Oriental studies and in general non-Indo-Germanic philology. The other name is Christ, a philologist and archaeologist, who had a determining influence on Klopstock, Goethe, and particularly Lessing.

The great students of these great scholars were the ones who were entered into the book of history. I have already mentioned the names. Especially Lessing, who was the first true writer in German, attained his worldwide renown outside the life of the university while also mastering the academic science. And it was especially Goethe, this universal man, whose work and influence so greatly exceeded the realm of academia. It is characteristic for the situation of Leipzig in the seventeenth and eighteenth centuries, that the honor roll, which named the most famous sons of the university for the jubilee of 1809, included as well a number of names which we recognize not as professors but only as students of this university. This monument was dedicated to (—always in the dative case—): *Leibnizio, Thomasio, Fabrizio, Christiano Wolffio, Mascouvio, Geller-*

to, *Rabenero*, *Cornelio*—the lawyer—, *Ernestio*, *Lessingio*, *Reizio*—the philologists will remember the *Reizianum*—, *Cornizio*, *Garvio*—Kant's renowned colleague and correspondent—*Gutschmidio*, *Hedwigio*, *Fischero*, *Kestnero saeculo octodecimo decoribus huius academiae quondam alumnis*.

The third phase of the history of the University of Leipzig, which I will characterize with a few words, is closer to us in so far as its direct effects reach up to our time. This is the university of the nineteenth century. During this time, Leipzig's development, as those of all German universities, was determined by the model of Berlin, which was founded by Wilhelm von Humboldt. The new ideal of education was education through scientific research and the University of Leipzig now sought to emulate this. The ethos of the researcher, the model he set in life and teaching, was to educate the students to a life in ideas, which could form the ruling elite of the nation without being influenced by the one-sided purposes of the state. It is no longer possible to characterize the research and researcher of the nineteenth century in the same sense as in earlier centuries where the unitary form of Western science could be encompassed by an individual person, as, for example, by Leibniz in the early eighteenth century. In the nineteenth century the specialization of research had forcefully begun.

If I might venture a general statement from the position of my own sciences, philosophy, and philology, then it would be: what is most characteristic of Leipzig in these sciences is, also, the perseverance of an intellectual physiognomy. Leipzig never actually became a city of philosophy, although within philosophy it acquired a very characteristic direction, to the extent that German Idealism and German Romanticism passed over Leipzig almost without leaving a trace. In the nineteenth century the school of Herbart dominated Leipzig and prepared for the development which led from Fechner to Wilhelm Wundt and Felix Krueger, i.e., to the great tradition of Leipzig psychology. When one traveled in foreign countries as a Leipzig professor of philosophy, one was introduced not as the successor and colleague of some professor of philosophy but as the successor of Wilhelm Wundt, even if one hardly deserved this honor.

Similarly one can say, for example, of classical philology that it adhered, in an unbroken continuity, to the tradition of humanism. In the beginning of the nineteenth century, Gottfried Herrmann was the leading intellect in this area. He was the person who crossed swords with Friedrich Creuzer in Heidelberg—the rationalist with the romantic—and who, opposing all the great academic leaders of the time, Wolf and Boeckh, and all the others, asserted with unrelenting pride that *he* knew Latin. His students were then the ones who established the great history of Leipzig's classical philology: Moritz Haupt, Otto Jahn, and especially

Ritschl, who transferred from Bonn to Leipzig in the middle of the century, and who for another two decades most fruitfully advanced the school. His name is known in many circles because Friedrich Nietzsche was counted as one of his students and Ritschl created for him the unbelievably fast ascendency to a professorship in classical philology at the University of Basel, even before the completion of his doctorate. I do not mention Nietzsche's relationship to philology at Leipzig because the magnificence of this philological school was especially apparent in him. Rather, to the contrary, because the crackling in the beams of the belief in science, which supported the great research of the nineteenth century, was first expressed by Nietzsche. And because this crackling indicated the much discussed and doubtful form of science which the humanities would adopt in the twentieth century. Friedrich Nietzsche's skepticism while he belonged within Leipzig philology may be demonstrated by an excerpt from a letter to Erwin Rohde from 1868:

"That we received all enlightening thoughts in the history of literature from those few great geniuses, whom the educated speak about, and that all the good and advancing achievements in this area were nothing other than practical applications of those typical ideas, and that consequently the creative in literary research came from such persons, who themselves never or hardly ever carried on such studies, and that, on the contrary, the celebrated works in this area were written by such persons who did not have the creative spark—these strong pessimistic views, in which a new cult of genius lies hidden, occupy me continuously and entice me, for once, to test history for this."

It is not sensible in general to individually name here the renowned researchers of the nineteenth century, who are still counted today by those knowledgeable in the particular disciplines as masters: the great doctors, the great jurists, the great natural scientists. Rather we will have to concern ourselves with the question of what lesson we should learn from this last and most splendid phase in the history of the University of Leipzig. What were the forces which enabled the university to ascend to a world university at the time when the University of Leipzig was placed under exclusive state care and administration?

Leipzig's unique advantage, then, was that it had a scholarly royal house which was genuinely attached to its university. The Saxon kings cultivated personal relations with all Leipzig professors and occasionally attended their lectures. And the royal house and its government successfully supported the basic principle: that in the appointment of professors to the University of Leipzig, native Saxons were not to be favored but rather the best researchers were to be obtained. This freed Leipzig from academic and political inbreeding, which had limited it in the eighteenth century.

The second condition for the rapid ascendancy, which Leipzig was to have and whose effects can still be noticed today, was the enormous love of science of the Saxon people. Only this enabled the generous funding by the ruling house and its government, which the University of Leipzig experienced at that time. For it was just the provincial diet who created the material basis for Leipzig's development into a world university, just as it was the intelligence of the Saxon people who guaranteed its intellectual basis. The facts speak for themselves. This generous legislature and sympathetic government permitted the University of Leipzig to participate to a far greater extent than all other universities in the large economic growth in the last decades of the century. If one compares Leipzig's budget at the end of the nineteenth century, when the university had approximately 3,000 students, with those of other universities, then Berlin, of course, was at the top with a yearly budget of about 2.4 million marks and a personnel budget of 890,000 marks. However, the University of Leipzig was already second with almost 2 million marks and only about 10,000 marks less for the personnel budget. When one compares this to the University of Tübingen, for example, which was nevertheless the most cultivated state university in southern Germany, one sees it had a budget of not nearly one million and a personnel budget of not even one quarter million. Modesty forces me to be silent concerning the University of Heidelberg.

The lesson which we may draw from this aspect of things is not obsolete: only by means of the participation of the whole public may a university develop its true powers. When Wilhelm Wundt, in the proud self-assurance of being sustained by the forces of the time, held his famous address, to which I have already alluded, he also referred to Leibniz's old prophecy that the academies would at some time become the true research centers and the universities merely centers for teaching. Wundt dismissed this with ironic self-confidence by pointing to the grand institutions of research and teaching which the University of Leipzig had united and to the modest three rooms that the Saxon Academy of Science had within this whole.

Ladies and Gentlemen! It is not just as a curiosity that I refer to this. It was rather the experience which I had as Leipzig's rector when the Russian occupying forces took over our administration. The Russian occupying forces and the German forces, united with them, brought us the idea of a university from the eighteenth century, where the teaching and educational interests of the state were to be served, and not primarily free research. It was characteristic, when the representatives of the Russian occupying forces commanded me to see to it that history would be more strongly represented in the curriculum of the university and that not so much would be said about Oriental studies (in the cultivation of which the utilitarian political thinking of my partners spied a secret imperialism). I was to convince some professors of oriental studies to lecture in history.

In the eighteenth century such a request would not have been so peculiar—just as today it would not be unusual in the secondary schools where one is merely concerned with the communication of scientific results, for this communication requires only the teacher and not the researcher. But for us, who knew ourselves to be supported by the superb development of the thoroughly specialized research and teaching of the nineteenth and twentieth centuries, this request opened a chasm. We too were an institution supported by the state, nevertheless the services provided by the institution to the state were only a result of the fact that it was a free research institution. The Russian politics of science, on the contrary, give this function not to the universities but to the academies, in the sense of Leibniz.

This policy is reflected in the reconstruction of Leipzig which is presently occurring. The forces of research and teaching, which are still active within the University of Leipzig, have to resist the idea that the university is to serve the construction of a new state. For this would lead to academic education being completely controlled by the purposes of the state, as interpreted by each current state leadership.

In those decisive years of reconstruction, during which we defended the traditional form of our university and naturally were the ones defeated, the portraits hanging in the office of the rector of the University of Leipzig were enormously fortifying for us, not only the painting of Joachim Camerarius, but especially the unbelievably vivid portraits, which Anton Graff had painted of Gellert, Ernesti, and Garve, as well as the portraits of Hornung, Beck, and other great men of the University of Leipzig. The weight of the historical tradition that stood behind us gave us our dignity. It is a legacy that we may also build upon for the future of the University of Leipzig.

Now the decisive question is clearly raised: to what extent will we ourselves be in the position to fulfill our own task—the task of creating from the present German universities something which may again realize the idea of the unity of research and teaching. Students and teachers at this university, as at all other German universities, are well aware of the desperate difficulty of this task. We see how differently the universities in other countries have been structured. We know that we have been delegated a special type of educational task, which only can be effectively realized by participation in research. The work of the university in educating the academic youth is, in any case, only a contribution to the process which will be determined by various other forces: by the home and the school, which form the youth during the actually pliable ages, by the living community, which surrounds the students in cooperative groups, in the dorms and not least in their dealings with their landladies. The contribution which the university as the community of scientific research and teaching can make to this educational process can only be that something of the educational enthusiasm of research crosses over to the youth. However, this can occur, as we must acknowledge, only in small and the smallest circles. The old idea of the German university can be realized today only in the community of research that we find in an institute or in small circles of students gathered around a teacher. Let us, therefore, seek together the means—and appeal to the whole of society for this—which will permit the educational powers of research to shine on the whole academic youth in the midst of the modern mass university. These means are not only financial; the sufficient guarantee of such means would rather be the result of public consciousness truly identifying with its universities. And so not only would the academic profession of teaching preserve its old power of attraction, but this would especially awaken and nurture in youth the awareness that the old forms and paths of scientific education would be greeted by the recognition and pride of all. Everything will depend on whether one can again successfully transmit in a reasonable approximation and in contemporary style that old unity of research and teaching. If we are successful in this, than one day, what I stated at the beginning will also be true for the University of Leipzig: that we can never know what we are, because the powers, from which we live, reach into a future which we cannot foresee.

Chapter 4

THE UNIVERSITY OF HEIDELBERG
AND THE BIRTH OF MODERN SCIENCE*

The spectacular success of the Bibliotheca Palatina exhibition this year, in connection with the six hundredth anniversary of Heidelberg University, informs us of what the historical depth of one's own past can mean to people today. No individual can wish to compete with the comprehensiveness of this documentation, although it can only attest to the older history of our university. Our Ruperto-Carola has, however, a special justification of its double name 'Ruperto-Carola.' It alludes to something like a second founding, to the initiation of the university's reconstruction in the beginning of the nineteenth century. At that time, after a period of decay, a new epoch opened which would raise Heidelberg to world renown. This epoch will be our subject in so far as time limitations permit.

That modern Heidelberg and modern science, one of whose centers is here, belong to the great movement of the Enlightenment does not require explication. We recognize in the reconstruction of Heidelberg University, as the first university of the newly formed state of Baden (beginning in 1803), the fundamental victory of the Enlightenment's central demand to guarantee intellectual freedom in opposition to throne and altar. Admittedly it still took a long time until censorship and politically motivated interference stopped having a massive influence on the intellectual task of science.

The reconstruction of Heidelberg University occurred at the same time as Heidelberg blossomed as one of the cult centers of Romanticism. Enlightenment and Romanticism—one asks oneself how these forces could cooperate. Clearly the negative, pejorative tone in the expression "Romanticism" is a result of the later development of the pragmatic, dispassionate way of thinking, an antagonistic image propagated by the new religion of hard currency. In any case, the relationship between the two concepts 'Enlightenment' and 'Romanticism' remains an expression for a precarious antagonism. There will always be something unreal in the invocation of the Romantic past, although the Romantic movement saw this as its final goal. Against this, I maintain: the spirit of Romanticism belongs itself to the Enlightenment movement in the West. This is

---

*Essay first published in Heidelberg, 1987.

proven in a negative way by the productive critique which Romanticism exercised on a fossilized and scholastically sterile rationalism, and positively in one of the greatest achievements of modernity, in the new acquisition of historical thinking. The discovery of the people's soul in songs and the vision for what constitutes a people and their culture were just the prelude and accompaniment to a greater event whose power would be released in the French Revolution. Of course, Germany was just barely touched by the dying wave of the French Revolution. The dynastic form of government remained for another century. Nevertheless, the bourgeoisie (the urban culture supported by the surrounding farmlands) raised art and science to a new level through their business activity. In this process the universities were institutions rich in tradition with their own inertia and by no means leading. So the Romantic movement in Heidelberg remained at first for the university only a provocative peripheral issue.

However, the epoch in which Romanticism blossomed in Heidelberg was in general rather stormy. There was the proximity of the French Revolution. There was Napoleon's politics for the Confederation of the Rhine. There was the rise of the national wars for independence and the following disappointment of the national and democratic expectations—all this enabled the aesthetic religion of Romanticism, which had developed in Jena, to become a politico-historical movement in Heidelberg. The future would belong to it. Even the restoration politics of the post-Napoleonic era was finally limited by the new reality of the nation-state and people's identification with it. Characteristic for the small model free-state, to which Heidelberg owes its particular blossoming, was that the pressure of the reaction remained mild and especially that no new repression occurred after the quieting of the storms of the year 1848. Rather a tolerant state, supporting culture, embraced Heidelberg University. It was by no means the self-determination of the professors, as the University had had in the late Middle Ages, but rather the cultural will of the sovereign and his advisors, that was at work here. In this manner the new science was born in Heidelberg. Not only from the spirit of the Enlightenment but also fanned by the spirit of Romanticism, a new historical thinking in theology, law and the historical sciences unfolded into a school of thought concerning the living spirit. Mythology and a science of Pandects, constitutional law, economy, and a politically accented universal history, in addition a theology department where besides the Hegelian Daub the rationalist Paulus taught, and a philosophy department where next to the Romantic Creuzer the sober Voss taught—they created the climate in which the new grand cultures of natural science and scientifically based medicine would in time reach maturity. In the end, it had to affect the whole when the speculative dreams of natural philosophy were shattered by the spirit of sobering experimental research. The new era of life saving chemistry began with Liebig; physics and physiology dissolved the caloric and the wonder of life into fields of scientific research; and even music, which is perhaps the highest expression of German Romantic genius, revealed its fundamental and natural lawfulness in the hands of a Helmholtz.

One must remember what this natural philosophy was according to its own foundations. It was clearly not a summoning of the spirit of nature which slumbered in the tomb of the sorcerer Merlin, like the romantic and poetic dreams of a Novalis. It was much more itself a part of the last grand venture of philosophy in the time of the Enlightenment, to reconcile modern science and traditional metaphysics and to create one rational and total science. Philosophy sought for the last time to encompass all that is and could be known into a 'doctrine of science' [*Wissenschaftslehre*] and to raise the whole of reality to the order of thought. For the Greeks, only nature, and especially its observable order in the heavens, appeared as a proof for the intellect and the good. Now the changing world of history, with all its wild confusion, and finally even the mysteries of religion should also come to themselves in the concept. How universal the reaction to this had to be! How the rejection of a constructive apriorism, which had dared to say: 'All the worse for the facts,' had to influence the whole line of advancing research! It is true that Schelling and Hegel were not so provokingly present in Heidelberg as in Berlin. The two years of Hegel's Encyclopedia were short. Nevertheless, the whole tendency of the new sense of research made itself known in Heidelberg at that time not so much in the still backward natural sciences as in the totality of the sciences of this decade. They were characterized by the slow dismantlement of pseudo a priori elements: dismantling natural rights in favor of thinking about historical rights, from historical construction to historical research, from theological dogmatic to refined historical exegesis—this can be seen by looking at the influential representatives of rationalism in Heidelberg at that time: Thibaut, J. H. Voss, Schlosser, Paulus, later Eduard Zeller, and many others.

Today, we may perhaps have reason to proceed from a methodological and scientific basis in order to retrieve much which in nature and culture was then affirmed by the romantic spirit. At that time, it was important to first establish the value of the standpoint of experience, controllable observation, experiment, method and critique over and against mere speculation. That this could happen without falling into the one-sidedness of a technological pragmatism and without misunderstanding the sciences of society and history in their uniqueness and equal stature, is due in great part to the awe-inspiring figure of Hermann Helmholtz.

With this we are already in the middle of the second phase of the reconstruction of Heidelberg University, in which the university received an international reputation unknown to any German university at that time. During the first half of the century when natural scientific research in Heidelberg was still little developed, the scene was dominated more by the lawyers and historians. But now, with the move of Helmholtz from Bonn to Heidelberg, a development reached its zenith which established the modern image of the natural sciences in Heidelberg. Helmholtz came together with such important natural scientists as the chemist Bunsen and the physicist Kirchhoff.

It is interesting enough to note that when, in 1862, Helmholtz held his vice-chancellor's address, "On the Relation of the Natural Sciences to the Whole of Science," one could still clearly detect the old primacy of political science and theology—because of their human subject matter— over the science of matter. It sounded like an apology when Helmholtz warned that one should not separate the sciences essential for the technological control of nature from the totality of the academic sciences and place them in technical schools, or even that one should not disintegrate the whole university into technical universities. In this one recognizes what is truly new and revolutionary in the new science. The important pioneering breakthroughs of science in the seventeenth and eighteenth centuries were accomplished mostly by outsiders and against the universities. The opposition of the universities to modern science was strong and long-lasting. The essence of Helmholtz's argumentation in his address acknowledges the victory of the critical method for the empirical investigation of facts. John Stuart Mill's inductive logic became foundational for this understanding of research. Helmholtz also expressed a new self-confidence. He almost explicitly stated that the unrelenting work of self-confident argumentation in natural science came closer to resolving the scientific task than generally in the other sciences. This did not hinder Helmholtz from acknowledging the scientific nature of the other sciences. In them he saw another kind of thinking at work, an artistic induction, which proceeded by unconscious comparison and generalization. In its results it could, of course, never attain the quality of natural law as being without exception.

One understands something of modern science, when one observes how 'what is established by convention' is part of the meaning of the concept of law (also in the Greek word *thesei*). In modern times, strict lawfulness, its concept having been derived from the secularization of the theology of creation, became a characteristic of nature, therefore of what was not *thesei*, but was *physei*. In the original German sense of language, there is in the expression 'law' [*Gesetz*] the sense of having-been-placed [*Gesetztsein*] and especially not the sense of having been given [*Gegebensein*] by nature. One asks oneself where is the place of mathematics in this relationship. Mathematics certainly does not conduct an empirical examination of facts. Nor are simple psychological facts revealed in the wonder of numbers and the puzzles of number theory.

This way of describing the foundation of mathematics, as Helmholtz attempted, cannot be the correct one. So the struggle against psychologism, which became characteristic for philosophy at the turn of the century—one thinks of Frege and Husserl—, had already been initiated decades before in Neo-Kantianism, above all by Cohen. More correctly, one might describe as psychological facts what was occurring in the historical process and in social reality, and thereby justify that rational explication had been set a boundary in those areas. However, is it only that? Only a boundary? Only a boundary of the ability to know? Or can an essentially different type of rationality be found here, one which also requires another knowledge?

For the last hundred years philosophy has struggled with this question. In truth, the question had already been raised at the beginning of modern science. For a time, law and political science as well as the historical sciences could be classified as 'practical philosophy' according to the traditional system of the sciences. Even German Idealism continued this with Hegel's *Philosophy of Right*. But as science became more and more dominant, and that was in the middle of the nineteenth century, one returned with a renewed commitment to Kant, in whom one saw the liberator of science from all the metaphysical slag of rationalism and the guarantor of scientific philosophy. This means: philosophy became epistemology. Here in Heidelberg, Eduard Zeller championed and established this expression and this interpretation of Kant, which even today is the ruling and all too one-sided image of Kant in the Anglo-Saxon world. In opposition to this we must remember: in truth, Kant subordinated his critical work in the final analysis to a moral metaphysics, in order to thereby show the Enlightenment its limits. The autonomy of practical reason is, according to Kant, grounded in freedom, a fact of reason, which cannot be confirmed nor contradicted through the empirical investigation of facts.

For the concept of science which Helmholtz intended, this was not informative. Even though the historical school wished to base its scientific-theoretical justification on categories of freedom; even though in Heidelberg the late-Hegelianism of Kuno Fischer wished to interpret Hegel's absolute idea as development, as what already is what it is in each of its stages—like nature; and even though the Neo-Kantian school in Heidelberg in our century wished epistemologically to ground the cultural sciences on the concept of value, —Helmholtz, for his part, would have probably agreed with Max Weber, another genius of Heidelberg University. He was clearly the greatest mind in Heidelberg in the twentieth century. He had just sharpened his weapons in the critique of a late

Romantic second blossom, the organic theory of the state, in order to develop a value-free sociology and to remove all value decisions from science.

And yet the human sciences will remain underdetermined in an evident manner if there should be no other rationality than that of the lawfulness of empirical facts. Certainly there are also experiential stabilities in the social sciences and not the least in economics which exhibit something like lawfulness and which may be presented using rational means, perhaps by constructing mathematical models. Such knowledge would then even make predictions possible, although specifically uncertain ones. It is fruitful to ask why they are uncertain. Is this due to a still insufficient set of data, as is the case in meteorology, which John Stuart Mill had already compared to the human sciences—hardly to the honor of both? But what would be a sufficient set of data? One will say, if it permits the calculation of the unpredictablility of human behavior in these processes in rough approximation. But if too many would allow themselves to draw practical conclusions from the rational predictions in these sciences? Then the rationality of these sciences would be contradicted exactly by the fact that humans using rationality would take those predictions into account.

Here, it appears to me, one must speak of the limits of the objectifiable, and this is true for many other cases where natural science is applied to complex life-situations, especially those concerning humans. This is fundamentally true in, for example, the science of medicine, which limits itself when it relies on the 'art' of the doctor. Even the scientifically trained doctor cannot construct health, as otherwise a skilled craftsman is able to fabricate something. He can always only lend assistance, so that nature can help itself. So we say that the sick person can join in healing or not. That may be a figure of speech which expresses the limits of the doctor's possibilities. But one would hardly wish to call it just a figure of speech, when a person after careful consideration decides to act in one way or the other. Another may have ever so correctly (or incorrectly) predicted how he would decide. He himself did not 'know' this. The one who chooses sees himself as free in his choice. He can even regret it and that proves in all cases that he takes responsibility for his own actions.

So it gives one pause, that such a great admirer of Max Weber's scientific rigor as the psychiatrist and philosopher Karl Jaspers would not be satisfied that the final existential decisions fall outside the area of the rational. Max Weber appeared to accept this limitation to our knowledge with his unflinching courage when he insisted on the value-freedom of science and limited it to pure goal-oriented rationality. But wasn't Jaspers correct when he tried to find reason in existence itself and directly spoke of the clarification of existence? Or take another Heidelberg example: When the promising young sensory physiologist Viktor von Weizsäcker chose his place to be that of a doctor at the sick bed, he made a most consequential decision. When he ultimately dared to question the fact of sickness itself, claiming that it was a self-chosen evasion by the soul, he was primarily concerned with knowledge. Whether correctly or not, he believed he had discovered actual facts when the psychosomatic relationship of a disease revealed itself to him in a conversation between persons—beyond the whole area of counting, measuring, and weighing. And perhaps he could have helped the patient in that he himself 'understood' in this way.

One may mock the Icarus-flight of speculative philosophy as much as one will, when they tried to think nature as spirit or when they, in the form of identity philosophy, denigrated the exploration of facts to an external activity—Hegel had called it 'external reflectivity,' whose unending process never reaches the self of the entities nor of spirit. The experimental sciences had to defend themselves against this. For them nature is a methodologically well-defined area of research. We today are quite unable to accept an idealistic equating of nature and spirit since we were introduced to the inner entanglements of nature and spirit by Nietzsche, Freud, and the further investigations of the neurologists. However, the human way of life contains its own rationality, as do all creations and structures which crystallize out of it and which we call culture. This obviously distinguishes it from the rationality of nature. Therefore the science of this human life and its manifestations must be different. It will be much less concerned with the secure control of the facts of experience. It will be concerned with more: with partaking [*Teilhabe*], with participation [*Teilnahme*], and with involvement [*Beteiligung*] of the one with the other. There will always be a grain of self-recognition involved in all encounters of humans with humans and with their creations. This strain of speculative identity is innate in humans. It is involved in all of their efforts and even influences the researcher who thinks to follow only "the iron laws of rational reasoning"—to quote Helmholtz. Presentiments, expectations, and recognitions must surely exist in all sciences and enliven the imagination of the researcher. He will accept nothing untested. However, each one finds oneself already in a world, wherein one has received a previous world-orientation long before taking the first steps as a researcher. He learned to speak and began to learn from others, and has never completed this tutoring. Here lies the primacy of language and the experience stored within it, which governs the hermeneutic universe. From the communality of tradition and during the process of communicating in language, insights and surprising conjectures flash forth. What is suggested by the words may often mislead—we know the warning concerning *idola fori*—

but sometimes it will point out the direction, like a hint of primeval origin. Not to speak of the schematization of all experience by grammar, which Nietzsche valued as being so important for living and which Werner Heisenberg valued so much for the investigation of nature. The Romantics knew something about this, and it appears that all authentic researchers in all areas of knowledge know something about this.

Helmholtz described for his time the common ground of all cognition using the contemporary inductive logic wherein one recognizes the influences of Aristotelian logic. However, when he attributed to the humanities the superior role of memory, he certainly overestimated—or even underestimated?—what its true achievement is. Not merely the storage of knowledge as is accomplished in a dictionary, a catalogue, etc. Memory corresponds much more to the acquisition of experience, which the natural scientist has acquired in his area—often after years of preparatory work for his experiment. What leads astray in both cases is to see exclusively psychological facts involved here. Memory, not just an automatic pinning down of what was previously present, is a intricate living system of retaining and forgetting, of preserving and suppressing, in short: a behavior. One has a memory for some things and not for other things; one can even honor and foster memory, and one knows why—just as we do in this hour of celebration. Equally true: the formation of concepts is not an accomplishment of conscious or unconscious inferring. There is no inference from many cases to all cases. The dogmatism of this concept of induction, which in this manner is not in Aristotle, appears to me to have been correctly demythologized by Popper. But one must go further. There is rationality at work in conceptualization. It is a process of life itself in which selection, differentiation, and identification occur. All these are processes which are not led by blind inspiration to a fixed result, but which produce fruitful and more rational conjectures through the difficult labor of thinking, as in logical deduction and in the testing and proving of inferences.

With this we enter into the area of *Inventio*, which precedes all *Deductio*. *Inventio* comes from *invenire*, and *invenire* means 'to come upon something' [*auf etwas kommen*], to find it. What is it however that one should find there? I say: The *question*. Wherever the unexpected presents itself, whether within the expectations of practical life or in science, it is always important to find the questions which one has to ask. The unexpected always belongs already to a horizon of expectation, within which possibilities are sketched. To come upon the correct questions here, to find the questions which may truly be asked and to which there is an answer, thus or so, this has its own rationality.

In life we know these possibilities as what is feasible. Only among them and not in a utopian domain, and yes, not even in the infeasible, can the practically correct answer be found. It is not different in the area of theoretical cognition. In science it is important to ask the correct questions. There is, in science or life, no answer to a senseless question which concerns nothing questionable. What a good or correct, a well-aimed question is, can be corroborated only through its rational testing. But to find fruitful questions is itself an art, no, an ability which has its own rationality. It is no less rational than the discovery of the feasible within the decision process of living activity. We practice this art during our whole life. We practice it daily, in seeking the correct word when we wish to communicate something to another, as in deciding on the correct choice in acting—and even if it is a researcher acting.

Even given new developments in the philosophy of science, the model of pure constructivity and its testability does not appear to be an exclusive ideal of rationality. One only has to realize what types of problems and insights constitute the foundations of system theory, crisis theory or catastrophe theory, whose mathematical execution lie well beyond my comprehension.

We are approaching the end of a century where the field of rationality in the sense of the well-calculated organization of life has broadened more and more. With this, the freedom to structure and restructure things has been necessarily restricted. This is also true for science which has learned to use new computer technologies and to unlock new data and relationships among data. These require all the more the correct questions of a competent researcher. The area where the rationality of calculation is practiced has necessarily continued to expand, thereby narrowing the free space of that rationality where ingenious improvisation and innovation occur. We have to preserve this free space and thus bring research to fulfillment. Then one recognizes what research actually is, and how unusual and how fortunate its occurrence is. Nevertheless, to provide close contact with research is the task which justifies a university's existence, especially also in the education of the teacher, priest, lawyer, and doctor, all of whom are subject to the constraints of a completely organized society. More than a century of scientific and social experience has intensified the situation which previously led Helmholtz to argue for the university as a whole. In spite of all the significance which the natural sciences have achieved through their results for the survival of modern humanity, it is important to recognize the inner interwovenness of one field of research with another and its development out of the immeasurable fields of teaching and learning, even the most remote.

We are not concerned with great plans. Our concern is the cycle of life, its preservation. To overcome instabilities and to discover new equilibria is the task in all areas of our so frightening and increasingly pressured life. The task is the same in our own area of research and teaching—yes, it especially belongs to our own area. Two things are required of us, both to possess and to teach: 'ability, which is restrained, and wisdom, which is humble.'

Chapter 5

THE IDEA OF THE UNIVERSITY—
YESTERDAY, TODAY, TOMORROW*

The theme which was proposed to me for today was specifically introduced to this university by the model and precedent of my predecessor, Karl Jaspers. So I will follow the suggestion to reflect upon how we today evaluate the university in terms of its idea and reality. In discussing this subject matter I would claim a double justification. One is the detachment of age which allows me to view the university of today from a distance of almost two decades during which I have not been an active member of this university. The other is that the universal concern of the philosopher is to seek distance, to preserve this as a basic value and, yes, even to recognize this as a fundamental human responsibility.

I wish to present my reflections as a free sequence of remarks and not as a commemorative speaker. I wish rather to express what affects me. When I chose the title, "The Idea of the University—Yesterday, Today, Tomorrow," I did not intend to undertake a historical review or a prophetic prognosis. Rather I will try to order my thoughts from the perspective of today which always stands between yesterday and tomorrow. Although I repeat the title of Jaspers' three public statements concerning the idea of the university from the years 1923, 1945, and 1961, that also does not mean that I will follow this sequence nor hold the same position. Everyone must come to terms with reality in their own way and I believe that whoever wants to come to terms with reality has to recognize that ideas and reality always belong together and are always apart.

I would like to briefly remind you that the specific structure of the university which developed in our German culture has, in the meantime, become a model for universities in many countries around the world. Humboldt's founding of the University of Berlin expressed a Prussian-Protestant critique of the more or less orthodox style of teaching and learning during the Enlightenment. We are conscious of this model as embodying this critique. That however implies that we are conscious of the critical situation in which this idea began to seek its reality. Knowing this, we may be convinced that it is not something completely new and perhaps also not something completely bad when a nation—or even humanity—knows itself to be in a critical situation. At any rate it was

---

*Address given in Heidelberg, 1986.

truly a critical situation when, at the time of the most pitiful and darkest degradation of the Prussian nation, Humboldt's reform of the university undertook the political and cultural renewal of the university and provided for academic freedom. It became the model for the nineteenth and twentieth centuries. Certainly there were and are ideologically influenced universities, for example in the Catholic tradition and in places of state-funded atheism. But that does not at all change the fact that everywhere the idea of the university, as it has developed in the last two centuries, concerns the transition from *doctrina* to *research*. Or as Wilhelm von Humboldt defined it: the transition to 'science, which has not yet been completely discovered.' We call it research and find the idea of the university to be closely connected to participation in research. Taking part in scientific research is not however a preparation for a profession in which science is to be applied, but rather means "education" [*Bildung*]. This word is, of course, not a very popular word any more, and it has forfeited its true meaning when it began to mark the class difference between the educated class and the uneducated.

Humboldt himself was not so much concerned with the teaching achievements of the professors or with the output of scientific research when he founded the university on the idea of education. What he wished to denote with this word was not opposition to the uneducated, but is explicable as being against developing the university into a professional school. It meant, therefore, opposition to the expert [*Fachmann*]. The word, education, signified a distancing from everything profitable and useful. In its elevated sense, the "science, which has not yet been completely discovered," means "living with ideas." This should unify the youth at the university and is intended to disclose through knowledge the horizon for all of reality and thereby also to open the possibility of surpassing this reality. Two things are required for this, solitude and freedom. Humboldt, one of the most introverted great intellectuals, understood solitude particularly well. And freedom, the struggle for which has constituted the world-historical fate of humanity, was supposed to especially become possible by this "living with ideas" at the university. The freedom to structure one's studies and the solitude of research were the important founding values of this idea of the university. That one is always also concerned to make these values productive in preparation for the professions of political life was self-evident for Humboldt. Lawyers and doctors were clearly the ones in whose professional preparation at the university the humanistic idea of renewing classical education was first formulated in our history. This occurred in order to enable them to work together with the clergy and teachers on the new task. To transmit to them the idea of education was exactly the point of Humboldt's new action. That this could occur through participating in research was certainly an ideal which could be accomplished by a greater number of students in the earlier stages of Humboldt's reform than is possible today. And nevertheless today it is still the goal of our actual efforts.

We have thereby reached our own problem. We must become aware of the critical situation in which the university finds itself today. We live in the time of industrial society. The time, which I would like to review with you in order to understand our situation, is the time when industrial society formed and when the task of the university found itself placed in an unusual and new relationship of tension with practical living. Today research is not conducted exclusively at the university. It has even become difficult to conduct research at a university in such a manner that the student can at all participate in the formative ideas. We will need to discuss the reasons for this critical situation and we will only be able to look to ourselves for help. We must recognize that industrial society through its structuring of the whole way of life indirectly affects the university. This is particularly due to the enormous explosion of the costs which are required for research today. And because of this, industry has made funds available to the universities for some time. In order to justify universities and research institutes, and what they can and should be, besides responding to the dominant interest in the economy, one has used, for decades, a differentiation which does not exist. I mean the difference between applied research and basic research. In truth there can be no other research except basic research. That means there is no other type of research except research which in its own activity is not concerned about the practical and pragmatic purposes which may be related to it. The freedom of the will to know consists exactly in pursuing to the end all possible doubts and one's own possible self-critique. So it is already indicated that the situation of the university in modern society is necessarily a critical one. It must seek to discover a balance between the duty to prepare students for a profession and the duty to educate which lies in the essence and activity of research. Not without reason has the characteristic word for industrial work, namely the word "industry" [Betrieb], been extended into the research sector. We speak unreservedly of the research industry and regard our place of work as an industrial institution. In fact, all the professions we know are dependent upon the research industry and teaching industry—the doctor, the lawyer, the economist, the minister, and not to forget all the teachers who through their profession indirectly have the broadest area of influence in the modern state. We need to think through the continual opposition between the educational task of the university and the practical utility which society and the state expect from it.

Yesterday and today. Let us look at yesterday from today. I do not mean to refer to the long history of the university but to the particular development of the university in the industrial epoch and that means at the same time the epoch of the alienation of education [*Bildung*]. Naturally this does not concern just a particular German phenomenon. The question is posed within a world process. However, we must examine and explicate this general problem from the particular conditions of our own history, our own academic institutions and our way of life. This is the central question of the industrial epoch of the nineteenth and the slowly ending twentieth century. So for a long time the continued effect of Humboldt's university reform was directed toward a university for the bourgeois elite. We should recognize that for such an elite this institution was excellent, recognized throughout the world and often used as an exemplar. But we should also recognize the developmental law of our civilization: increasing scientific specialization has to be paid for with a decline of education [*Bildung*]. Finally, we must recognize that the place of the "academic world" within the whole society has become doubtful.

Recalling my own university days, I began during the First World War while Wilhelm the Second still ruled and then continued my studies in the difficult first years after the war. We all know how difficult the living conditions had become then in Germany. With honorable exertion the Republic attempted to make available to all parts of the German populace the old and traditional form of elite education, which had been supported by the bourgeoisie and in part by the nobility. The academic profession became the legitimate goal of all those who felt their intellectual capabilities and talents would enable them to study, at least in principle. That was the end of the old traditional form, which a social class had established for itself. When I became a student, student life still occurred in traditional fraternities with all their old customs which had survived from one generation to the next in the fraternities' associations and their ideals. But fundamentally it was not the fraternity student but the free student who sought his form of life and his friendships at the university. Along with this, we should remember that the emancipation from the parents' home, which had always been associated with the initiation of one's studies, had also delegated a certain educational role to the landlady of the student, which earlier had been accomplished in the corporate forms of military service and the fraternities. Since this education no longer exists, it appears to me that we have lost something today. The youth today are presented with a new task of self-education which is not supported by any institutions. At this point I must relate my experience in other countries, for example, how impressed I am with the level of self-education in American students. It is astounding how these rowdies, whose parents may not even completely trust them, become in a few years polite, disciplined, and very reasonable young people. Never during a visit has an American student not asked me after ten minutes if he would be permitted to have just a moment longer of my time. American students have always done this—a German student does not in general say this. Certainly it pleases me when one wishes to speak with me longer. But I also admire the degree of reciprocal education which has been accomplished there, where every visitor has learned to show consideration for other possible visitors and for the time taken from the professor.

Clearly, at that earlier time, one studied under different conditions. I remember that when I was a student at Marburg the 3,000th student received a gold watch from the city, because one was so pleased over this increase. Today we are rather in the opposite situation. Today we would be willing to present much more than a golden watch to that student who would symbolize a decrease in the number of students from 30,000 to 3,000. We would reward in him the return to a sensible relationship between teachers and students, and therefore, the return to an actual chance for education which would be truly compatible with our teaching and research duties.

It is not my intention to romantically portray my own academic youth. The difficulties which the young Weimar Republic had to overcome are well known also in the sphere of the university. Especially at the university one could clearly observe how little German society was prepared for its task of parliamentary democracy and how a system for selection was missing which was truly supported by all classes. Not a very encouraging aspect of life at the university then. On the other hand, as a student in the university, one could have experienced, perhaps better than at any other time, how the unmastered weight of tradition encumbered the German university, which before had formed an elite society. Nevertheless, one can say that in the Weimar Republic a living tension existed between the ideological preconditioning through the earlier German tradition and the searching and creating of new ideals. This created a genuine freedom which found expression in the free choice of interests for the teachers as well as for the learners. The false nationalistic and reactionary ideology, which was already developing at the universities during the Weimar era and which then led to Nazi control, is known. What one does not know so well, either abroad or in the younger generation which surrounds us today, is how this fascist ideologizing at the universities, which came to dominate with Hitler's seizure of power, was defeated after a few years by the students themselves. This led to the use of terror by the party and secret police. Due to the insanity of the war and its criminal continuation, this terrorizing became ever worse, especially for the academic youth. On the whole one should not be misled: only in extreme cases was there an ideologizing of science and academic teaching, about which one now would prefer not to be reminded. But these cases were avoided by the reasonable student who sought education and knowledge.

Now we have reached the present and its most recent history, i.e., the epoch which began with the reconstruction of a free university and society. Clearly at that time the problems of today's university had already emerged. At first a kind of restoration madness dominated, namely, the idea that in modern industrial society there could be something like a "pouvoir neutre," a neutral position, for the academic institution of the university within the state. The major point of my presentation will be to demonstrate that that is not the case. Freedom will not be guaranteed us, if we do not know how to use the small space of freedom which has been left us. So the reconstruction of Heidelberg University began with the incentive not to again be dependent upon a tradition which no longer sustains and is dead. On the other side, the incentive was to transpose what was alive and valuable in this tradition into new forms. Therefore, we in Heidelberg have attempted—I have also participated in this since 1949—to give a new structure to student life, the living together of the student body, and thereby to create a new tradition. This failed due to the students themselves—for very sincere reasons. The gap between those who had returned from the war and the inexperienced young people who came to the university as greenhorns at the end of the 1940s, did not permit a unification, from which a tradition could have developed within student life. Thus the leadership was missing which could have created a common life for the students according to their own desires. Finally, the real problem of our academic existence erupted with the enrollment explosion. No one in the whole world was really prepared for this. This as well was a worldwide event. In our German tradition we were especially poorly prepared. Because we were still guided by the idea that academic education meant to direct one toward research and at least to participate in research. This was an ideal that had been preserved within the bourgeois culture of schooling and education in the nineteenth century, although by the beginning of the twentieth century it had already degenerated into a mere system of certification. With the change to a mass university, structural problems had to occur for which, in the sheer quantitative expansion of the universities, we have not found the institutional forms.

The result is a threefold alienation which has afflicted the community of teachers and learners and their position in society. First is the obvious relationship between the academic teacher and his students which characterized the previous *Universitas Scholarum*. The address "fellow-student" [*Kommilitone*] is derived from the existence and functioning of this community, because we all understood ourselves to be in the same "militia," whether professors or students. This has clearly become a problem which can in principle no longer be solved. Fortunately, surrounding each professor who has something to say, there are those who gather around him not just for the purpose of achieving a grade and completing a good examination but who also come into personal contact with him. The circle which forms around each academic teacher in the natural sciences and medicine is prescribed to some degree by other regularities. Here the place in the laboratory or in the internship allows a direct relationship among the researchers, teachers, and students. However, even in this case, the availability of research directors will be lessened by the administrative bureaucratization to which one must devote too much of one's time. But wherever such restrictions, caused by the means and modes of work, prevent direct contact between the teacher and student, it has become an unsolvable problem to handle the unlimited number of students. Statistically it is almost impossible to express how poor the relationship between the number of teachers and students is in Germany and in a few other similarly under-developed European countries. I do not exactly know the situation in the East. In any case, the adherence to forms of academic teaching, which we still defend for carefully considered reasons, confronts the teaching professor of today with overwhelming problems—and naturally the student has to pay for this, for he is not able to find the proper access to his teacher. Therefore, the student encounters the truly didactic, namely the role model, almost exclusively as standing behind a rostrum. In most academic disciplines, the augmentation of teachers by using assistants cannot be considered a solution to this shortage.

The second alienation, which affects professors just as much as students, is the alienation of the sciences from one another. Where is the *Universitas Literarum* considering the fragmentation and departmentalization which has become unavoidable due to the large size of institutions? Obviously this fragmentation leads to the disintegration of the university into professional schools, which are more or less tightly sealed from each other. One tried everything possible so that the organization of the newly formed departments would not become too meaningless and the organic relationships would not be too greatly sundered. But a disruption of the intellectual communication which belongs to a university unavoidably occurred. In the daily routine of teaching, the sciences know all too little about each other; in the area research it may be better. Again the students have to foot the bill.

The third is perhaps the most serious problem. I remind you that Humboldt viewed the actual purpose of studying at a university not to be attending lectures or completing good essays on small research assignments for a seminar or something similar, but "living with ideas." This has become enormously difficult for today's student. The alienation occurs especially between student and student and between oneself and the society in which the students live. It is almost as if a new profession has been created for being a student. There are economic and social reasons for this. But anyone who takes his studies seriously certainly knows that his position as a student is only the preparation for a real place in society, and that means for a profession. In our German society, because of its structure and history, this is also a unique problem which grew from the peculiar merits of our scientific culture.

Let us now attempt to look from today toward tomorrow. Not as a seer does, although the Homeric seer, the Greek seer, was one characterized by not being able to know the future without knowing the past and present. Here we are concerned with a fundamental problem: I mean the independence [*Abseits*] of the academic world. What happens to the idea of the university in a society which induces in those who are growing up an ever increasing distrust in its way of life, so that every appeal is only heard with mistrust? How should the idea of education through participation in research, which may still be the actual attraction to academic studies, be made possible in reality?

Where else can the idea be if not in reality? There is a thought in Plato which we need to consider in this case. It states: one cannot even imagine a city where the idea of a city is completely lost and no longer recognizable at all. That is surely also our task, not to imagine an idea as a distant guiding image but to learn to recognize it in concrete reality. That includes in our case the task of recognizing and justifying the independence of the academic world. It would be an illusion, to which the German academic has all too long succumbed, to still dream of a *res publica literaria*, a republic of intellectuals, which would be an autonomous world based on old privileges from the Middle Ages or established with the formation of nations in modern times, and so embodying and guaranteeing the idea of academic freedom. Our task is rather to give a new definition to academic freedom. We live in a modern industrial world, in a modern bureaucratic state, in a thoroughly organized system of social life, upon which we all depend, and in this system we have been allotted a modest space of freedom. Within it occurs our effectivity as inquiring teachers and inquiring learners, and it is truly a privilege to be exempted in various important matters from the tight net of modern professional life and from political calculations. Here romantic ideas of guarantees for academic freedom are out of place. We will need other justifications for our activity, and we must develop them.

There is still another independence which is no less vital and unavoidable, even if it may appear to be precarious in the social reality of our time. I mean the distance from practical activity, which is implanted in the essence of this large institution of research and teaching. One understands the transition from this world of research and teaching to the practical activity of a profession and the unique relearning that must then occur. It is therefore common to accuse the university of being divorced from real life, and one contemplates improvements. However, I do not believe that this independence of the academic world is something which we could or should alter through reforms and modifications in the institutional arrangement of the whole or through an opening of it to so-called real life. We are concerned here with a much deeper problem. It is not limited to teaching and learning nor to knowledge and ability at the university alone. I am here approaching a subject matter which I may partially claim as my own. This does not mean that I will now conduct a technical philosophical lecture. I will also not lose sight of the fact that we are concerned with a special case of learning and teaching when we consider the uniqueness which characterizes human social life. This no longer concerns just the situation of German education and the idea of the German university, but concerns a basic anthropological problem which exists in all schools and educational institutions in all cultures. It concerns the position of humans in nature. The central point is that humans, as opposed to animals, are in a special manner social beings which have moved beyond the impulses, instincts, and hierarchies which otherwise determine life in nature. Nevertheless human beings and their life processes are also undeniably part of nature.

Aristotle attempted in his politics to point out the constants of our human nature which constitute the foundations for the political task of ordering and directing human life. He declared it to be a decisive step in nature when it granted humans language, a system of communication which surpasses those used by animals of so many species. And with language we received distance and thereby pretence, lies, self-deception, in short all the great ambiguities of our human existence. Evidently they are connected with the distinctive characteristic of human beings: to find means and ways for distant goals, to sacrifice for distant goals, and in general, to be able to subordinate instinctual impulse, fear, or desire. To use our own concepts: to accept the whole asceticism connected with work. We may actually perceive work as something specifically human because it is achieved by a continual denial of impulses. It appears to me that all this is implied by the unique human possession of language. We live this dangerous distance to ourselves, which possesses an eery presence in the impulses of the human soul as, for example, the phenomenon of suicide shows, or is seen in the terrible legacy of war against one's own kind not known elsewhere in nature. If one recognizes this, then one understands that the exceptionally dangerous characteristic of humans— to achieve distancing and the bridging of distance—has the effect of blocking natural impulses and instinctual urges. But it also demands we construct the possibility of living together and the structures for living together. All this is demanded of us. The Greeks had a word for this, which Aristotle used in such a context; it is *syntheke*, the common establishment of common values. The whole legal system with all its limitations, the whole of our institutions and morals, the whole of what modern psychology calls "socialization," all this grows from this difficult distinctive characteristic of humans. A never-ending process of learning occurs which does not end in knowledge. To remain incomplete is the fate of our desire to learn and know. Religions have known to seek and find their emotionally powerful answer. In the history of the Western world an answer has developed, the Greek answer, which is continually being revived by us. It is the answer connected with the concept of *theoria*, theoretical knowledge. This ideal of *theoria* presents itself to the Greeks through the model of the divine, a spirit which perceives and finalizes itself and everything else. However, the Greeks never forgot that this ideal of theory—of living in pure observation or thinking which sees the things as they are—is not a straightforward human inheritance but, in the best case, a possible accomplishment which always remains restricted and bounded. Given their constricted practical and political life, there was no need to tell the Greeks how limited the free space of theory was. It is the same for us. Society offers and grants us a free space of a limited type. The free space of theory is not offered as a privilege to a particular class but as a human possibility, which is never totally unrealized in any person and which we have been given to develop to a higher degree for everyone.

It is not a new problem that persons having received a theoretical training are often disappointed when they have to face practical life. This transition always entails a new learning and often a renunciation of the abstract, exotic, and unpragmatic knowledge which one had absorbed. This problem appears to me to be necessarily connected to the fundamental problem of desiring to know and needing to know, which is the very essence of human nature, and implies a dislodging from the path of natural life. In a famous allegory Plato presented the whole problem to us in an unforgettable manner. It is the story of the cave where humans are chained. They may only look at the wall where shadows are passing. Through careful observation they learn the series of ever repeating forms, which are depicted there. Experience means for them that one begins to know and to say what comes next—until one who is so chained is set free, turned around and led out of the cave—to the sun and bright day of the true world. But, if one is then finally forced to return to the cave from the bright day, then he will be ridiculed by those who have remained chained because of his dazed and blind state which prohibits him from finding his way about due to the sudden darkness. The story which I tell has its point for our circumstance. It portrays the insurmountable tension between true knowledge, which is knowledge in the bright light of the universal and binding, and pragmatic correctness, adroitness and prudence, which we practice in specific situations. In both cases insurmountable prejudices threaten. From the side of those who always followed only pragmatic adroitness, that they will perceive the newly arrived from outside as completely blind. The others, who may believe that they have understood the truth, may be tempted to scorn the thankless enterprise of attempting to discover order within the darkness of this cave existence. In this story it is already understood with total clarity: a free thinking, which is bound by no political, economic, psychological, or emotional restrictions, cannot even exist. Life must always enter into new restrictions. Within the restrictions of our social life, in the fateful framework into which each one has been placed by birth and experience, it is important to preserve the free space which one has been allotted. I believe we can draw conclusions from this story for our own thought and perhaps also find an answer to the questions which afflict our youth: how can the free space be found where they can realize their own possibilities?

The modern mass university imposes three forms of alienation upon us all, teachers and learners. I wish to discern the positive possibilities which still remain for us. The first thing that we must learn is that the freedom which permits us a theoretical orientation in our life must be seen by us as a task and not just as a bestowed present. This task is enormously difficult. For we live in a society which, in order to preserve its own order, teaches and rewards adopting to and fitting into its institutionalized structures of being. Society trains us in all that—to use the image—like shadowy forms pass on the cave wall and where discovering order is the pragmatic wisdom of all. What can the university be in this situation? Considering the large number of students today, I do not overestimate the extent to which participation in research is an actual possibility. But even a faint awareness that there are people here who as participants in research speak to them and take a position in questions which concern everyone, is already something. The alienation between teachers and learners may become a little less when we understand what it means to nevertheless see in existence a kind of *universitas scholarum* as opposed to the molding of social consciousness by the powers of the present, accomplished as it is through the struggle of ideologies and interests, the struggle of competitive life in a modern society. That is, when we encounter the existence of the *universitas scholarum*, still free in its seclusion. Here one can still participate in research out of theoretical interest and without asking *cui bono* (whom does it please?). Thus one is free from censorship and reprimand, be it by a government which already knows the truth or be it by the economic system for whose flourishing and functioning everything else is concerned. This participation in research does not so much mean, as the novice may perhaps think, that one is actually able to make one's own contributions to research. The most noble mediation between us few teachers and the great mass of students consists of all those who at least attempt an authentic accomplishment of their own in research. Success is perhaps not granted to all, but a professor without students who attempt to enter science would be robbed of his best interpreters, best mediators.

What I mean by this is especially that inquiry and research produce poor television viewers and newspaper readers. We always ask: What is the motivation? What interests are being expressed? Why are we being informed about this? Is the aim to keep us within the limits of an administered social order? The interaction with research, even in the limited forms which are today still possible for everyone, assures that one can again risk one's own judgment and need not simply agree to opinions. I see this as the most noble task presented the student of today. And yet this is exactly what one criticizes in us and in him—that we give no ideological direction, not even instructions concerning how to act in the future concrete situations of professional life. Of course, we already know and think it appropriate that the educated student will be exposed to a new shock when, after his studies, he has to enter into professional life and come to terms with pressures to conform. Fellow students, every student who has taken his studies seriously, should be aware that he has received something: to risk his own judgments and not simply to allow himself to be manipulated.

The second alienation which I discussed concerned the specialization of the sciences and the separation of the whole field of knowledge from skill, even in the field of the "Litterae." The contemporary university is disintegrating into many specialties. Here as well I have no illusions. The researcher himself is influenced by the pressure to specialize. He is thereby enclosed within the boundaries of his own knowledge. And teaching is even more deeply affected. Becoming older one especially experiences this. One may still take note of the development of new tendencies in the research of one's own discipline, which one may still observe with the open-minded attitude of a genuine spirit of research. But one is nevertheless excluded. Already it is not easy for the researcher and the one who lives with science to keep up with his own discipline. Nevertheless, it remains true that only those teachers who can freely question their own prejudgments, and who have the capacity to imagine the possible, can help students develop the ability to judge and the confidence to think for themselves. That we criticize ourselves and that others criticize us is the authentic breath of life for every true academic and researcher. This is not always comfortable. I do not propose that to be criticized is comfortable. Every person is then a little distressed and doubts himself still more than he usually does. This is true for teachers as well as for learners—and to have chosen this is our lot.

Now for the third question. What I find to be most dangerous in our situation is that it has become so unbelievably difficult just to discover an existing authentic solidarity. I believe it is important to keep one's eyes open in order to discover where it exists. To a limited extent and for a time in the family; nobody who has been embraced by a family for an extended time should discount that he has once known solidarity. Also the emancipation from the family usually, if not always, means entering into a new solidarity by making friends, becoming acquainted with the working milieu, or whatever else it may be. In short, the free community of those who come together in solidarity has not ceased to accept us, even if we, as citizens in our state, have this general position of independence, which is not always appreciated and does not qualify us as good democrats.

Let me conclude. We should have no illusions. Bureaucratized teaching and learning systems dominate the scene, but nevertheless it is everyone's task to find his free space. The task of our human life in general is to find free spaces and learn to move therein. In research this means finding the question, the genuine question. You all know that as a beginner one comes to find everything questionable, for that is the privilege of youth to seek everywhere the novel and new possibilities. One then learns slowly how a large amount must be excluded in order to finally arrive at the point where one finds the truly open questions and therefore the possibilities that exist. Perhaps the most noble side of the enduring independent position of the university—in political and social life—is that we with the youth and they with us learn to discover the possibilities and thereby possible ways of shaping our own lives. There is this chain of generations which pass through an institution, like the university, in which teachers and students meet and lose one another. Students become teachers and from the activity of the teachers grows a new teaching, a living universe, which is certainly more than something known, more than something learnable, but a place where something happens to us. I think this small academic universe still remains one of the few precursors of the grand universe of humanity, of all human beings, who must learn to create with one another new solidarities.

PART 2

Hermeneutics, Poetry, and Modern Culture

Chapter 6

INTERVIEW: WRITING
AND THE LIVING VOICE

This text is based on interviews with Hans-Georg Gadamer carried out on two different occasions. A first interview took place in Hamilton, Canada, at McMaster University, in November 1985. The second interview took place in the garden of Hans-Gadamer's house in Heidelberg, July 1, 1986. Translated by the editors.

QUESTION. Professor Gadamer, you have written a memoir of your academic and intellectual life which has been published in English under the title *Philosophical Apprenticeships*. This book includes portraits of scholars and philosophers whom you knew well. But you say little about your own writing from the 1920s till the 1950s, where you conclude the memoir. You also do not tell your readers much about the genesis of *Truth and Method*, the book for which you are best known. Would you care to tell us about the origins of this book, where and when you wrote it, and how plans for it emerged from your own academic and intellectual history?

GADAMER. Oh yes, but I am not someone who can lay out a program for his thought, and so I shall tell you how this work grew out of my teaching. I always have been a very dedicated teacher and I remember that my students frequently complained that they lacked a text of mine which corresponded to my teaching. They were often asked who they were studying with in Heidelberg. And when they mentioned my name, they were asked: "but who is that"? And so I decided that I should try to write a book which was indicative of my practice of the interpretation of texts and my teaching generally. But, of course, the first ideas of the book were formed when I began to teach and I remember that my first notes toward it were taken in 1933. Then it became apparent to me that the spirit of optimism typical of liberal civilization was collapsing and I gave a lecture called 'Art and the Public' in which I tried to demonstrate that art can convey truth and therefore form public opinion, that art stood for more than giving aesthetic pleasure. Here was the germ for *Truth and Method*. But then there was a further circumstantial reason for continuing to write. Once the first recording technology was available, my lectures were recorded and transcribed. To me this appeared to be a distortion of my lecturing. For machines do reproduce vocal speech, its noises. But they do not reproduce the whole of speech, gestures, and the like, which make up a good speaker's performance, *all* the circumstantial factors, so to speak, which accompany the spoken word, for a lecture is addressed to an *audience*. Writing therefore is a complete transformation of the spoken word, somewhat like the transformation of the princess, in the famous fairy tale of Hauff's, who is changed into a frog and then when she hears the word "mutabor" (I will be changed) she comes out a princess. So it is with speech changed into writing. Thus it went for ten years. Because I was the only one teaching in my field, I would then begin again during every vacation, every break: "Non nullum imperator in annum." This old maxim was really fulfilled in my book.

QUESTION. This was in Heidelberg during the 1950s?

GADAMER. Yes. But the first part of the book was outlined in the lecture of 1933 or 1934, which I mentioned. Then lectures on Husserl and Heidegger became material for Part 2, and the same holds for Part 3 on 'Language and World.' But then the whole thing grew together.

QUESTION. Did you teach courses on the history of hermeneutics? Or did you announce seminars and lectures in hermeneutic philosophy?

GADAMER. No, no. I never announced lectures or seminars under this title. I only did so once the text was finished. In fact, I did so little thinking in terms of it that it first became a reality for me, when my publisher asked for a title for my book (later to be *Truth and Method*). I suggested *Philosophical Hermeneutics*. And they asked "what is that"? My wife and I pondered a little, like a cook who lets his imagination roam when he draws up a menu, thus giving different names to one and the same dish, so we came up with *Truth and Method*. Ambiguity is the secret to a good title and promptly some reviewers would comment correspondingly. Some would say that the book discussed the method for finding truth, others said that I claimed that there was no method for finding truth. The ambiguity of the title is its key quality.

QUESTION. Did you already in the 1930s have a notion of *wirkungsgeschichtliches Bewusstsein*?

GADAMER. No, no. But as a classics scholar I was practicing it. My interest in the classics focused on the tradition of rhetoric, which kept the classics alive and was the way through which antiquity remained alive. The doxographies composed by the later philosophers interested me less. Generally, in writing all this, it was a bit as Paul Valéry described the making of poems: The first verse is most difficult. For me it is like that. I need to overcome my hesitations and then, slowly, I forget my fears and hesitations. But that's still the exception. Really, I am not a good writer, I am a speaker, a lecturer.

QUESTION. But other books, e.g. *Plato's Dialektische Ethik,* clearly were written as books, is that true?

GADAMER. Yes, *Plato's Dialektische Ethik* was completely written as a book. But this is due to the fact that I had to write it in order to acquire the licence to teach, to become "habilitiert," to become "Privatdozent."

QUESTION. Could one claim then that you have a theory of speech and writing and of their relation?

GADAMER. Yes, this I think has not been well considered yet. What does it mean, for example, that in all of antiquity no silent reading was done, and what does it mean that we no longer hear a real voice when reading? This has implications also for writers. I would say this is a good topic for research, research into the history and styles of writing, research which should respect the different conditions, such as that during antiquity the aristocracy and the educated employed others who recited for them.

QUESTION. Are you then reasserting the primacy of speech and resisting the preeminence of the literary?

GADAMER. I would say, literature and writing must take note of the different conditions under which they occur. I would define hermeneutics as the skill to let things speak which come to us in a fixed, petrified form, that of the text. So one has to modulate, use intonation. And things have to be written so that they can help us in this. It is, for example, striking that punctuation is only needed when something is badly written.

QUESTION. It wasn't used at all in ancient Rome or Greece, or in old High German?

GADAMER. No: There were professional recitalists—of poems, and epics. They possessed the skills required. Their audiences did not possess them.

QUESTION. But can we ask you a question about you yourself and your own work once again? It appears, for example, that your work has a strong continuity, more than is the case with Wittgenstein and Heidegger where the early and the late work are completely different. Do you agree?

GADAMER. Heidegger and Wittgenstein would probably protest and say that there is much continuity. For they are thinkers and their identity is to be found in the continuity of their thought. Thus biography is normally marginal to them. As Heidegger said: A thinker only thinks one thing all his life. Well, probably I am not a thinker in this emphatic sense. But as my work comes from my teaching, something like this must hold as well. Writing is my secondary form of self-presentation, as Plato thought it should be. So I am not such a bad Platonist after all.

So I didn't really change directions, not at least before the appearance of *Truth and Method*. And that was very late in life, and this is largely due to the fact that during the Third Reich, it was almost a matter of prudence not to be very public. I tried to have a career, and I succeeded by publishing little. My publications appeared in very specialized journals which were not very public. So I got called to my first chair in Leipzig on the basis of an article about "theories of the atom in ancient Greece" (*antike Atomtheorie*). And this came to Heisenberg's attention, and the voice of Heisenberg was very strong, even against political opposition which was obviously there in my case.

QUESTION. You have described that *Truth and Method* only emerged very slowly for you as an entire work. Was this also due to the fact that you worked quasi-underground during the Third Reich?

GADAMER. Yes: but I was free to teach. The secret police, you know, they were so stupid. They sent observers to my classes and reported my work was boring. Therefore you must realize the effects of a long period of silence: I published books in 1931 and then in 1959. Twenty to thirty years of relative silence. The changes which I underwent during these years have already been reworked to produce an effect of continuity. My first book was an attempt to emancipate myself from the style of Heidegger. But there are obvious traces of it in this book. And so I developed a style of my own by speaking freely (not reading to an audience) and teaching this way. I learned to develop the melody of my own thoughts and although I do not think I am a bad writer, there always is the living voice behind the writing. At least I hope that it does not disappear.

QUESTION. Your view of speech and writing has in part been produced by your political experience?

GADAMER. Yes, but also by my personal experience, my difficulties with writing. I am a dialogical being. When teaching, I was very shy at first, I never looked at the students. This was the case in lectures. But when I held seminars, I myself was present from the first day: I had a real talent for listening and replying and believe that that remains my talent: to listen even to the silent voice of an audience.

QUESTION. The hermeneutical talent?

GADAMER. Yes, and if I compare myself with Heidegger, if I may be permitted to do so, there always was his deep religious commitment, attempting to find more adequate self-understanding, to distance himself from the dogmatic faith of the church and from public opinion. That was Heidegger's deepest concern. This insistence, not so much to liberate oneself from inauthenticity, but to make visible the ambiguity inherent in authenticity. No, Heidegger was not a moralist, he was not like Jaspers. He was always captivated by the tension

between his real inspiration and the covering over of that by his own
tendency to adjust to the public. The inseparability of authenticity
and inauthenticity, the sliding into ruination as the tendency of
everyday existence, that was the early Heidegger's concern.

QUESTION. There is another complex of questions which we wish to
raise with you, Professor Gadamer. Are the universities today still
entrusted with the inheritance of antiquity and classical philosophy?
Does there still exist a continuity between the practice of philoso-
phizing in our times and the practice of philosophy in antiquity?

GADAMER. Well yes, of course we encounter the origins, the fathers of
our culture, with the Greeks. For them philosophy was the totality of
what could be known theoretically. But they didn't call this philosophy. A term having this meaning was only introduced by Plato, and
it was accepted as a word designating theoretical knowledge only at
the point where theoretical knowledge was distinguished from the
empirical sciences, that is, in modern times. Thus we may well ask
whether there is any continuity. I believe there is continuity, for
example, in the sense that the famous Socratic inquiry into the good,
his claim that no one in society had the expertise to give a satisfacto-
ry answer to this question, remains significant for our times, for we
face the danger of becoming too dependent on experts. Thus
Socrates' critique of the sophists, and of the status and competence
claimed by citizens in Athens who were chosen to be members of the
legislative and executive bodies of the city state, remains valid. No
one is in a position any more to speak to all citizens, so in this sense
we have to expect limits. Yet there remains the question of the common good which must be faced in all the specialized organisations
which make most of the relevant decisions.

QUESTION. You emphasize the Socratic aporia, the recognition of not-
knowing as a quality to be attained by the philosopher, a quality
endangered by the claim to expert knowledge in public affairs. But
beside this continuity between Greek thought and yours, you also
emphasize the uniqueness or singularity of the classical authors.
Why is this the case? What makes these texts unique?

GADAMER. This is a complicated matter. But probably these writings
appear to us this way because they have formed our understanding,
our anticipations of what makes sense so profoundly, that they
remain ultimate reference points for us. We can show this through
studying the history of key terms, those derived from Latin and
Greek. Heidegger in particular has uncovered the consequences of
the translation of Greek philosophical concepts into Latin, their
latinization; he has also shown how significant German mysticism
has been for the development of the German language. And he him-

self is unthinkable without German mysticism, just as Hegel remains incomprehensible without reference to his Swabian predecessors. Our philosophical language is Greek and Roman in its substance and uncovering this enlivens our understanding of our own concepts. Who today would think of "substance," of *hypokeimenon*, when they hear the word "subject"? They think of "consciousness" or "soul." That *subjectum* means something quite different, that an understanding of time is involved, the Greek one, which was different from the Christian understanding of time, that therefore the Greek understanding could do justice neither to the understanding of human existence nor to Christian existence, all this Heidegger has revealed by way of this inquiry into the history of concepts.

QUESTION. Is it true, then, that the texts of the Greek philosophers would not have the same significance for people from India, China, or Japan?

GADAMER. Yes, quite correct, but at the same time this is changing for us. We live in a culture of exchange and interpenetration. Occidental scientific culture and its philosophical presuppositions are becoming effective everywhere. What this will lead to, what will result from the assimilation of Greek philosophy among the South Asian or East Asian people, how it will differ from the result so far of all of occidental history, namely the technological era—all this I leave open, and cannot anticipate. The day may yet come where we have to study their poetry, for example, for our own reasons. And as to the uniqueness of the Greeks, Greek art, sculpture for example, when I experienced Mexican sculpture for the first time, I began to think differently. These wide-open eyes and open hands of those sculptures oriented toward the rising sun, the basic religious attitude expressed in them, that is quite impressive. I would no longer dare to say that Greek culture is unique, exceptional. But then, of course, sculpture is independent from language as is music. Therefore European classical music now is widely listened to and played in East Asia.

QUESTION. Then you seem to believe that there are special difficulties involved in the translation of literary works, that they will not easily be accepted in other cultures, for example, modern European literature and philosophy?

GADAMER. Yes, there is a barrier, the barrier of language. Direct translation is not possible. It is possible perhaps with the novel and drama. Thus Shakespeare may be accepted in Japan and China. But the obstacles are much greater in the case of lyric poetry. It is the originality of language which constitutes a barrier.

QUESTION. So actually you are skeptical about the possibility of translation?

GADAMER. Yes. In the case of great prose texts I can put my skepticism aside. Thus I read Russian and Danish prose in translation. But in the case of poetry, only bilingual editions are useful. Translations make the reading of the original possible. And with respect to philosophy: here I am also skeptical. The language of philosophy is so evocative, full of connotations. Only linguistic analysis believes that one can say everything that one means or knows. One can never say fully what one wants to say. A statement always falls short of what one wants to say. Which is not to say that translations do not help sometimes; they do, precisely because they are flatter. Thus Christopher Smith, who has translated much of my work, has sometimes persuaded me to change a German text, so that it could be translated. It just wasn't clear enough.

QUESTION. Could one say that your hermeneutics is a European hermeneutics, that one cannot think about hermeneutics in the same way when one teaches the classics in Salt Lake City or Winnipeg?

GADAMER. I'll answer somewhat indirectly. This isn't how I experienced my presence as a teacher in North America, where I also feel that I am well understood now, when I speak English. But I think of the interest in Heidegger among the Japanese who come to study with us in Germany. You must know: half of all the editions of Heidegger go to Japan these days. The way Heidegger has made the Christian history of the Occident go up in smoke, so to speak, so that there is only this vague talk of the divine, of a God, or of Gods, all this suits them. But then I wondered why there wasn't an interest in my work. It is because they confused the category of historically effective consciousness with the real content of effective history in the Occident. Thus it was not understood that when I make use of Augustine's trinitarian speculations, (the theme of "verbum"), I am not defending Christian claims, but identifying their categorial significance. Obviously, these kinds of categorial investigations have a particular significance in the face of the instrumentalist understanding of language prevalent in North America. North America is the technologically most advanced society and against this background I can understand your question. At the same time there is a real interest in my work, not merely due to a general openness toward all that is foreign, but because a consciousness of history and of traditions specific to North America is developing. There is a developing historical consciousness in North America among the intellectuals. And the interest in what is other is not always dependent on an experience with a variety of languages, as it is still the case in Europe.

QUESTION. Is hermeneutics primarily concerned with what is old, e.g., literature of the past, or does it also apply to contemporary literature?

GADAMER. It is entrusted with all that is unfamiliar and strikes us as significant. That is why I have written about Celan, one of the most inaccessible poets of world literature. For I was disappointed in what the experts had to say—they gave sentimental, diffuse interpretations. And I thought that here applies what the mathematician Hilbert said about the physicists: "Physics is too difficult for them." I would say that in this sense literature (or philosophy) are too difficult for literary critics and philologists. By the way, 10,000 copies of the little book which I published on Celan *Who Am I and Who Are You?* were printed in Germany. So people must have thought, for once we can understand something. Thus hermeneutics is the art of employing methods where they belong, not where they don't belong. It isn't another doctrine of method.

So, for example, the literary scholar may want to explain a love poem by comparing it to all the love poems which existed at the time. And then he or she may go on to compare these poems to love poems of another period. This certainly is following a scientific procedure. But the poem itself is not understood at all. It has been subsumed under a class concept, that of 'love-poem in general.' Celan once put it beautifully: When a 'stone' is mentioned in a poem, it is, of course, important what can be meant by 'stones'; but what matters in the poem is *this* stone, the one the poem mentions. This is the secret to the capacity for judgment: that one makes something general concrete with respect to the given situation. This is missing in literary criticism and therefore I can see why creative people are upset and feel that their work is used up like cannon-fodder in literary criticism.

QUESTION. Thus hermeneutics is also criticism, e.g., of literary criticism?

GADAMER. I practice this critical attitude. I don't compete with professional students of literature, and I do learn from them. But I also learn from others, e.g., in the case of Celan, and because of the special vocabularies which he uses, I have learned from people who sail, from fishermen, mountaineers. But then, with respect to art: how much knowledge can one really cope with? One still has to be able to make the work one's own. So there are no rules, other than one: only as much knowledge is useful as one is capable of forgetting, that's the measure. As Plato said at the very end of the *Phaedrus:* give me as much gold as a reasonable man can carry. One should not let oneself be deformed by knowledge. That's a crazy way to proceed. But that's what literary criticism does. Thus hermeneutics is a protection against the abuse of method, not against methodicalness in general. In this sense it builds on Socrates, Kant's critique of judgment, and Hegel's critique of the abstract universal.

QUESTION. It appears that you always emphasize the possibility of reaching agreement, that you take an intermediate position between those, on the one hand, who believe in the possibility of rational enlightenment by means of communication and who deny the inescapability of untruth and irrationality, and those, on the other hand, who believe that there is only misunderstanding, thus succumbing to a new irrational skepticism about truth.

GADAMER. I began by objecting to the modernist prejudice that certainty, the possession of criteria, is more important than truth. I objected to this old skeptical argument. I have argued that communication in language is a rhetorical phenomenon, not subject to the rules of logical demonstrability. It is more important to find the words which convince the other than those which can be demonstrated in their truth, once and for all. We can learn this from the Platonic dialogues. Here the one partner in dialogue speaks to the other, having him yield to the truth of what is said. Retrospective examination can, of course, show that these concessions are logically unsatisfactory. But this is something we can do with any speech. Alexander Pfaender already demonstrated in his logic that argumentation does not follow strict rules of logic. Social life depends on our acceptance of everyday speech as trustworthy. We cannot order a taxi without this trust. Thus understanding is the average case, not misunderstanding. And Derrida, for example, when he takes a different view, really is speaking about literature. In literature there is a struggle to bring something to expression beyond what is already accepted.

Chapter 7

ARE THE POETS FALLING SILENT?*

In our society, which is increasingly ruled by anonymous mechanisms and where the word no longer creates direct communication, the question arises: what power and what possibilities can the art of words, poetry, still have? For the poetic word is essentially different from the perishing forms of speaking which otherwise support the communicative event. What is special in all these forms of speaking is the self-forgetting within the words themselves. The word as such always disappears in the face of what the word engenders. The poet Paul Valéry, who must have known, formulated a brilliant metaphor for the difference between words used in spoken communication and the poetic word. The spoken word is like a coin, i.e., it means something that it is not. The gold coin of the past, however, had as well the value which it signified, since the metallic value of the gold coin equaled its value as a coin. So it was itself at the same time what it meant. Clearly, the distinctive character of the poetic word is exactly that it does not refer to something in such a manner that one is directed away from it, in order to arrive somewhere else, as the coin or bill needs its backing. In poetry, when one is directed away from the word, one is also at the same time directed back to it; it is the word itself which guarantees that about which it speaks. That is the experience which we all have with the poetic word. The more intimate one is with poetic conjoining [*Fügung*], the richer in meaning and the more present the word becomes. The distinctive characteristic of the poetic word lies in the manner in which it presents itself by presenting something.

I wish to ask our age and the literature of our age: Is there still a task for the poet in our civilization? Is there still a time and place for art in an age where social unrest and the discomfort with our social life in an anonymous mass society is felt from all sides and where the demand for rediscovering or reestablishing true solidarities is advanced over and over again? Is it not an escape when one claims art or poetry to still be an integral part of human being? Must not all literature be now *littérature engagée*? And like all committed literature quickly become outdated? Is there still a stable framework in the art of words, when only the constantly changing contents in their instability constitute the center of legitimation for literature in general? Where consciousness is fulfilled by nothing but

---

*Essay first published in 1970.

science, i.e., by the idolatry of scientific progress, does there still exist such a conjoining of words, wherein everyone could be at home?

Without a doubt, the word of the poet in such a time must be different. It will be related to the reporting, casual nature, and dispassionateness of technical language. But is the poetic word thereby truly a reporting? Or can one demonstrate that even today one can still build a lasting image out of words, which is not passé but present and forever? And which, therefore, still permits the "common spirit" to be expressed in a poem? Perhaps the best general characteristic which distinguishes lyrical poetry today is a phrase that Rilke once wrote. He writes in a letter (to Ilse Jahr on Feb. 22, 1923) concerning his relation to God: "There is an indescribable discretion between us." In fact, God is not even mentioned in his later poems, for example in the *Duino Elegies*. There is only mention of the angel, who is, perhaps, more a messenger from humans than from God. Rilke's phrase, "indescribable discretion," describes exactly, it appears to me, the tone of the contemporary lyric poem, about which it is important to become more aware. Two poems to be interpreted here may clarify this discretion and its challenge for us. One is a poem from Paul Celan:

> In den Flüssen nördlich der Zukunft
> werf ich das Netz aus, das Du
> zögernd beschwerst
> mit von Steinen geschriebenen
> Schatten.
>
> In the rivers north of the future
> I cast out the net, that you
> hesitantly weigh down
> with stone-written
> shadows.

One can often doubt, in the case of modern lyrical poetry, whether the division of lines still has a true justification. When one reads long-lined constructions of free rhythm, as in the *Duino Elegies*, this division surely is not convincing. One should remember that in the first edition the lines were typographically longer and the division of lines therefore less frequent. Through the division of lines which the later editions have, one inadvertently accepts a rhythmic form of the text which certainly is incorrect. With Celan, in contrast, there are short lines which constitute a true poetic division of lines. That is especially true for the final verse, which is often only a single word. One could also demonstrate that it nevertheless has a distinct meaning. Here it is the word "shadows." Completely independent of the sentence structure of this poem, what "shadows" means becomes directly present in the word itself. This arduous word always makes present as well that which casts the shadow.

We may now pose the general question: What is being spoken abou, and who is speaking here? Which I casts out the net? The I of the poet? However, in a composition belonging to the lyric genre, it would not be the I of a poet, if it were not to become the I of everyone. And this I is a fisherman. He casts out the net. The casting out of a net is an act of utmost expectation. It is not said when this act of the I is performed, and I think, it can also not be said. For when is this act not performed by an I? What I is not always an I of expectation? Fishing is pure expectation. When a fisherman has laid out his net he can do nothing more than wait. But here, a waiting, an expectation, is evoked in such a manner that the I clearly does not wait for something determinate, on whose appearance one can count; so it is unlike the experienced fisherman who has cast out his net in the proper place in the waters. This becomes quite clear in these lines of the poem. In the rivers north of the future, the fisherman, who is an I, casts out his net. That means: there, where otherwise, no one else fishes. The image evokes the clarity and frigidity of ice cold waters and the sun which shines through the water down to the bottom: it speaks of shadows cast by stones. Just as the casting of the net occurs in an imaginary place and in a gnomic, and so permanent, present—therefore always—so too, the weighting of the net is something which occurs always. The weighting of the net, which permits it to "stand" and thereby promises a catch, is itself also an imaginary act. It is the shadows and not the stones themselves which weigh down this net. In order to make the imaginary nature of this completely clear, the shadows that should weigh down the net are not cast but written by stones. Shadows written by stones: that guides perception and imagination in a particular direction. Written shadows, like anything written, have a readable meaning. And if it is a shadow-text written by stones, then the meaning which is forged in this imaginary space of the word is evidently a burdening, by means of its weight a burdening meaning, and yet a meaning which makes a catch possible. For one must see the image that the poet evokes here entirely sensuously. "Hesitantly weigh down"—what does "hesitantly" mean here? It is not the inner hesitating of indecision or doubt, because possibly you—in a moment we will speak about who the you is—would not share the confidence of the fishing I. It would be a complete misunderstanding, if one were to assign this meaning to the hesitating. Here an actual act is very carefully described. Here the one who weights the net, which is to bring the catch, may not add too much or too little: not too much so that the net would sink, and not too little so that the net would float. The net must—as the fisherman says—"stand." That is the hesitating of the weighting: one must, so to speak, weigh with one's finger tips whether something must still be added or not, in order to achieve the necessary labile equilibrium. The procedure of net fishing is being exactly described. In fact, there must always be two. No one alone can do it. When one carefully adds stone after stone in order to weight the net, as one does in weighing something in a balance by carefully adding one weight after another until the correct moment of equilibrium, then one helps to insure that the catch can succeed at all.

What does it mean that the "I," therefore the human, casts out the net? Now it is clear: No human can look into the future except as always hoping. North of the future—always beyond any justified expectation concerning what comes next—that is how we humans live. That is the principle of hope. However, for the one who wants to catch, who wants to succeed, and to whom should occur that which he hopes, for him the weighting is indispensable. What is to be weighted, is the opened net of expectation. How are expectations weighted? Evidently, by means of the shadow cast by experiences and disappointments, which one brings along. No human hoping can be optimistic, unless one's own hoping is weighted by these shadows. And, it almost appears that someone is there who would know how unfathomably much one can burden a hoping heart without allowing the hope to sink.

Such a transferring of a completely sensuous image into its spiritual meaning allows everything to become somewhat overly explicit. Interpretive words should, however, disappear after they have evoked what they mean. If one reads the poem again, then one should not remember what has been said about it, but rather one should have the impression: there it stands. It is there in the words of the poem and not in what someone has said about it. Interpretation is completed when the interpreter disappears and only what one has interpreted is there—an ideal which understandably is always only achievable in approximation.

Let us examine more carefully the meaning of the balanced tension which is clearly evoked. Two actors are exhibited in their interaction—in two actions: the casting out of the net and the weighting of the net. There is a secret tension between the two actions, and yet they build a unitary activity, the activity which alone promises a catch. Between the freedom and agility of throwing and projecting, and the pull downwards to the boundary, towards the limited, there stretches the opposition, which belongs to success. Here a "pure" expectation is not being clouded by the recognition of boundaries, but rather it is only made actual by this and only becomes in this way a prospect, i.e., the unreal utopia of this projecting, which reaches into the unpredictable, is transformed into an exact and skilled activity.

What is it, however, that is the "catch"? One can call what is so depicted, using today's popular expression, the word-event. For this poem may first be related to itself in that what is to be joyously caught is the poem itself. The poet relates how he, like every poet, casts out his net into the pristine and not yet clouded waters of language—they are like rivers carrying along all sorts of things from unknown mountains—and waits for a successful catch. One should remember Stefan George's penetrating word-poems, in which, for example, he recounts that after each journey he bends over the spring to lift the jewel from its ground. And it is his painful experience that sometimes there is no answer. For the poet, it is always an anxious question whether from the deep spring of human experience, sedimented in language, the radiant word which illuminates all will arise and endure—that is: become a poem, which we repeat until it completely sounds in our inner ear and from whose rhythms we may live for half a life. In a first approach, one can certainly understand these verses from the point of view of the poet and as the expectation of the word which would succeed.

However, what is said here about the poet who hauls in his catch, reaches again far beyond the particular poetic experience. The poet is the archetype of human being. This is one of the powerful central metaphors of modern times. Therefore, the word, which the poet catches and causes to endure, does not mean just that artistic accomplishment through which one becomes or is a poet, but it also represents the essence of possible human experience. This allows the reader to be the I of the poet because the poet is the I which we all are. So, who is here the I and who is the you? Which you is with the I in such a secret unity of accomplishment? It is not the I of the poet alone, and the you is not just some encumbering being, man or God, laying down word shadows confining one's freedom. This poem expresses who the I and you are, here and always: Kierkegaard's "this single individual" who each of us is. Who then is you? To begin, there is a simple and clear answer justified by the grammar: it is the one addressed. The you is the one who is there with the speaking I. Who that is, we are not told by the poem—and just because of this the answer is not left to our interpretive wish. Whether I am myself the you or he is another close person, or the Closest or Furthest, God, is initially not to be determined. It is exactly like the Christian Love Commandment, which also does not offer the alternative: to love your neighbor or God. If I may concern myself here for a moment in the area of theological exegesis where I have no expertise: Also in the Christian Love Commandment, the differentiation between our neighbor and God, or the question of who our neighbor is, is already a misinterpretation of what the commandment states. One must see there, as here, that this you is the you of the I. And that one can first comprehend what is being said when one understands himself to be the one who should always already know, here and now, who the you is: everyone.

Therefore, the poem is an expression of us all. When we have verses, so to speak, present within us, we all, everyone of us, enter into a relationship where each one of us has his part to do for its completion.

One will note here that the you is in a place of emphasis, i.e., at the end of the verse as in a question. It is exactly the question concerning the you: who is it? Only the one who understands the poem to be his own expression has an answer to this. Only an I has a you. The whole is an example that should indicate what discretion is and that in discretion there is also the involvement of the individual. Especially because nothing is being pronounced here in an affected form of language, but one discovers oneself confronted suddenly by a simple expression; one thinks at first, "this is a very trivial sentence," but then one ponders the positioned words in their relationships; and the more these relationships are realized the more one is involved; and finally one knows who the you is, since it has become apparent that the I is I myself. The question is not whether the poets are silent, but whether our ear is acute enough to hear.

In order to reduce the arbitrariness of such a choice of poem and in order to discover a less incidental answer to the posed question, I will present a second example. I choose a poem of Johannes Bobrowski. It is "The Word Man":

> Das Wort Mensch, als Vokabel
> eingeordnet, wohin sie gehört,
> im Duden:
> zwischen Mensa und Menschengedenken.
> Die Stadt
> alt und neu,
> schön belebt, mit Bäumen
> auch
> und Fahrzeugen, hier
>
> hör ich das Wort, die Vokabel
> hör ich hier häufig, ich kann
> aufzählen von wem, ich kann
> anfangen damit.
>
> Wo Liebe nicht ist,
> sprich das Wort nicht aus.
>
> The word human, as a term
> ordered where it belongs
> in the dictionary:
> between cafeteria and human remembrance.
> The city
> old and new,

beautifully enlivened, with trees
also
and vehicles, here

I hear the word, the term
I hear here often, I can
recount from whom, I can
begin with that.

Where love is not,
do not speak the word.

One also perceives this poem to be almost hermetic. What does it actually mean? What kind of unitary statement is there in it? And this is exactly why so many speak of the growing silence of the poets, since they, if I may put it so, are no longer able to listen to the discreet.

Let us begin the interpretation where all interpretations must begin, namely where it first becomes comprehensible to us, and here that is without a doubt in the final stanza. It says something quite clear: Where love is not, do not speak the word. That means—and this must have been realized before—that everywhere where the speaker has heard the word "human," there was no love. Now everything becomes clear. The first stanza is full of bitter sarcasm and an almost acidic acuteness. It may be true that the term "Mensch" [human] is between "Mensa" [cafeteria] and "Menschengedenken" [human remembrance] and that the poet once noticed this by chance while using a dictionary—that the word just before was cafeteria and just after was human remembrance. But when he says this in a poem, it is purposeful. The word "cafeteria," well-known to young people, means a place where one feels probably most strongly the anonymity of life and the lack of relationship after leaving the family. The cafeteria somehow recalls continually to memory what the family is, so to speak, by way of privation. The word which follows is "human remembrance," a word which we now use in only one phrase: "as long as anyone can remember." What this phrase evokes is something almost no longer having truth—it has been that way as long as anyone can remember. Concerning this, one does not have the possibility of justification. When one says, "it has been that way as long as anyone can remember," this will be treated as something which has become completely self-evident. Therefore, on one side, we have what is anonymous, on the other side what has become obvious, and between these two extremes is the term human, as if trapped.

The second stanza concerns the city: "old and new." Anyone who listens, knows immediately: this was written after the war which devastated our cities. "Old and new" clearly means this tension which penetrates the image of our cities. "Old and new" is perhaps intended even more universally and portrays not only what has been revitalized after its devastation and destruction. For the third verse "beautifully enlivened, with trees" leads one to the wonderful, monosyllabic "also" which constitutes a complete verse and thereby obtains an unusual weight. What sounds like an added treasure: "also trees," attests to the complete misery of life in the cities. Trees are certainly also there, but what constitutes a city is its traffic, the vehicles. Therefore, this "also" becomes a moving expression for the hastened destruction of nature which we experience in the streets of our cities. This "also" is an emphatic example of true poetic discretion.

And then, in the series of words "here / I hear the word," the "here" also receives special emphasis. It is at the end of not only the verse but also the stanza and therefore is a so-called enjambment. That means the thought continues and the conclusion of the stanza is not deformed by the enjambment nor does the verse itself become inaudible, as the amateur thinks. Such a false appearance arises simply out the obsession to deny the verse as a verse. That surely sounds like very trivial prose when one reads "here I hear the word," i.e., here in the city. But one must listen to the "here" all by itself! The enjambment allows the verse and the break in the stanza to be clearly observed. Since the sentence continues and yet there is a metric break, the "here" receives, as it were, a rhythmic exclamation point. "Here" means then: just there where right from the beginning it is doubtful that man can still converse and interact as man with men. One often hears the word—in order to make unmistakable the unreality of such talk about humans, the text continues as if a correction: "the term I hear here often." The change of expression from word to term implies that with such a use of words one is concerned not with the topic [Sache] but merely a word, which has been torn from its real use and no longer has any life. Not matter how often it is said, it is an empty term.

Now comes the part in the whole poem which is most difficult for me: "I can recount from whom / I can begin with that." The first part is easy. One hears it everywhere, and so I can recount from whom. Here, here, here; everyone says it continuously. I hear it continuously. But what does the remainder mean: "I can begin with that"? That is peculiar. If I can recount from whom, then I can of course begin with that. What then does the verse mean? "I can begin with that" appears to imply a similar restriction as the "also" above. Everyone uses the term. It is senseless to enumerate all of them. I would get stuck—that lies in the limiting "I can begin with that." However, I would get stuck not only because there are too many, but also because it would soon become clear to me that there is no sense in counting how many use the dead word without it becoming alive.

The final stanza demonstrates that this is correctly interpreted and that this part is, as it were, the turning point of the whole. For now it is explicitly stated, as in the failure of the counting search and like a reprimand: "Where love is not, do not speak the word." That seals, as it were, the meaning of the whole: The word "man" should not be just a term. There is no exclamation point after this poem. Accepted punctuation will miss it, for it is certainly an imperative! But that is exactly the discretion with which today's poets speak.

Both examples are to have made clear why I believe that it is false that the poets are becoming silent. They have necessarily become quieter. As discreet messages are spoken quietly so that an unintended person cannot overhear them, so has the poet's voice become. He shares something with the one who has an ear for it and who is sympathetic. He whispers something to him in his ear and the reader, who is all ears, nods finally. He has understood. Therefore, I believe that for the poetry of our time one can verify, in the same way as always before, Hölderlin's statement "the thoughts of our common spirit are completed quietly in the soul of the poet." One, who allows oneself to be reached by their word, accomplishes thereby a verification. One certainly also understands that, in an epoch of the electronically amplified voice, only the quietest word still confirms the communality and therefore, the humanity, which you and I find in the word. What is required for the quiet word, for the speaker as well as for the listener, we know. It is similar to the slow passages in a symphony—in them the true mastery of the composer and conductor is best demonstrated. And who will determine which experiences of skillfulness reach out from the life of technical civilization into these word constructions and are captured in them, so that we are able to suddenly meet and welcome, in this our house, the powerful foreignness of the modern world as something familiar?

Chapter 8

THE VERSE AND THE WHOLE*

With hesitation I stand before you. I wonder about my qualifications and I wonder about the possibilities of analysis which one who has devoted himself to the art of concepts has in facing a poetic work. I also wonder what I should say at all after a number of introductory remarks in which the tone and echo of the intellectual reality and effect of the poet Stefan George was to be heard.

Nevertheless a kind of qualification may exist in the desire for justification, which is—I believe—especially incumbent upon the so-called philosopher. Justification, *logon didonai*, is the old Socratic requirement which no thinker can completely escape. And it is, I believe, such a desire for justification which gathers us all together here. Our gathering does not signify a following in the sense of developing a community or founding a church nor does it concern establishing a political organization. As an individual speaking to you I am one of many, who since their youth have been a witness to the fascination which has emanated from this poet and his poetry. We have also witnessed the provocation with which this poet confronted the consciousness of the era by means of a conscious separation from and through a radical critique of the ideals of modern mass society.

Now justification is always conditioned by its own time and its future. We already know the various changes in evaluation which have occurred to great intellectual and influential persons: consider the time between the nineteenth century and today, the last quarter of the twentieth century, and examine the changing constellations which, for example, Schiller and Geothe exhibited: How Schiller led the way by lending his voice to the patriotic feelings of the developing German national state; how Goethe's broad and encompassing influence was first made possible at the end of the nineteenth century due to its liberal ideals; or how Hölderlin advanced from a *poeta minor* of the Romantic period to a true classical figure in our century. Reciprocally we see countless figures of central and influential importance becoming controversial or of lesser esteem. And even among the greatest preferences shift. For example, think of Richard Wagner as opposed to Verdi or of Beethoven as opposed to Bach. Living tensions express themselves in such comparisons. Or—to approach our

---

*Address to the Stefan George Seminar in Bingen, 1978.

theme more closely—think about the surprising renaissance of *Jugendstil* in our day. The young Stefan George took part in this as he was developing his own style. Stefan George and his work have certainly not yet received in the public consciousness of our time a corresponding new attention as *Jugendstil* has. The opportunity that brings us together here was not created without a consciousness of this circumstance. One must expect that the old familiar provocation, which Stefan George hurled against mass society, awakens a new resonance in us today—in all of us without regard to age, conviction or political disposition. For, in all of us, the idea begins to awaken that nature and environment are more than a field for exploitation and transformation into a single, monstrous industrial enterprise; that our human, social, working environment must care much more about reintegration into the greater totality which supports and nurtures us. Therefore it could be that the prophecies of a poet like Stefan George slowly disengage themselves from the short-sighted applications which they have been given in the last decades and that they demonstrate their true value as a gauge that can measure with criteria which are just as true for the future as for the past.

The theme "the verse and the whole" to which I would like to draw your attention, is to be understood in this broad and radical sense. It points to a question, which basically encompasses three questions. These I would like to discuss and shed light on one after the other.

It concerns the questions:

"What is the way from the verse to the whole,"

"What is the separation of the verse from the whole" and,

"How, finally, is the whole in the verse to be comprehended"?

The first of these questions is well known to every scholar of Stefan George's poetic work and life achievement: the way from the verse to the whole.

When Stefan George appeared for the first time to a limited public with the series *Blätter für die Kunst*, he articulated in his preface the guiding theme, saying that these pages of art wish to serve especially poetry and literature "excluding everything political and social." He explicitly called it a spiritual [*geistige*] art, an art for art's sake. Now, the essence of poetry is most certainly not only a protected preserve within society which should serve cultural self-satisfaction. The essence of poetry rises always somehow out of the spoken language and finds its echo in the ears and souls of all who can listen. Another word from our poet may already anticipate how beginning with poetry may lead to the whole. The sentence states: "The essence of poetry as well as the dream: that I and You * Here and There * Once and Now endure next to each other and become one and the same." This word speaks from the end of the nineteenth century; it speaks into the beginning of this century, in the time before the First World War. Suddenly, "Once and Now" also slide very close together for us, i.e., this time before the First World War and our time, which—as we hope—will not someday be called the time before the Third World War. Times draw together and in this unified time there stand then, for example, the poems of the *Stern des Bundes* [*The Star of the Covenant*] with their prophetic intensity. There one encounters a poem such as this from which I will quote a few verses:

> Und an der weisheit end ruft ihr zum himmel:
> "Was tun eh wir im eignen schutt ersticken
> Eh eignens spukgebild das hirn uns zehrt?"
> Der lacht: zu spät für stillstand und arznei!

> And at wisdom's end you cry to heaven;
> "What to do before we suffocate in our own waste
> Before our own ghostly image consumes our mind?"
> He laughs: too late for halt, and medication!

And then come the three famous verses:

> Zehntausend muss der heilige wahnsinn schlagen
> Zehntausend muss die heilige seuche raffen
> Zehntausende der heilige krieg.

> Ten thousand must be defeated by holy insanity
> Ten thousand must be taken by the holy plague
> Tens of thousands by the holy war.

What a distance from "excluding-of-everything-political-and-social" to these verses. George asked himself how to bridge this distance and how a justification of his own activity can arise from it. The actual theme of my present discussion is summoned forth in the great poem of *The Star of the Covenant* where one reads:

> "DA DEIN GEWITTER O DONNRER DIE WOLKEN ZERREISST
> Dein sturmwind unheil weht und die vesten erschüttert
> Ist da nicht nach klängen zu suchen ein frevles bemühn?"
> "Die hehre harfe und selbst die geschmeidige leier
> Sagt meinen willen durch steigend und stürzende zeit
> Sagt was unwandelbar ist in der ordnung der sterne.
> Und diesen spruch verschliesse für dich: dass auf erden
> Kein herzog kein heiland wird der mit erstem hauch
> Nicht saugt eine luft erfüllt mit profeten-musik
> Dem um die wiege nicht zittert ein heldengesang."

"SINCE YOUR STORM, OH THUNDERER, TEARS APART THE CLOUDS
Your storm wind wreaks havoc and shakes the fortresses
Is it not an unblest task to search for verses?"
"The sublime harp and even the supple lyre
Tells my will through advancing and falling times
Tells what is unchangeable in the cosmic order.
And secure this saying for yourself: that on earth
No prince, no savior will be who with first breath
Will not draw in an air filled with prophetic music
About whose cradle will not vibrate a hero's song."

The question arises by itself: Could the poet—who so strongly insisted on always remaining the poet and who, even when he was the master for so many, wished always to be it as the poet—wish to reawaken through poetizing what this time so missed, e.g., the heroic epic? George resolutely saw the poet above all, even in his friends, even in men of great scientific talent like Friedrich Gundolf. And he addressed them accordingly. Education was for him educating toward poetizing. In the much criticized molding and instructing of his young friends concerning his own superb style of composition, education was to be through poetry and the reading of poems. Further, it strove to reawaken and strengthen— quoting George—the "ability to dream." The cult of Maximin, the new myth of the George circle, was finally to serve the awakening of the ability to dream. As a memorial cult and through the living memory of a meaningful human experience for the poet, it was to unite a group of humans and fill them with a new spirit.

Let us ask ourselves: How can this path of a poet be taken as a path to the whole, when the whole is so different and so alienated from the verse, as was the case in George's youth and as is especially the case in our time. Let us ask first: how did the separation of the verse from the whole occur? Can poetry express something other than the thoughts of the common spirit? Poetry is the retelling [*Weitersagen*] of the myth. A myth is a 'Saga' requiring no attestation. But where in our unromantic world is such a saga requiring no attestation? I call our world unromantic and thereby use an expression which already carries a particular accent since German Romanticism differentiated between the Classical and the Romantic. At this point I must recall Hegel, that great thinker of the Romantic period. For everyone today, Hegel forms one of the pertinent strands in one's spiritual and linguistic web of rational justification, even if one does not know it. It concerns the famous teaching, which is less a teaching than an ascertainment, which Hegel termed the past character of art. This means that art is no longer the highest form of spirit, but rather belongs as a whole to the past. Without a doubt this means that the unity of sensible appearance and the reality of the divine was unquestionably present in classical Greek culture. We, however, no longer bow down before these powerful sculptures of the Greek gods, even when we honor and admire them as the highest expressions of human creativity. For us, they are no longer united with our own being and desires. In addition to sculpture, where it is most visible, the same applies to the evocation of the divine in poetry—in the epic, the tragedy, and finally also in the Platonic myth of souls as well as the Aristotelian or Stoic world-god. They are themselves still like final sensuous appearances of the nonsensuous. With Hölderlin's "Bread and Wine" we think in this sense of Christ himself as the last God who was present in the sensuous-experienceable world and reality. And we see in him the parting of the last God, the departing God. Christianity, however, led to the demythologizing of this world. It replaced the worldly appearing of the divine by another message from the divine. Its essence is the Transcendent which, as worshiping-in-spirit-and-in-the-truth, became the new Christian attitude toward the divine. Everything which then appears during the Christian Era, for example in art or in Christian poetry—recall the great Christian epics of Dante or Milton—everything which has come together in the magnificent humanistic-Christian unity, which we call the Western tradition of our culture, presents a type of first pastness measured against the unity of the classical sketched above. What has passed away is not art but rather its religious immediacy. It is experienced as 'art' precisely because it lost its religious immediacy, and because the authority for intellectual comprehension, which the Christian message had once claimed for itself, was now also claimed with reference to the perceptual nature of all artistic creation. Hegel meant the whole Christian Era.

However, we feel at the same time that Hegel makes us aware in his teaching of something else and something very specific, which we cannot deny: at the end of the eighteenth century a second pastness for art begins. What occurred was the dissolution of the mythical tradition as bound by Greek-Christian thought, wherein art had lived. What follows is like a free echo of this mythical tradition. When Goethe, in his *West-östlicher Diwan*, indulges in Eastern characters; when Hölderlin teaches us to see, by means of the unprecedented intensity of his prophetic vision, the secret code of our native landscape as the presence of the divine; when Kleist invokes the God of inner feelings; when Immermann, in a crazed and materialistic world, praises the chiliastic expectation for salvation; when Mörike plays his youthful myth of "Orplid my Land," whose song we recognize as the Weyla's Song in Hugo Wolf's rendition; when then—more dubiously—the German Middle Ages or German Prehistory return, for example, in Hebbel's Nibelungen drama or in Richard Wagner's colossal musical phantasies for theater; when very remote characters are evoked as Zarathustra is in Nietzsche's thought; and, finally, when Stefan George invokes the tone of the mythical in the Maximin cult in order to preserve in memory and to unite his friends in memory—what is appealed to in all such invocations of the mythical, is no longer the whole, is no longer the church, and is no longer the knowledge of a whole people. It is a type of playful variation of what was once obligatory. The religious vocabulary still transmits the eschatological atmosphere and an expectation which deeply influences the political and social. But all this is clearly only—no matter how positively it is evaluated—the capturing and preserving of an echo.

And yet poetry remains always a recitation of the truth. This appears to me to be the other side of the development just presented. The disintegration of the unity of verse and whole does not prohibit that something pervades our own spiritual and human totality as an event of tradition, i.e., as an event of continual reawakening and reappropriating. This does not concern the question of aesthetic irresponsibility or historical relativising, as one has become accustomed to think in the age of a dogmatic belief in science. Rather it is as George's preface states: The essence of poetry, as that of the dream, is that "I and You * Here and There * Once and Now" become one and the same. What occurs in human being through the event of tradition is a continual reacquisition. This is not that diffusion and distancing caused by a continually changing light wherein the values of a culture split apart, as Nietzsche sensed in the historicism of his day. Something else is happening here. Thus I come to the highest legitimation which we are able to claim for ourselves in our time—Plato has presented it in the *Symposium*. There Diotima instructs Socrates that Eros, the entrancing universal power of love, should not be praised as the quintessence of the beautiful but rather as the demonic being who everywhere aims at procreation with the beautiful. We are this Being-outside-of-ourselves. In this way Plato informs us with a decisiveness—which, it appears to me, we are always again forgetting—that the human essence and knowledge come to be realized only through practice, through *meletán*: only through always new creation, continual reacquisition, continual renewing, or continual re-creating does the stable come to be. The Greek expression for the retention of memory, *mnéme*, connoted for the Greeks perhaps something from *ménein*, from remaining, from becoming stable. In any case, *memoria* has for us the important sense of the inner treasure houses of our soul, which Augustine first expressed. However, Plato says this process of reacquisition, i.e., this continuing new procreation, is the way, *mechané*, mortals participate in immortality. Everything living, including the human race, is able to preserve itself only through physical propagation. But there are also humans who procreate in souls. Of these Diotima lists first the poets and all other humans who we call creative, including the great lawmakers; she lists Homer, Hesiod, Lycurgus and Solon. They all renew the whole.

It should have become clear, how what could have appeared as simply an echo of a previously immediate and religiously formed culture is, in truth, a continuing and essential human task, i.e., an essential possibility of humans. Therefore, in the end, the separation of the verse from the whole is superseded and it becomes possible to recognize especially the whole in the verse. *Mnemosyne* rules everything: to keep in memory means to be human. We are taught this, as well, by the religious tradition of all peoples and by the innumerable graveyards and grave finds which return to us from prehistoric time. *Mnemosyne* rules especially in poetry. *Mnemosyne* is the basis of all epic poetry, which has been passed on to us through the activity of the rhapsodists, who conveyed our oldest epic literature. And we realize today, due to American research in the 1930s in the Balkans, that even in our civilizations there was, and perhaps even today is, an oral epic tradition based solely on *memoria*, on memory.

Nevertheless, it is true that this important possibility of a natural way of living in remembrance of one's own tradition comes to an end with the second past—about which I spoke with reference to Hegel. No epic, nor drama, which we count as literature, is any longer a true allusion, i.e., a continual replaying of the mythical tone in which tradition resounds. What reaches us is only a multiply shattered echo. The epic of today, the sociological novel, expresses already in its name who its hero is and that no one is a hero any longer. Inasmuch as theater and opera are not just an echo, the same applies. Nevertheless, these literary forms of narrative or dramatic prose still have their place in the history of literary genre. This decomposition of poetry corresponds to the new subject matter which is depicted. So it must also be seen as a consequence that the narrative content in lyrical poetry is reduced more and more. In the end, its pure lyrical power is proven not by transmitting a mythical inheritance but by creating its own mythopoetic incantation. One calls this symbolism. Thereby lyrical poetry fulfills the full law of its genre, i.e., to be a whole of sound and meaning which does not tell us a saga but does tell us how we are. The lyric is its own saga. It resonates of itself and becomes the dominant form of poetry in our time, far from the mythic. Therefore, in spite of all insistence upon the choral forms of poetic expression, we discover in the poet Stefan George that the lyrical is in the foreground.

I would like to support this possibility of capturing and retaining the whole in the poetic word with a few philosophical reflections, familiar to all of us. One should not be too frightened by the word philosophy. It means that thinking justification which each one of us requires of himself. The only difficulty is to find communicatively effective words which would satisfy everyone's endowment for justification. And this brings the philosophers their difficulty and disrepute.

Let me now ask, what is it that makes something which is nothing more than a linguistic construction, a poem, so important to us? What is language? According to the great teacher Aristotle, whom George had also given that name, it is the distinguishing characteristic of humans that they have language. Language and the use of tools differentiate humans from other animals. However, for humans language is more than just a tool or just a sign system for the purpose of communication. In the meantime, we know a little about animal languages, as we commonly call them. We observe that dolphins have their own means of communication, without being able to understand them. We know something about the language of bees. Also Morse code is just a means of communication and nothing else. But the possibilities which language allows us humans, the possibilities of language which we all use, surpass the possibilities of a tool and the use of tools. Language signifies memory. *Mnemosyne* is, however, the mother of all the muses and so the patron of art. Art—whether picture, word, sound, song, or whatever its origin was or its present social function may be—means, in the final analysis, a way of confronting ourselves in which we become mindful of ourselves. In word as in picture, in petroglyph as in the song, and still in the refined and mediated forms of later literature, the world as a whole—the whole of our world experience—has become present. And even the most silent forms of modern painting, which radiate a brooding silence, evoke in us the "you are that." Such an experience of the whole, in which we confront ourselves, occurs through the continual new-awakening of the echoing of art. In this lies the actual distinguishing characteristic of humans. Philosophers express the fundamental situation of finitude by transforming into concepts the old Platonic teaching concerning human 'immortality,' to which I have referred. This finitude determines us so completely because it is our distinguishing characteristic to know about it. It constitutes our essential futurity. We live inasmuch as we orient ourselves to our future in expectation and hope. In our daily activity and inactivity and, above all, in our work, we continually forgo our desires. We do not seek direct satisfaction of desires, instead we work.

On the other hand, however, this human state of having-been-forced-out of the living creation bounded by nature, implies a continual task of return and self-communion. But, the return to ourselves is always a return to what we have been allotted, i.e., a return to the whole in which we are and who we ourselves are. The most profound symbol for this fundamental human task is perhaps *nómos*. A generation who is losing itself in its belief in progress must always and again be reminded of this. *Nómos* is not just law and man-made order. *Nómos* is the allotted

[*Zugeteilte*], the measure [*Maß*]. To know about it is human. Not least the poem teaches one to accept it. So, in the *Blättern* George quotes the poet Verwey who once wrote: "Only when the movement of life becomes measured in words, does it attain its highest power." Therefore, I think it understandable that poetic reading and speaking were the appropriate form of education used by the master' Stefan George in relating to his followers. Poetic reading is more than an ability or an art. It is learning how to submit to the measure [*Maß*] which gives freedom. It is the "Christ dancing." The natural and thorough rhythmization, which the reading of a poetic creation demands and transmits, articulates, and orders not only the recitation but also the breathing of the speaker. One acquires an experience of the whole and of ourselves in the whole. For in the verse, in the gliding, and if I may put it so, in the gracefully dancing self-movement of the verse, there presides a Resting-in-oneself. From every direction a return occurs. The verse participates in the roundness of all creations and is like a circle, that good infinity about which Hegel speaks and which he opposes to the bad infinity of an unbounded movement and of the continual self-over-reaching-of-oneself. This good infinity is the whole. In as much as the verse and art are themselves such a whole, they incorporate us in themselves. They are, philosophically speaking, reflections in themselves. We are ourselves encompassed by the whole, which we are and which is in us; but not encompassed in such a manner that the whole would be present for us as the whole. We encounter it rather as the totality and the vastness, wherein everything is, only through adhering to what has been allotted us, i.e., the *nómos*, whatever it may be. Our civilization will have to learn this again. However, a step on this path of learning is living in poetry. It is more than a kind of exercise in relaxation, occurring within the helter-skelter and pressures of our performance-oriented life. Living in poetry is rather one of the ways through which we experience being moved within ourselves. In this only are humans able to find their self-fulfillment. Our education will again have to return to and acknowledge what inner value is and what living in poetry means, and certainly also what for the devout living in prayer means and what for all of us living in the unutterable word means. It is the rediscovery of the abundance which *memoria* is able to grant to human life. *Memoria* is preserving [*Bewahren*]—not external orders or institutions, but all of what we are. Preserving is not an unquestioning clinging to what is. In the end, we have to learn from Plato that we must continually renew what we hold to be true. The poem of a poet does not permit us a superior-critical judgement. Critique means, in reference to a poem, to acknowledge it as such and to allow it to be true. It depends on us to preserve it. Preservation is certainly always and finally the authentic manner in which the true can be for us humans.

Chapter 9

HÖLDERLIN AND GEORGE*

The theme "Hölderlin and George" is not an ordinary comparison where the particularity of one poet is to be contrasted to the other, but rather a truly historical theme. In a surprising manner Hölderlin and George have achieved a true contemporaneity in our century. Certainly Hölderlin's poetic work was already known and prized a century earlier by the generation of romantic poets. However, the Romantic reception of his poetry placed him in a context where the understanding of his works was determined by Romantic criteria. As the interest in Hölderlin's poetic work came alive in the beginning of this century, it was a true event when the late work of the poet became available for the first time through a new critical edition—as always, and in this case as well, a constellation of the literary present was decisive—namely the desire to oppose the ruling naturalism with a new sense of style. It was like the rediscovery of a lost work, no, it was like the discovery of an unknown poet, when Norbert von Hellingrath, who was preparing a dissertation at the University of Munich on Hölderlin's Pindar translations, examined the manuscripts in Munich, Stuttgart, and Homburg, and compiled in their totality the great hymns from Hölderlin's late period, of which only parts had previously been known.

The particular access which the classical philologist Norbert von Hellingrath found to the poet was therefore important. It was through Pindar. At that time the work of classical philology had placed the poetic form of Pindar's victory odes in a new light, which also provided a new perspective for the poetic style of the later Hölderlin. Pindar had long been recognized as an important example of poetic freedom, especially after Goethe, under the influence of Herder, had chosen Pindar as his model and had refined the form of free rhythm through his own significant poetic creations. That one saw in Pindar the ecstatic poet of exceptional hymns, not bound by strict meters,[1] agreed with the aesthetic theory of genius, which had selected Shakespeare to oppose to the rule-aesthetics of French classicism. On the other hand, as heir to a long tradition of philological research, which had in particular clarified Pindar's meter, Norbert von Hellingrath was impressed by Pindar's great artistic sense and the grave formality of his compositions.[2] This opened

---

*Essay, published in the *Hölderlin-Jahrbuch*, 1967–68.

for him a totally new access to Hölderlin's late work, which even in its fragmentary condition attested to a similarly rigorous sense of artistic form. What one had earlier viewed in these late creations of Hölderlin as a sign of decay, mental disintegration and dissolving intelligibility, were now, suddenly, discovered to have a stringent compositional structure. This structure in his completed pieces was constituted by a binding precision of stanza structure and parallelism. It had nothing to do with the flow of free rhythm which Klopstock, Herder, and Goethe had promoted. Using this contemporary sense of form, Hellingrath came to see what he, along with Dionysius of Halicarnassus, called 'austere conjoining' [harte Fügung] of words. This he encountered in Pindar's as well as in Hölderlin's poetry.

Moreover, he also encountered the same stylistic ideal in the later works of a contemporary poet, Stefan George—especially in the poems of *The Seventh Ring*. In this way the philologist and editor of Hölderlin was able to empathize more and more with the poetry of Stefan George, becoming deeply affected by the personal power of Stefan George. This is clearly expressed in his correspondence with his teacher Friedrich von der Leyen. In 1907, before this change occurred, Hellingrath wrote in a seminar paper that George was primarily a technician and, therefore, an ideal translator since he was an artist with words although not a poet. Further, in a kind of dispassionate admiration for George, he emphasized the grand gesture, mask and stilted formality (*cothurnus*) of his poetry and called him cold and unmoved. However, only a few years later, on May 7, 1910, he wrote to Friedrich von der Leyen,[3] "and so at present, I certainly associate my next hopes for the future of the world with the name Stefan George." He reports how he was moved by the later work of George to overcome his aversion to the earlier works and how he learned to appreciate the important development of George "from the aristocratic decadence, aestheticism, and self-assured pose of Mallarmé, to the almost awkward greatness of today's Pindar-like austere purity."[4] Without a doubt this recognition awarded to Stefan George was decisive for Hellingrath's Hölderlin interpretation and his enthusiasm for the poet, even if this does not mean that he had joined George's "circle." It was decisive, not in the sense of George influencing Hellingrath's discovery of Hölderlin, but certainly in the sense of confirming what Hellingrath saw in Hölderlin through a contemporary poet and in the sense of encouraging the recognition of Hölderlin's poetic vision in its religious significance.

In this context the decisive question may be posed. Hellingrath's correspondence clearly demonstrates that he also affirmed the Maximin cult, which had been dedicated in the circle around Stefan George to his deceased young friend. He writes: "The fundamental fact demonstrates

that it concerned not a literary, etc., but rather a religious movement."
Further he sees a Protestant narrowness in the refusal "to take the matter
at issue here beyond literature."

So it appears that Hellingrath completely follows the religious interpretation, which Stefan George had programmatically established in his
prose hymn to Friedrich Hölderlin. This is a short essay which became
known to a broader public just after the First World War when it was
published in the eleventh and twelfth issues of the *Blätter für die Kunst*.
There George sees Hölderlin as the great seer for his people, who suddenly, as in a miracle, stands before us. George praises him as the pro-
claimer of a new God. In this hymn George emphasized Hölderlin's
unique stature and especially that he ought not to be confused with the
romantic movement of German poetry. Instead, he saw in Hölderlin a
kind of anticipation of Nietzsche's discovery of the Dionysian under-
ground of Apollinian Greek culture and also his discovery of the stream of
secret Orphic religious tradition in the background of Homeric religion.
"He alone was the discoverer," is written there, and this means: it was not
Nietzsche, raving in insanity and despair, but the great poet who invoked
the return of the Gods in his patriotic odes. It was the poet who had seen
the religious darkness behind the Apollinian clarity and thereby overcame
the classicist image of Greece. No matter how controversial the question
of Hölderlin's religious intentions is and may remain—as is also the case
with Stefan George himself—one point which George had programmatically predicted has completely come to pass: Hölderlin has been elevated
to one of the very great poets of the German language. No one would now
relegate him to the Romantic school. George prefaced his essay with a few
selected pieces from Hölderlin's poems which were only a few verses from
very different hymns. This selection announced, as well, the perspective
from which George would celebrate Hölderlin. It is the eschatological
mood, the hope for an appearing and the suffering due to the not-yet-
appearing of the gods, which speak in all these verses. It is clear enough
that George claims Hölderlin's poetry as a kind of harbinger for the
prophecy of a new god, which he himself honored in the "spirit of the
sacred youth" of his people.

The crucial volume of Hellingrath's edition, containing the late work,
appeared just before the First World War. The 1914 preface presents the
perspective through which Hellingrath examines Hölderlin's work. It is
peculiarly hesitant, when one compares it to the statements in the 1910
correspondence. Further, it is reported that George dismissed it because
of its half-heartedness.[5] Hellingrath, to be sure, presents in his preface—
in the same tone as George in his hymn—a religious interpretation: "the
great hymns were understood by the poet himself as the word of God."
However, he differentiates the patriotic turning in Hölderlin's late work

not only from the Romantics' nationalistic withdrawal from the classical model but also from the "re-paganizing endeavors which are essentially just a renunciation of our Christian past." Thus, the claim to a religious prophecy is also restricted here. Hellingrath writes, "And here as well the prophesying itself is the warrant for the prophecy. The resounding and sincere words about life and the return of the heavenly ones, prove something almost unbelievable: that in our time a childlike true belief can still call the gods down...."

Here it is important to examine exactly what Hellingrath in fact meant by this—and perhaps also to examine what George actually did with his Maximin cult. What does 'the religious' mean here? It appears that Hellingrath knew very well what separates forever the poet from the actual cult founder. But he knew this in the sense that he did not want to know about it. And he concentrated completely on the inner affinity of the artist to the religious movement. He wrote, "Since quite possibly the cultic, or a tendency toward it, is an integral element of religion, I believe that the artist, who has given himself form and thus has become a model, may be more directly the bearer of a religious movement in its complete realization: Klopstock, Hölderlin, Marées, George." A highly instructive list. To begin, it is clear what the painter is doing on the list. Hans von Marées, the painter, was known to Hellingrath through the beautiful examples of his art in the former Munich state gallery. He was a friend from the circle of Konrad Fiedler and Adolf von Hildebrand. His work breathed an exceptionally bold and glowing classicism. His canvases invoked a heroic world of classical-Hellenistic as well as Christian forms and scenes in monumental compositions, some as triptyches. One may ask whether the painter of the *Neapolitan Rower* or the *Evening Forest Scene* may truly be seen as the transmitter of a religious movement. However it appears to me, the same is true for the other names on the list: Kloptstock, Hölderlin, and even George. Is it true, as Hellingrath's context suggests, that the path or movement toward the cultic was prepared for in the poetic form? Is this true for Klopstock? Is it true for Hölderlin? Is it true for George?

What these poets have in common, it appears to me, is the legacy of Pindar: the hymn. The literary genre of the hymn, however, is a form of its own. The hymn serves exclusively to praise the gods and heroes (whereby heroes in its Greek meaning must be understood as deified men). The hymn is not a poem of honor. The Greeks carefully distinguished between honor [*Lob*] and praise [*Preisung*] (*Makarismos*) as well as between a poem of honor and a hymn. And correctly so. In the final analysis honor presupposes an equality with the one honored. Not anyone is permitted to honor another. For he who honors cannot avoid setting himself as an equal. On the other hand, praising and so the hymn, which is its art form, presupposes the recognition of something completely higher, something which surpasses oneself and whose presence fulfills one. This reflects a scale of attitudes which run from acknowledgement and admiration through veneration [*Verehrung*]—a word we have completely worn out—to worship of something holy. That is Greek religion. The hymn is the art form corresponding to it. We can now see how this poetic form achieves an incomparable completion in the late work of Hölderlin, and we then understand what is thereby implied: not only is a literary form—which remains directly connected to Greek religious life—used and transformed in an exceptional manner by a modern poet, but here also the experience of something higher made this literary form possible and necessary.

What was this higher? Let us ask this question with respect to Hölderlin in order to then answer the respective question for George. Hölderlin encountered the higher in the forced departure from Diotima, a separation which destroyed a living happiness. It was the experience of the divine as present in its own withdrawal which brought the new tone to Hölderlin's poetry. And our century stood before this as before something totally new. It is important that it was the experience of departure which made the poet certain of the Being of the divine. Hölderlin's poetic tone was basically changed by the 'divinity' of love, which had become an experience for him.

Hölderlin's poetry acquired now the tone of naming, i.e., the invocation of what is. He no longer used the rhetorical-allegorical ornament of poetic speech as he had previously, following Schiller. Hölderlin wrote many poems after the separation from Diotima in which he expresses how song became a 'sanctuary' for the homeless and uprooted—the real shelter from the emptiness and coldness of a world without love.[6] What he develops in his poetic work is not a new religious prophecy legitimated by a divine revelation, but rather an interpretation of what exists and the world resulting from his knowledge of the gods' *withdrawal*. What exists are 'the angels of the fatherland,' which the later hymns treat. These hymns too praise the transcendent, invoke witnesses and interpret signs and messages, all of which attest to the Being of the divine. "Of divinity we surely received much."[7] The new grand tone that Hölderlin finds brings him close to Pindar's tone, which invokes what is well-known as the living part of a cult. Assuredly there is an austere conjoining (of words) here, but beyond that there is an innermost and fervent stammering, which knows its own insufficiency with touching resignation.

Hellingrath is correct, and there can be no ambiguity about this, when he calls "prophesying itself the warrant for the prophesy." Language and what the poet accomplishes in his language certify a common reality which requires no further legitimation. If one looks more carefully, however, one will recognize that Hellingrath treats the acknowledgment of the poetic in his preface, as well as in his correspondence and last lectures, as only a minimal demand, which even a sceptical reader of Hölderlin cannot avoid. Hellingrath himself follows George's interpretation when he interprets the warrant for the work to be a promise to the "secret Germany," which reached an inner fulfillment for him in the patriotically charged hour of the Great War.

It can also not be overlooked that Hellingrath is filled by a kind of salvational certainty. In his last lectures he alludes to the greatest living being, who is clearly Stefan George, as to one whose immediate and future presence means fulfillment and salvation and to whom the word of the poet Hölderlin offers a legitimation created by temporal distance. One must grasp that point when one reads the sentence: "Only as a prophet, not—and not even in his most secret thoughts—as the bearer of salvation, in this way Hölderlin stands unknown and hidden among his people."[8] This agrees with George's interpretation of Hölderlin's mission. George's *Lobrede*, which we have already honored, is complimented by the tripartite poem in *The Kingdom Come* which is entitled "Hyperion." There Hyperion, Hölderlin, and George flow together to form a unitary poetic mirroring.

Certainly, one should not fail to recognize that the "master" always saw himself as a poet and seer, and never as kind of savior. No matter how he "portrayed" himself, his actual character was formed by an experience of something higher, similar to the one Hölderlin experienced with Diotima: the encounter with Maximin. The evidence clearly shows that the religious temperament in his work was caused not so much by the enchantment which he experienced in the youth's presence as by the separation and mourning caused by his early death. To that extent the Maximin experience corresponds to Hölderlin's Diotima experience. The analogies are quite clear: Just as Hölderlin, the tutor, torn between thought and song, and distorted by unskilled ambition, was changed by his love for the beautiful wife of his Frankfurt patron, and just as the breathtaking urgency of his hymns grew out of the pain of separation, so too did Stefan George experience a new foundation for his whole endangered existence in the encounter with Maximin. This finds poetic expression in his work, especially in the more austere conjoining of *The Seventh Ring* and *The Star of the Covenant*.

The extent to which the whole of the Maximin cult relied on the departure of Maximin can be seen in George's own verses. The early death of the youth affected George deeply—one suspects that the poet's elevating of the maturing youth to such tremendous heights might have appeared to him to be like a sin. This death inspired him to collect anew his own life in remembrance of his young friend and also to give a new character to the lives of his friends by binding them together in a kind of community of remembrance. This is expressed, for example, in the verses from *The Star of the Covenant:*

> Der sich und allen sich zum opfer gibt
> Und dann die tat mit seinem tod gebiert
> Die tiefste wurzel ruht in ewiger nacht...
> Die ihr mir folgt und fragend mich umringt
> Mehr deutet nicht! ihr habt nur mich durch ihn!
> Ich war verfallen als ich neu gedieh.

> The one who sacrifices himself to every one
> And then births the act with his death
> The deepest root rests in eternal night...
> You who follow me and surround me questioning
> More is not meant! you only have me through him!
> In my decline I flourished yet again.

If one considers Hölderlin's Diotima poems, then one clearly recognizes the difference within the analogy. To begin, one may remark that Hölderlin advanced by means of the Diotima experience to a completely new dimension of poetic speech, which first justified his high poetic rank. In George's poems, on the other hand, the Maximin experience and its poetic form are more a consequence, toward which his life and poetry pointed. The unique tone of his poeticizing, which from the beginning distinguished his work from the contemporary scene, receives thereby only a new accent. Further, one realizes how Hölderlin's new certainty of the presence of the divine lost itself in an overflowing of new visions. He is completely taken with interpreting the nature surrounding him and the past made present in nature, which are for him the holy, and so he himself becomes almost inaudible in "blissful silence." On the other hand, George makes himself and his circle of friends the object of a new poetic self-portrayal. The memorial cult for Maximin, which George established for himself and his friends, is the poetic testament of his own experience. It is his person which he portrays in its own appearance and form as the focal point of life for his group of friends. His poetry ascends to the form of religious self-interpretation and climaxes with the expression:

> Ich bin ein dröhnen nur der heiligen stimme.
> I am only a resounding of the sacred voice.

This most clearly determines the manner of speaking in which George's tone differentiates itself from the hymnical poetry of Hölderlin, i.e., by moving always more forcefully in the direction of the liturgical and the choral. One can formulate the difference in the antithesis of two words.

It is well known that George, who avoided foreign words and above all rejected the foreign thing called recitation, used the expression *Hersagen* (recite) for the reading of poems. Without a doubt the enormous power of edification which emanated from George expressed itself in the exercise of reciting poems. Hölderlin presents the complete antithesis of this.

One cannot recite [*hersagen*] Hölderlin. Hölderlin can only be uttered [*hinsagen*]. He speaks uttering to himself—there is a meditative element in Hölderlin's late poetic language. So one can doubt whether one can read Hölderlin's hymns aloud at all in front of a larger audience. Whoever would do so would perhaps misunderstand in the end the Protestant-meditative element in this lyrical form. On the other hand, it appears to me that George's tone is formed by the Gregorian chant. It is the melody of the chant which gives George's use of language the character of a liturgical activity. These are enormous differences which must have conferred a special tension upon the appropriation of Hölderlin by George.

Therefore, with the great disruption which the death of Maximin brought for George, the assimilation of this experience indicates a change not so much in his poetic tone as in the complete form of his poetic existence. His own life, which he had constructed anew, and the life of his circle, acquired new directions. A turn toward the inner realm began at that time. One can also call it the growing direction of the poet's own energy toward the education of his young friends, which caused, more and more, his poetic creativity to take second place. An intellectual expression for this shift in emphasis has been found by Friedrich Wolters. It can be condensed in the phrase "Rule and Service." The honor of serving and the consecration of ruling were invoked by Friedrich Wolters following the tradition of the Christian Middle Ages. So the 'circle' acquired more and more an institutional charcter. This character was not constituted by empty ceremonies or by ostentatious behavior, such as wearing special clothes, for example. It was constituted rather by a consciousness of being summoned, which filled the members of the circle and granted them awareness of salvation, comparable to a church's means of grace. One must consider this if one is to understand properly the new poetic tone of George's speaking. This speaking is completed only by the response of those addressed, not however, in the sense in which a religious document proper receives its completion through a believing community. For example, the language of The New Testament, which was certain of its community, did not possess the higher type of style that great poetic prose otherwise does. George's late work, on the other hand, is without question of a choice linguistic style. Nevertheless, in George's *The Star of the Covenant*, there is not only a need for completion but also a power toward completion at work. It burgeons within the poetic discourse, but is not completed in it.

One would not be just to George if one were to base the change in his tone in this sense on his religious self-interpretation—where he presents himself as the founder of a new cult. It cannot be denied that *The Star of the Covenant* in particular, because of its overstylization, affects one as cooler and more cramped than the earlier books of poetry. Nor can it be denied that many admirers of his work find *The Year of the Soul* or *The Tapestry of Life* to be the apex of his poetry. But also in the later books of poetry, which seek a cultic tone, there is an enormous artistic ability at work. Although the prophetic gesture and the ceremonial style of the high cothurnus repel some people, this is not because of an esoteric religion which does not reach poetic validity. In these books of poetry we find nothing usually associated with founders of sects, who are able to collect a community around them by means of their oratorical fascination, yet whose literary style—I am thinking, for example, of Rudolf Steiner—makes us shake our heads in puzzlement how such literary texts could hold a community together. George's later poetry is not based on a pre-existent community ritual, as such texts are. Instead it is poetic means that give the poetry its 'cultic' effect, and that awaken a readiness for fulfillment. In a religious community, however, such a readiness does not come from the word, but is brought to the word.

We cannot discuss the different means for community building in George's poetic language.[9] We must be satisfied with a comparison of the language by which Hölderlin and George realize the genre of the hymn, i.e., the celebrating of the higher.

Therefore, it is most important to see how different the presuppositions were which Hölderlin and George encountered...both as artists working with language. Hölderlin began his poetry when German poetic language was still relatively fresh and clean—expecially due to the unique flexibility and naturalness with which Goethe could handle the German language. Therefore, Hölderlin could take this lithe fabric of the German language, let it fall like natural drops, and direct its flow into the most artful cascades without losing its fervent and singing tone. He endeavored to make the enormous freedom, which the German language permits, productive for an art of composition which left all imitation of the classical behind, although it was formed according to the meter and literature of the classical ideal. In George's time, however, artistic convictions predominated which were alien to authentic poetry. At that time, naturalism dominated and completely focused on using words as the speaker's expressions for his character and his emotions. Beyond this, George was also consumed by such a hatred of verse that he permitted verse only as a parenthetic, even unnoticed, support for intense use of language. So George's will to form and will to style had to lead to a purposeful use of language, whose force of will one was certainly supposed to notice. This is not to be measured against a song-ideal of melodic naturalness as in Goethe or the Romantics.

It would be a mistake to see in George's choice of exquisite words and far-fetched images a decorative aestheticism or a cultivation of the strange. The violence of his language is poetically demanded. And it expresses the provocative outsider position which the poet took against the dominating poetic realism and its sense of life. With George, rhyme—a characteristic expression of the time—attains a new presence in the tradition of the French symbolists. He employed the most various linguistic means to tilt the balance of meaning and sound, which all lyric has to preserve, far over toward pure sound composition. Therefore, there is no form of world literature, not even Dante's (which George greatly admired and imitated), which sounded so like his own as did Roman Augustan poetry. Horace especially influenced the "austere conjoining" of his late poetry. Horace's technique of verse composition, especially the use of assonance and the inversion of normal word order, is a model for George to heighten the tension in the verse and to diminish the singsong of the end rhymes. A novel rhythmic and musical lawfulness is set free by means of the vowels, which attain their own life following the model of *poésie pure* and which are commingled into artfully composed assonances. The austere conjoining which Hellingrath speaks of, following Dionysius of Halicarnassus, in order to characterize the style of Pindar and Hölderlin, applies to George as well, even if not in exactly the same sense—because austere conjoining does, in truth, dominate his art of composition. The principle of inversion, which rules Horace's word order, is repeated in George's placement of sounds. Here it creates a similar unity of tension which is also not meant to go unnoticed, but, as in Horace, forces itself into the foreground with increasing awareness. The mature art of George avoids, thereby, direct alliteration and seeks instead to interlace, in a carefully balanced form, the harmony of the consonants and vowels.

For the musicality of George's verse struture, the sentence form is also of particular importance. He avoids the double subordinate clause and prefers above all the short main sentence and simple sentence part. By means of this, the unity of verse and unity of meaning occur so often together, that the rare cases of severance create a special intensity of expression. This constitutes what I would like to term George's enjambment technique [*Bogenführung*]. For it is the hiatus of meaning which emphasizes the balance of the metric movement and unites the verse sequences into larger wholes. In this way, similarly built, analogous, or analogously sounding verses are created, which are positioned one above another, and thereby create the effect of repetition which is linked to an effect of intensification. This produces the incomparable and often ecstatic flight, to which George's verses rise.

In spite of all the similarities which the background of Pindar's poetry has for George and Hölderlin, it can be demonstrated, exactly here, that the discovery of Hölderlin by the poet George, and those contemporaries inspired by him, was one-sided. When Hellingrath calls Hölderlin's voice "the resounding and sincere voice" that is hardly an accurate characterization of Hölderlin. The sincerity admitted, but resounding? What is resounding? Surely the type of sound which diminishes all articulations in favor of the identification of vital harmony. We all know something of the vitalizing effect of the great resounding which can belong to brass instruments which also play a corresponding role in religious cults. And we know it especially as a characterization for a voice and for the charisma which a resounding voice has. Of this, there is little in the great enjambment technique of Hölderlin's poetry. It always contains something meditative—an increasing immersion and hampering of the voice up to the point of silence.

> Jetzt aber endiget, seeligweinend,
> Wie eine Sage der Liebe,
> Mir der Gesang, und so auch ist er
> Mir, mit Erröthen, Erblassen,
> Von Anfang her gegangen. Doch Alles geht so.

> Now however ends, joyously weeping,
> As a saga of love,
> For me the song, and so also it has
> For me, with blushing, paling,
> From the beginning happened. Yet, everything happens so.

For George's versification, however, the characteristic of resounding is completely correct, if only not falsely understood. Naturally his verse is built upon the play of meaning and sound as is all poetic verse. However, within the range of the play allowed by the balance of this poetic power of language, his verse stands under the priority of the sound's power. For that reason his verses are somewhat hammering, somewhat the return of the same, which is connoted by the word resounding. In resounding, there especially lies the directness of charisma, which does not come from the intellectual content of the linguistic structure, but is rather like the transmission from one will to another will. And it is more a permeation by sound than a speaking. Therefore George can say of himself

> Ich bin ein dröhnen nur der heiligen stimme.
> I am only a resounding of the sacred voice

So the unique character of George's poetry must have also influenced the reception of Hölderlin's poetry and stylized it in a voice which, as we see today, is not completely adequate.

Nevertheless, we must question the religious self-conception as expressed, for example, in the above quotations of Hellingrath, and which is generally found in the vocabulary of the George circle. And we must recognize a deeper similarity between the inward stammering in Hölderlin's art of hymns and the disciplined rigor in George's verse composition. This similarity lies, if I have correctly understood, in the conception which the poet has of himself. In spite of all the differences between the pompous self-presentation, which George gives himself in his poems, and the reserved renunciation, which the "poet in an impoverished time" is ready to muster, the conception of the poetic tradition and of being human forms the common background of both. They are incorporated into a nexus of modern themes, which began with Renaissance poetry. It was the renewal of the Prometheus figure and its application to the artist as the second creator, the *alter deus*, which was first expressed at that time by Bovillus[10] and then led, as is well known, over Shaftesbury to Goethe's extraordinary metamorphosis of the Prometheus symbol.[11] The essential element of this symbol is that the poet, no matter how much he is ostracized and exceptional, nevertheless represents humanity in its creative activity.

The poetic I is less often than usually recognized the I of the poet and almost always that universal I who is everyone. It appears that even the interpreters of George, not to mention those of Hölderlin or Rilke, did not pay enough attention to the ambivalence in the use of the first person by the poet. They should listen to George himself. Nowhere "as much as in this book [are] I and you the same soul."[12] That is certainly a unique distinction of *The Year of the Soul*, that nowhere so much as in this book are I and You the same soul. However, one should certainly also infer from this that for the poet, I and You are the same soul in all of his books. That should especially be recognized for those poems in which the poet speaks about poets.

One of Hölderlin's poems, which seems to have been of special importance for George, may serve as the basis for this discussion. It is the fragmentary poem "For Mother Earth."[13] A longhand copy by George of this poem was found in the poet's posthumous papers in Minusio. Also one of the fragments, with which George prefaced his prose essay, was taken from this poem. Hölderlin's poem speaks, as do almost all of the poems of his later years, of the fate of the poet in an impoverished time. I wish to demonstrate here how the fate of the poet in its representative meaning expresses the universal fate of humanity.

It is the well-known trio of the brothers Ottmar, Hom, and Tello. The song of Ottmar constrasts in three stanzas the lonely singing poet to the people's choir, which is still absent. But this does not occur to emphasize the separation. Rather, the first phrase states

Statt offner Gemeine sing' ich Gesang,
Instead of the open community I sing a song,

and the third stanza exhibits the actual communality which supports the
poet and the people: it is language,

Doch wie der Fels erst ward,
Und geschmiedet wurden in schattiger Werkstatt,
Die ehernen Vesten der Erde,
Noch ehe Bäche rauschten von den Bergen
Und Hain' und Städte blüheten an den Strömen,
So hat er donnernd schon
Geschaffen ein reines Gesetz,
Und reine Laute gegründet.

Yet as rock first became,
And in a shadowy workshop were forged,
The brazen fortresses of the earth,
Even before brooks roared from the mountains
And groves and villages bloomed along the streams,
So had he thundering already
Created a pure law,
And founded pure sounds.

That one is concerned with language here could be corroborated by several parallels in Hölderlin.[14] The poet and the people together have
received in a, so to speak, precreation before creation the pure sounds
through the thunder of the Highest. Language is the answer that mortals
find. However, it is also the authentic and only warrant which we possess, even when the gods are distant and no common spirit arises to sing
the common song.

The song of Hom expresses this absence and the representative
function of the poet. These are idle times, in which the memory of a
heroic time is preserved, and the great rules of the temple "are abandoned in days of despair."

If we now turn to the third song, the song of Tello, which has been
preserved only as a fragment, it will, I hope, become clear why I associate
this poem with George's poetic self-consciousness. Although in the first
two stanzas one could still concentrate completely on the difference which
exists between the conscious loneliness of the poet in Hölderlin and the
orientation of the poet to his surrounding community in George, the third
stanza makes a most intimate proximity between George and Hölderlin
detectable—a proximity lying in the common poetic experience.

Wer will auch danken, eh' er empfängt,
Und Antwort geben, eh' er gehört hat?
Ni[cht ist es gut,] indess ein Höherer spricht,
Zu fallen in die tönende Rede.
Viel hat er zu sagen und anders Recht,
Und Einer ist, der endet in Stunden nicht,
Und die Zeiten des Schaffenden sind,
Wie Gebirg
Das hochaufwoogend von Meer zu Meer
Hinziehet über die Erde,

Es sagen der Wanderer viele davon,
Und das Wild irrt in den Klüften,
Und die Horde schweifet über die Höhen,
Im heiligen Schatten aber,
Am grünen Abhang wohnet
Der Hirt und schauet die Gipfel.

Who would also thank, before he receives
And give an answer, before he has heard?
Never [it is good], while a higher one speaks,
To interrupt in resounding speech.
He has much to say and another law
And one is, who ends not in hours,
And the ages of the creator are,
As mountains
Which billowing high above from sea to sea
Stretch across the earth,

Many wanderers speak of this,
And the game errs in the canyons,
And the herd roams over the heights,
In the sacred shadow however,
On the green slope dwells
The shepherd and looks at the peaks.

The fragment breaks off. That the prose-draft, which begins with "O Mother Earth," should constitute its continuation, is not believable. Despite its fragmentary condition, the conversation of the three is, for the most part, completely composed. And it is not to be seen how the content of "O Mother Earth" could have been incorporated. With reference to the content, it appears to me highly doubtful whether the two pieces have anything at all to do with each other. (I think that Beissner has correctly concluded that they cannot be reconciled with each other as two phases of a single creative project.[15]) Is the theme at all the same? In the prose-draft, mother earth is addressed and she is to be the object of all future odes. Here she is not addressed. Here she is spoken of as the fortresses of the earth. They are the pure law of language, out of which the poet sings and out of which also the song of the community can only come. Earth and language are mirrored in one another here in order to say: The ages of the creator are not in the power and at the disposal of the poet, any more than the mountains, toward whose peaks—toward what is above him—the shepherd looks.

However, be that as it may: George, in any case, did not copy down the prose-draft but rather our poetic fragment. In this he recognized his own life-consciousness as a poet. This may be supported by George's poem from the eleventh and twelfth issues [of the *Blätter für die Kunst*]:

> Horch was die dumpfe erde spricht:
> Du frei wie vogel oder fisch—
> Worin du hängst * das weisst du nicht.
>
> Vielleicht entdeckt ein spätrer mund:
> Du sassest mit an unserem tisch
> Du zehrtest mit von unsrem pfund.
> Dir kam ein schön und neu gesicht
> Doch zeit ward alt * heut lebt kein mann
> Ob er je kommt das weisst du nicht
>
> Der dies gesicht noch sehen kann.

> Hear what the murky earth speaks:
> You are free as bird or fish—
> Wherein you hang * that you do not know
>
> Perhaps a later mouth discovers:
> You sat with us at our table
> You ate with us from our meal.
>
> To you came a beautiful and new vision
> But time was old * today no one lives
> Whether he ever comes that you do not know
>
> Who can still see this vision.

The background of this poem is the motif of resignation, which is well known through George's work. In *The Seventh Ring*, the poet bends over the mirror of the spring, seeking acknowledgement after a great experience for which he believes to have found the poetic form, and the shapes always answer him "We are not it! We are not it!" And nothing else is meant in the poem from *The Kingdom Come*: *Kein ding sei wo das wort gebricht* ["No thing is where the word fails".] One has to read our poem from the background of this constant motif. Its key is (and I believe that with this its interpretation is no longer difficult) the ambivalence between being a poet and being human. For what the poem says, and therefore, that it says something to us, is finally this: The poet is not master of his inspiration and creation, but remains like all others also dependent in an insurmountable and inscrutable way. I wish to put the emphasis on "like all others also." That sounds in our ear through the "wherein you hang...that you do not know," especially since it is taken up again in the penultimate stanza and lends the whole poem its meter. It is the "murky earth," something which one can in no way clarify and from where each one of us comes, which proclaims to us this essential ignorance about ourselves. Not only the poet, but each one of us, can listen to the following words. For always a later voice will know what we do not know. Certainly these verses intone the *parousia* forms from the Christian tradition. Not that Christ was meant, who remains unrecognized among His own and is first recognized in breaking bread. But it does speak of the Being of him who would speak the healing word, but still remains unrecognized. It is the essential theme of this poem and it is present in these verses: The poet reckons himself among the ignorant. He also does not know. However, he knows that he cannot know whether a vision that he has will ever be apparent—will ever be there for all. That means, however, he does not know whether a word will be. The deep trembling, which goes through these verses, is not limited to those others who would stand opposite the I of the poet.

If we return from here to the third stanza of "For Mother Earth," then we recognize the communality of the theme. One should not fall into the ringing speech, one ought not be over hasty, not reach with a sacrilegious hand for the fire. That is a central motif in Hölderlin.[16] So the poet must also here endure that he is the lead singer of a not yet answering community. The ages of the creator, which go their own way, dislodged by nothing, influenced by nothing, like the mountain range from sea to sea, say the same: "That you do not know" as in George's poem. It is the inner communality, which constitutes the position of the poet to time and the world, and which unites two poets very different from each other. It appears to be to be a sign of the greatness of George that his own poetic voice still sounds so completely different and authentic, and that his poetic voice presents no trace of imitating or reproducing Hölderlin's tone.

Notes

1. O. Regenbogen, *Kleine Schriften.* 1961, 520 ff.

2. F. Beissner, *Hölderlins Übersetzungen aus dem Grieschischen,* 2d. ed. 1961.

3. N. v. Hellingrath. *Hölderlin-Vermächtnis,* 2d ed. 1944, 226.

4. Hellingrath, 229.

5. See E. Salin. *Um Stefan George,* 2d ed. 1954, 19, 27.

6. Hölderlin. *S[ämtliche] W[erke],* 1, 307 (Grosse Stuttgarter Ausgabe).

7. Hölderlin. *S W,* II, 136.

8. N. v. Hellingrath. *Hölderlin-Vermächtnis,* 2d ed. 1944, 139.

9. J. Aler. *Im Spiegel der Form. Stilkritische Wege zur Deutung von Stefan Georges Maximindichtung,* 1947.

10. E. Cassirer. *Individuum und Kosmos in der Renaissance,* 1927, 299ff.

11. O. Walzel. *Das Prometheussymbol von Shaftesbury zu Goethe,* 3rd ed., 1932.

12. George. *Vorrede zur zweiten Ausgabe vom: Jahr der Seele.*

13. Hölderlin. *S W,* II, 123.

14. Hölderlin: *S W,* II, see 92 ("Brot und Wein").

15. *Kleine Sttuttgarter Ausgabe,* Hölderlin. *S W,* II, 1953, 426.

16. Hölderlin. *S W,* II, 120, 141, 155.

Chapter 10

UNDER THE SHADOW OF NIHILISM*

When I select two German poets, poets of the German language, for this subject matter, there is really no choice but Gottfried Benn and Paul Celan. If one wished to specify those writers in German literature since the Second World War who truly were able to express something of the basic emotional, mental and religious circumstances of that time, then one would have to search among the lyric poets. We Germans are not a people of great novelists. Even writers like Hermann Hesse, Thomas Mann, or Robert Musil are much too bound to the peculiar refinements of mannerist narrative style for them to possess the carrying voice of the natural narrative. Certainly we were deeply moved by Hermann Hesse's *The Glass Bead Game*, which reached us after the war, and even more by Thomas Mann's equally profound and yet rather contrived and esoteric reponse to the German tragedy—and—perhaps with the longest lasting effect—the ingenious retrospective of *The Man without Qualities*. Certainly, Heinrich Böll's brevity and Günter Grass's exuberance in narration also received recognition outside of Germany. But could any one of these compete with the great novelists of England, Russia, France, with Joyce, with Proust, with *The Possessed* or *Karamazov* or *Anna Karenina*, which do and which will continue to speak to us? On the other hand, one may well assert that German lyric poetry has for hundreds of years been an adequate expression of the German spirit, which was always bound to the great scientific and philosophic experiences and achievements of German culture. I only need mention Stefan George, who was surely the most significant artist in the German tongue in the last hundred years. I name Hugo von Hofmannsthal, Rainer Maria Rilke and Georg Trakl. Of course, politically speaking most of them were not German citizens, but the *Respublica Litteraria* does not recognize any borders which are not established by language. And we all endeavor to overcome even the borders of language, when we travel in foreign lands or when we listen to foreign guests speaking their own language.

Considering German lyric poetry of the postwar period there is really no choice. Gottfried Benn and Paul Celan are the two great poets who, in the time after the Second World War, adequately expressed in poetry something of the German sense of life, the German fate—the

---

*Essay, published in Amsterdam, 1988.

uncertain position between belief and disbelief, between hope and despair. Both are also well-known abroad. Both have been translated into many languages. But one who knows what lyric poetry is, knows that translations are only approximations and can hardly awaken an idea of what speaks in the original language.

To begin, a few words concerning Gottfried Benn. He was a doctor and lived in Berlin. After 1933 he had, for a while, false expectations for the developments of that time and then, like so many in his position, he sought refuge in the army in order to survive in a respectable manner. That was how one who was threatened in the Third Reich could most easily escape political persecution. He was a military doctor. As a poet he spoke up again immediately after the Second World War and, I must say, only then did we recognize him in his complete significance. We were aided in this because he was granted a special mature style which strongly dampened the provocativeness of his earlier poetry and flowed in a wonderful melody over his verses. The verses which I present come from his posthumous works.

> Dann gliederten sich die Laute,
> erst war nur Chaos und Schrei,
> fremde Sprachen, uralte,
> vergangene Stimmen dabei.
>
> Die eine sagte, gelitten,
> die zweite sagte: geweint,
> die dritte: keine Bitten
> nützen, der Gott verneint.
>
> Eine gellende: in Räuschen
> aus Kraut, aus Säften, aus Wein—:
> vergessen, vergessen, täuschen
> dich selbst und jeden, der dein.
>
> Eine andere: keine Zeichen,
> keine Weisung und kein Sinn—
> im Wechsel Blüten und Leichen
> und Geyer drüber hin.
>
> Eine andere: Müdigkeiten,
> eine Schwäche ohne Mass—
> und nur laute Hunde, die streiten,
> erhalten Knochen und Frass.
>
> Doch dann in zögernder Wende
> und die Stimmen hielten sich an,
> sprach eine: ich sehe am Ende
> einen grossen schweigenden Mann.

Der weiss, dass keinen Bitten
jemals ein Gott erscheint,
er hat es ausgelitten,
er weiss, der Gott verneint.

Er sieht den Menschen vergehen
im Raub- und Rassenraum,
er lässt die Welt geschehen
und bildet seinen Traum.

Then the sounds ordered themselves,
first was only chaos and cry,
foreign languages, ancient,
bygone voices among them.

One said: suffered,
A second said: cried,
A third: no prayers
help, God denies.

A piercing one: in intoxication
from herbs, from juices, from wine—:
forgotten, forgotten, deluding
yourself and all, including the dear.

Another: no signs,
no direction and no meaning,
alternating blossoms and corpses
and vultures circling above.

Another: tirednesses
a weariness without bounds—
and only loud dogs, who fight,
receiving bones and fodder.

But then in hesitating turn
and the voices stopped,
said one: I see at the end
a great silent man.

He knows, that to no prayers
ever a God appears,
he suffered through it,
he knows, God denies.

He sees the human race dying
from crime and racism
he lets the world go on
and shapes his dream.

The poem is not difficult to understand. However, in order to make clear the poet's prosody and rhyme, a few remarks may be required. At first, I would like to make a few—perhaps pedantic—remarks concerning lyric semantics, and then a few others on the lyric syntax of this poem. Naturally, I do not mean by lyric semantics the usual teaching of the meaning of words—I mean what is specific in lyric semantics: the manner in which a poet, as here, composes not only the sounds, i.e., rhyme, but also joins together sounds carrying meaning—words—and thereby creates new semantic and tonal unities. This is so clear in the case of Gottfried Benn that I only need to hear a line from Gottfried Benn in order to know: this is Benn. Using a few instances taken partly from this poem and partly from other poems, I would like to characterize Benn's lyric semantics. It consists mainly in binding together, using sounds, elements of contrasting meaning and, in this way, welding them together to form a new semantic unity.

I choose a few convenient examples:

> Ob Sinn, ob Sucht, ob Sage
> Oder:
> Ob Rose, ob Schnee, ob Mähre
> Oder:
> Die Fluten, die Flammen, die Fragen.

> Whether meaning, whether obsession, whether saga
> or:
> Whether rose, whether snow, whether mare
> or:
> The floods, the flames, the questions.

The means of rhyme are clear: alliteration, assonance, and melodic conjoining [*Fügung*] allow things as disparate as floods and flames to come together in a comprehensive gesture of meaning with something totally other: questions, which bring all into uncertainty. That is the lyric grammar of Gottfried Benn: he unites in one things that tend apart, that are semantically completely foreign. In this way, he opens up a type of cosmic breadth and distance. Also in the poem before us, there are examples of such an encompassing collection, as for example, in the beautiful verse: "from herbs, from juices, from wine, forgotten, forgotten..." Obviously it is the Dionysian component of all religion—herbs, juices, wine—although still relatively similar in meaning—which is evoked here. The other examples, which I presented, do not even have this relative unity of meaning. For example: "meaning, obsession, saga": how that suddenly comes together; how the tonal connecting here traverses the whole distance as a uniting figure and, as one must say, with immediate expressiveness. The distance reaches from meaningful speech over obsessive madness to the remoteness of saga in the unverifiable twilight. That is truly the unmistakable and original lyric semantics of Gottfried Benn and no other. One does not at all aspire to unity within the poetic image-world, but rather to a unity of meaning, behind contrasts, which exercises an indeterminate and, at the same time, all comprehensive evocative power. What is separated flows together into a new unified Melos.

The syntax, the conjoining of sentences, is equally original in style. The poem has a very poetic opening. It invokes the beginning by not starting with the beginning. "Then the sounds ordered themselves. First was only chaos and cry": This reference testifies to the beginninglessness of the beginning, i.e., the disappearance of the beginning (which is not a first moment) in the twilight of cosmic dawn and human prehistory. In this way these lines confront us, and then the poem tells us that when the sounds ordered themselves and language was first able to express something, this language was for human lamentation. That is the syntax of the poem: a single long sentence, with a clear intensification from cry to lamentation and from the lamentation which has grown faint to a vision of one who knows and no longer laments. At first, there is an inarticulate cry, then "suffered, cried," then "piercing, forgotten, intoxication," finally "despair, tiredness," and then the voices stop—and that means, they all listen and one 'speaks', one who no longer says something himself, but like a final verdict says; "I see at the end..." —so this last voice invokes a vision of a man who clearly does not repudiate God but who knows: "God denies." It appears to me, a magnificent and very good symbolic statement from the theology of the Hidden God, *Deus Absconditus*. It is the God who hides himself. In this respect it is a symptomatic poem from the time of Nietzsche's message of the death of God and the dawning of nihilism,—and, at the same time, a good and telling poetic proof for the power of the lyric word, not only to speak the truth, but to document it through its own being.

Much more difficult to understand are the hermetically coded verses which I have chosen from Paul Celan.

Paul Celan is a Jewish poet of German tongue, who grew up in Czernowitz, Bukovina, far to the East. After many bouts with fate he became, I believe, an English teacher in Paris. He was married to a French woman and wrote poetry only in German—a very peculiar circumstance. I do not know of any poems by Celan in French, whereas I certainly know some from George and Rilke. Obviously Celan was more at home in the German language, although Germany offered him no home, than those other poets who tried occasionally to write in another language. I select a poem from the latest period of this poet, who freely chose death in 1970. After a little explication, this poem's thematic affinity to the first presented poem of Benn will become apparent to everyone. It is doubtlessly a cryptic creation, a hermetic poem. It mirrors the great conversion to omission, to concentration, and so also to condensing, with which we are also acquainted, for example, in modern music since Schönberg and Webern. Since the war these changes have had an especially strong influence in German lyric poetry, not least because the German lyric speaks in a language where the freedom of word order is, as far as I know, only matched in classical Greek. This freedom is the basis for the exceptional possibility of concentration in lyric verse. The syntactical and functional expressions of speech—the prosaic-rhetorical means through which we normally accomplish the logical constitution of unity within speech—are almost completely eliminated. The poem relies solely on the gravitational power of the words:

> Wirk nicht voraus,
> sende nicht aus,
> steh
> herein:
>
> durchgründet vom Nichts
> ledig allen
> Gebets,
> feinfügig, nach
> der Vor-Schrift,
> unüberholbar,
>
> nehm ich dich auf
> statt aller
> Ruh.

> Design not ahead
> send not out
> stand
> forth:
>
> based upon nothingness
> without all
> prayers,
> finely enjoined, according
> to the pre-scription,
> unsurpassable,
>
> I accept you
> in stead of all
> peace.

One must read this in such a manner that the three stanzas and the enjambments could be anticipated. They are, precisely, verses. That means: even the one word verse has as much length as the other verses, a length which expands in our inner ear when we, listening and understanding at the same time, constitute for ourselves the rhythmic creation in language. This poem, as difficult as it may appear, is no more difficult than many other poems of the later Celan. In this poem, he has gotten closer to the deep sense of becoming silent than other poets who break off when they have lost their breath. To begin, a few examples will present the semantics of this poem. Again it concerns a language which has developed its own poetic semantics. If in Gottfried Benn the special conjoining of words essentially depends upon his placing next to each other and uniting together what is not related, here we have, in a sense, the opposite principle of poetic semantics: something which appears to be a word explodes, so to speak, and through its explosion into word fragments of different meaning evokes a new unity of meaning.

"Design not ahead"—the meaning context connoted by the word 'effect ahead' [*Vorauswirken*] is most likely that of predetermination and would bring into consideration the Christian and especially the Calvinist dogma of predestination. Of course, whether God is addressed or not, is a separate question left open during the first reading. In the next verse, however, the meaning context of "Send not out" is unquestionably clear. Without a doubt, it connotes the sending forth of the Apostles or the missionary commission which founded the Christian Church. One must and will hear this as long as one has some understanding of the Bible. More difficult is what is opposed to the sending forth, i.e., the "stand forth." The word 'stand forth' [*hereinstehen*] exists in Austrian also in an active meaning. As I have been told, one can say to someone 'stand forth' [*Steh herein*] and that means 'come in.' But that is not what the present speaker primarily means here; 'come in' would be a poor opposition to send forth. In addition, the "stand forth" is separated into two verses in the poem. "Stand" is a single word verse. "Forth" is a single word verse. Therefore, one must first hear 'standing' by itself, before it changes and completes itself in a "stand forth." In this way, the other intransitive meaning of the word comes into play. 'Something stands forth' means: it stands in the way so that one cannot pass around it. This one must hear. This "stand forth" means not really 'come' but 'be there in such a manner that I cannot pass by you.'

The 'stanza' ends here and the next one begins again with an audacious word destruction. "Based upon nothingness" permits two completely incompatible meanings to melt together. 'Founded upon something' [*gegründet auf etwas*] and 'governed by nothingness' [*durchwaltet vom Nichts*] are here suddenly thrust together into a unity, as in a phrase from Webern. Instead of being based upon something dependable in its being, what should build the firm basis is to be nothingness which disintegrates all entities. And it continues as before: "without all prayers"—one who hears "without all..." will immediately anticipate something completely different. Not exactly 'without any luggage'—but surely without any load or without any burdens, so that one is lightened. But then, prayer occurs instead. Naturally that indicates that the prayer itself was his burden. Without being weighted down, means a type of being free. And it continues as before: "finely enjoined" [*feinfügig*]—that word does not exist. There is 'accommodating' [*gefügig*], i.e., 'obeying' [*gehorchend*] and there is 'finely fitted' [*feingefügt*], i.e., 'finely fitting together' [*sich fein ineinanderfügend*]. Again, both are to be heard in "finely enjoined"—'fine' [*fein*] and 'submitting to' [*sich fügend*]. And finally "according to the pre-scription"—here we have, so to speak, the written proof for Celan's semantic practice. The word 'pre-scription' [*Vor-Schrift*] is written in the text with a hyphen: "pre-scription." One should not miss that here the Bible is intended and that the word alludes to 'according to scripture' [*nach der Schrift*]. This means however: what I so finely submit to [*fein füge*] is exactly not what is according to scripture but what is according to the pre-scription, i.e., something which is older than the oldest document of humanity—to use an expression of Herder. It is an experience which precedes what the Bible proscribes and nevertheless constrains like a rule [*Vorschrift*]. It says "unsurpassable"—it will never be revoked, whereas rules usually are; as even the Old Testament is supposed to have been superseded by the New Testament.

Therefore, this I, which is steeped in nothingness, says of itself: "I accept you instead of all peace"—what is extremely puzzling here concerns less the semantics and more the contents. And it is that in the end there is no peace, which is the tranquil acceptance of the Scripture's message. What is accepted here is not 'peace' but the continual unrest which you bring by your standing forth.

After these introductory semantic explanations, the interpretation begins with the syntax of the whole, which is the actual content of the poem, i.e., the statement which is made here. In Celan—and basically in any genuine lyric poet—one can never rightly say who is intended when the poem uses I. It is a poem because the poet does not just refer to himself. I, as the reader, cannot distinguish myself from him as the speaker. It is a poem since we are this I. What then is the you [*Du*] in relation to this I—the you which the I addresses as a you? It is an imperative: "Design not ahead"—who is this you? It is true, we are accustomed to refer also to ourselves as 'you' and it would not be grammatically and syntactically impossible to read the whole as a hermetic conversation with oneself. Someone is addressed and someone answers and both could be one and the same person. At first this question remains open. If one interprets this as an addressing of oneself, then one would be following, in one's preunderstanding, the Stoic principle, *eis heauton*, and would refrain from wanting to effect and prevail. This appears to be likely. However, the standing forth—in whatever meaning of the word—does not satisfy this interpretation. It is something from outside, which should stand forth, be or come.

The referent of what is said in the second stanza appears at first to be open. Does it refer to you—whomever this is—or to me? The colon closing the first stanza indicates that everything which follows belongs together and constitutes the request of the one standing forth. Therefore, it is not the addressed you, but the speaking I, that is expressed in what follows in its readiness to receive the you. That is the resulting syntax which unites the second and third stanzas.

A small problem occurs in the last verse of the second stanza, "unsurpassable." This attribute does not fit the description of this I. Here the meaning refers much more to the pre-scription. Many prescriptions are no longer in force; they have been surpassed. This prescription, which predates all, can never be surpassed. So this last verse is grammatically an attributive appositive to "prescription" and not an attribute of the I, as "finely enjoined" surely is. At most, one could suppose an indirect overlapping of meanings: because I myself obey the unsurpassable prescription, I can myself be called unsurpassable. That may be part of the meaning. However, the relationship to the prescription remains central.

In addition to these reasons based on grammar, there is in the suggested interpretation yet another and 'hermeneutic' reason to interpret God as the you of the completely other. The reason is the place which the poet chose for this poem in the last book of poetry he composed. In this, one is following the renowned hermeneutic principle, which Schleiermacher formulated, namely, the unity of meaning is also conditioned by its function within a greater context of meaning.

The famous poem, *You be as you...* [*Du sei wie du...*], precedes our verses and opens up the religious context. It speaks of the suffering of one who is tormented by his break with the Jewish community and the beliefs of his forefathers. "When I cut the bond to you" may refer to something biographical since Celan entered into a Catholic marriage in Paris. However, as before, one should not introduce particular private knowledge. The break with the beliefs of the forefathers means in the end, surely, everyone. It is the suffering of the search for God, which implies a separation from any particular religious affiliation, but which, nevertheless, cannot escape the question of God and to that extent the experience of the divine. It "stands forth." Therefore it is clear: The one addressed is someone different, the totally different one, God. But nothing of a religious promise of salvation is connected with this—no belief in a providence and nothing of the joyful message with which Jesus dispatched his disciples into the whole world. God should do nothing—only stand forth in such a way that I cannot pass by you. But that is precisely His Being and so the other transitive meaning of standing forth surfaces: He should just come in—I wish to receive Him and it should not be as in the prologue to John where the world did not receive the Logos. All the verses following the colon, therefore, constitute a justifying final clause for the request of "stand forth." Exactly because I am so deeply "based upon nothingness" and cherish no particular religious expectation or prophecy. "Without all prayers"—that I am. Prayer is like something which I can no longer endure. Just because I am in this way, I am not free. But I also know that I have to obey not a revelation 'according to scripture' but a prescription [*Vorschrift*], which is much more original and unsurpassable than all possible religions and all possible ecclesiastical communities of belief. The I which speaks does not even wish to pass by 'you': 'you' should stand forth like something around which one cannot pass. "Instead of all peace" means not that I would accept some new belief wherein I would seek and find peace, but rather that I cannot follow any present belief as compelling. It is exactly this disquiet [*Unruhe*] which does not allow me to pass by you and which I cannot keep from myself.

If one could call Gottfried Benn's poem a kind of negative hymn, i.e., a praising of Him who is mature enough to abstain from all lamentation, then one could call this poem a hermetic dialogue. This poem expresses for us all that the experience of the divine is unavoidable, even when "God denies" and refrains. For many, the experience of the divine may continue to produce commitment, solace and the promise of salvation—the I, who speaks for us here, expects nothing, but acknowledges the disquiet of the heart: *inquietum cor nostrum*. God denies—an internal concurrence exists between Celan's poem and the verses of Benn.

In his book of poetry, *Lichtzwang*, Celan includes a poem written after a visit with Martin Heidegger in the Black Forest. He also sent the poem to Heidegger.

Todtnauberg

> Arnika, Augentrost, der
> Trunk aus dem Brunnen mit dem
> Sternwürfel drauf,
>
> in der
> Hütte,
>
> die in das Buch
> —wessen Namen nahms auf

vor dem meinen?—,
die in dies Buch
geschriebene Zeile von
einer Hoffnung, heute,
auf eines Denkenden
kommendes
Wort
im Herzen,

Waldwasen, uneingeebnet,
Orchis und Orchis, einzeln,

Krudes, später, im Fahren,
deutlich,

der uns fährt, der Mensch,
der's mit anhört,
die halb-
beschrittenen Knüppel-
pfade im Hochmoor,

Feuchtes,
viel.

Todtnauberg

Arnica, eyebright, the
drink from the spring with the
starred cube on it,

in the
hut,
in the book
—whose name is recorded
before mine?—,
in this book
the written line of
a hope, today,
for a thinker's
coming
word
heartfelt,

forest sward, unleveled,
orchis and orchis, singly,

crude, later, while driving,
distinct,

> he who drives us, the person,
> who listens in
> the half-
> trodden log-
> path in the high moor,
>
> dampness,
> plenty.

The rumor is that this poem documents an unhappy conclusion to the visit. This may be left to the biographers' wisdom—even if it should include the autobiographer, the poet himself. The poem knows nothing of this—and further, it knows better.

I know this hut myself from many stays. It is like this. In the high Black Forest, one encounters these swards or high moors. High above, near the forest's edge on the Stübenwasen, there stands a small hut nestling close into the slope, completely covered with shingles, and very simple. There is no water. In front of the hut is a small spring, similar to a trough which one constructs for livestock in the Black Forest. A softly trickling spring always supplies fresh water. Heidegger and I have often shaved at this spring with the running water. The top of the spring's post is a cube carved into the wood, into which a star-shaped ornament is engraved. Naturally one need not know this, but one should recognize something meaningful in this situation, like a good omen, such as the stars of fate and the cast of fate. As the whole small premises, it is an "eyebright." The poem evokes this feeling by referring in the beginning to the name 'Arnica,' in German 'Augentrost' [eyebright], which is a native medicinal herb growing in the high mountains. It was Heidegger's custom to have all guests sign the book he kept in the hut. (Once in 1923, I also entered a verse. It was not by me, but by Stefan George: *Der wind der weiten zärtlich um uns braust* [The wind from afar blows tenderly around us].) Celan evidently went there, should have signed the book and did so. (A German-American philologist has meanwhile tried to discover without success what he had written. This is also a way to approach a poet.) In any case, it is clear which expectation or perhaps nonexpectation and which question moved the poet: Whether such a thinker as this one would perhaps have a word, a coming word, of hope for today. Carrying this secret hope in his heart, the poet wrote his line.

The scene is, then, evidently a walk over the Stübenwasen: "forest sward, unleveled, orchis and orchis, singly," "unleveled." That is truly how these swards are. But again, one should not drive to the Black Forest to study the landscape in order to better understand the poem. One should understand that there is no leveled path for thinkers or us who are thinking. An orchis is a small mountain orchid, but naturally the verse, "orchis and orchis, singly," does not say something primarily about the vegetation on the Stübenwasen, but rather something about the singularity of the two walkers, who walked together and yet remained apart, like the flowers which they passed.

The next scene is the visitor's drive home in the car. Someone else is driving and he is accompanied by another person with whom he speaks. They speak with each other and only now while they are conversing does the "crude" become clear to him. What Heidegger said and what Celan at first did not understand: Heidegger's words suddenly take on meaning for him and the other—not for the "person who drives us." That is, as it were, the end of the story of this visit. The first stanza concerns the comforting view of the modest premises. The second takes place in the hut, presenting the importance of the visited man and the secret expectation of the visitor. The third stanza is about the walking next to each other of two separated; then the drive home during which one's impressions are discussed. What follows this is no longer an 'action,' but something like a result, which was drawn in the conversation of those riding back, i.e., the risks of this attempt to walk in the impassable.

There are half-trodden log paths in the high moor. That is how it is in the high mountains. One makes the soggy paths along the moor somewhat passable by using logs. Here, there are half trodden log paths, that means: one cannot get through and must turn back. They are like "Holzwege" [woodcutter's paths]. It is a reference to Heidegger's not claiming and not being able to have a coming word, a hope for today—he tried to take a few steps along a risky path. It is a risky path. One who steps falsely steps into the moor and is threatened by sinking into the dampness. It is a description of the risky paths of this thinker's thought—and again, a situation in which we all, as humans today, more or less consciously stand and which necessitates our thinking to travel risky paths.

So it may well be that the despondent poet experienced no change in hope and clarity during his visit. It became a poem because the experience expresses him and us all. As a description of the actual visit, the poem is not unique in Celan's work. He has written many, so-called, autobiographical poems. In his Büchner speech he distinguished his own poetry from the symbolic poetry of Mallarmé exactly by means of this 'existential' reference. But this is not an invitation for biographical research. This reference to a situation, which lends the poem something occasional and appears to demand elaboration through knowledge of the particular situation, is, in truth, elevated to the realm of the meaningful and true, and thereby allows it to become an authentic poem. It speaks for us all.

Chapter 11

INTERVIEW: HISTORICISM
AND ROMANTICISM

This text also is based on two separate interviews. Both took place in Heidelberg, July 1 and 2, 1986. Translated by the editors.

QUESTION. We now would like to ask you some questions about your analysis of historical consciousness and the writing of history in Germany. You appear to regard the emergence of historical consciousness as something like a revolutionary break as significant as the scientific revolution of the seventeenth century. Do you look at this break as historians themselves do, or are your views different from theirs?

GADAMER. For me the historical sciences are merely an element or feature of the great process of the unfolding of historical consciousness which I addressed in *Truth and Method.* Here I followed the analysis given by Erich Rothacker, his *Einleitung in die Geisteswissenschaft,* published in 1920. Rothacker showed that the historians who belong to what we in Germany call the "historical school" and what you, in English, call the historicists, people like Ranke and others, really did have much in common with Hegel despite the fact that they denied it. There is much of Hegel, in their work, and we understand it differently since the rediscovery of Hegel at the beginning of the century. Following in the footsteps of Dilthey, Rothacker brought philosophy and history together. Since then we can see that the presumed pure concern with empirical facts claimed by the nineteenth century school of German historians (the *historische Schule*) was shot through by philosophical assumptions. Thus Ranke spoke of the immediacy of every historical era to God. There is much in this of Fichte, Humboldt, and Hegel although they had no real consciousness of that fact. We can see it now because of our consciousness of effective history. (Of course, there is never a full and complete consciousness of what has been brought about in and through history.) But we at least, in our times, can be aware of the metaphysical prejudices implicit in the concepts of science and objectivity which the historicist historians wrenched out of the system of German Idealism. The emphasis on objectivity in historiography and on proceeding scientifically leads to an impoverished form of historical consciousness, of the consciousness of what has been effected in and through history.

QUESTION. Would you therefore argue that there is a difference between historical consciousness and a sensitivity to history?

GADAMER. Yes, the aim of a sensitivity to history is the development of historical consciousness. The latter arose out of the famous *querelle des anciens et des modernes*. And it is not as if one side had prevailed over the other. We are still in this conflict, and have to regard the conflict itself as constitutive of historical consciousness which thus reaches beyond a sensitivity to history.

QUESTION. Could one say that historical consciousness is a phenomenon which emerged with particular force in Germany, more than in England or France, for example?

GADAMER. Well, first, one can observe that Romanticism primarily was a German development. Of course, there were parallels elsewhere, but never quite equal to it. And why is this so? Marx said, because the Germans did not make a revolution. That's quite true, in the sense that we Germans were never quite convinced of the transformative power of the Enlightenment; Burke has been more effective among us than Saint Juste and the concluding period of the French Revolution. And that is the case because a great revolution presupposes a centralized state. That didn't exist in Germany. There was the fiction in Germany, before Napoleon, of the 'Holy Roman Empire.' But in reality there were just small territorial dominions, many centers. There was no capital from which a revolution could start; the younger Balzac has shown how Paris was established as such a center in France against much resistance, due to the organisation of a centralized state and administration. And that is why you had the French Revolution and Napoleon. In Germany, even with Romanticism, we had a variety of regional forms. Everyone wanted to retain his own traditions.

QUESTION. So is German national consciousness, its formation, connected with events in France?

GADAMER. It was due to the occupation by Napoleon. The occupation stimulated the desire for national unity, a national state, and it grew between 1806 and 1813. That is a most important period.

QUESTION. Has German historiography been influenced by this desire for a nation-state?

GADAMER. Certainly. But even more so by the dominance of Prussia in the pursuit of national unity. Prussia and Berlin, led to the development of the historicist school of historians, such as Ranke, Droysen, Mommsen. And Prussia and Berlin were Protestant. And Lutheranism contributed, because it made an internal connection between the fostering of culture and of religion. The local rulers, the 'princes,' were entrusted with culture, because they were also charged with the administration of the church.

QUESTION. Can we turn to a different topic? Is it correct to say that the historicist school, historicism in general, gain in significance, when one accepts Heidegger's critique of the absolute, his radical historicization of truth? Leo Strauss and Emil Fackenheim, on the other hand, regard historicism merely as a form of scepticism, falling away from the claim of the absolute.

GADAMER. I have always argued with Leo Strauss about this. I have tried to make the point that one can only interpret historicism as a type of relativism or scepticism if one still holds to some concept of the absolute. But this does not commit me to a position like that of the historicists, because, in fact, they themselves believed in a form of absolute—their concept of objectivity.

QUESTION. Exactly what, then, has Heidegger contributed in the elucidation of this matter?

GADAMER. Here one must see the radical novelty of the questions that became possible after the period of the historicists. Think, for example, of how Nietzsche sharpened the question, especially with his critique of the various concepts of truth and his effort to reduce truth to the actions and reactions of the will to power. Now it is in this context alone that Heidegger can formulate notions such as the *Epoche* and the *Ereignis*. He means that there is no position that we can take, distant, objective, over against the things we see. This supposed observer who only says that which is, is standing in fact in the *Wirkungsgeschichte*, to use my own notion. This is what I have called historically effected consciousness, a consciousness which partakes in history without being able to fully account for its participation. Of course, even Heidegger in his later years was tempted to give an unduly systematic form to this vision of his, when he speaks, for example, of the growing forgetfulness of being, up to the all-encompassing sway of this forgetfulness. He introduced a kind of necessity into his ideas, which he then would also deny and say: But it is *Geschick*, destiny: It happens to us. It cannot be predicted in its necessity.

QUESTION. Would you still say, then, that what Ranke, Mommsen, Dilthey have done, is equally consequential for us (given the radicalization of this theme by Heidegger) as Galileo and Newton have been?

GADAMER. That I don't know. The problem is that we cannot really compare here. The historicist school of historians didn't really say enough about how history was to be understood as a science. There is no scientific method for establishing what counts as a historical fact. It is much more important to consider what it means that we are historical beings. Therefore our capacity to understand history is always also an expression of our self-understanding. That's more important than the cataloguing of historical facts. Obviously there is always the question in the human sciences too: "Now, what is the case here?" But that's not why we do them. We are always subject to the need to come to an understanding of ourselves. That is not the reason for the existence of physics as a science.

QUESTION. Did the historicist historians and historicism in general understand this?

GADAMER. Well, Droysen did, but Dilthey was confused about it, and Ranke didn't reflect on these questions. Thus they didn't have much to say on how each generation creates a new view of history; how it interprets expressions of life which are alien to it in order to understand itself better. That's not about neutral, objective facts. We can even say this when we examine historians of the past: Mommsen, for example, was a democrat. He wrote Roman history as such. And he could do so, because he came from a region not fully integrated into Prussia. He was not just a scientist, but a human being of his times. He could never finish his work on the imperial period of Rome. For he was a republican. That defined his interest.

QUESTION. To return to Heidegger and you: You don't use Heidegger's terms *Geschick* or *Schicksal*. Why is this?

GADAMER. I could see what he meant. As in the case of art: Works of art, as different as they may be in different epochs, still claim us. But the poeticizing mode of speech used by the later Heidegger, when he spoke of *Geschick* and the like—that bothered me. It made it easy to raise the charge of mythological thinking against him. I said: Here I can show what he means: Think of *Wirkungsgeschichtliches Bewusstsein*. The consciousness which we have of what has happened in history is never adequate to the real effects which have reached us. Therein lies a kind of fatefulness. I can't endorse formulations like: "Being reveals" or "Being sends." I am opposed to creating a special language and want to make the language which we normally use say what Heidegger speaks about. Yes, Heidegger knew this to some extent, knew of this danger; therefore he once interrupted himself when reading one of his essays to us and got quite impatient and said: "All of this is Chinese." And he was right. It is.

QUESTION. How do you then regard his interpretation of Greek texts? And of the words of the Greek philosophers such as *Logos*, or *Aletheia*? One just doesn't find what he says in the Greek philosophical texts.

GADAMER. I understand this much better now and can give you a good answer. Heidegger could only interpret words. He could not make sense of sentences. But how he has interpreted these words, that shows a depth of understanding which reaches beyond the recorded statements of the Greek philosophers. I once recently made the daring comment that the Heraclitus whom Heidegger has discovered is a Heraclitus of the year one thousand B.C. We have learned from Heidegger what it means that a word can *name*. Even his incorrect interpretations are more interesting than the correct ones of those who do not know about the power of the word to name something. Thus it is with the word *Logos*. When I first read Heidegger about this, I said: No, this is impossible, absurd. Now I believe he was right. We have to hear in *Logos* something like the *Lese*, a laying, and gathering. Previously, one was told that *Logos* meant 'flame,' 'speech,' 'reason.' None of this makes sense. Heidegger, of course, always read the Greeks for his own reasons. He was looking for the beginnings, for a nonmetaphysical way of thinking, something which might correspond to the structure of Chinese and Japanese as languages. In the end he understood this. He realized that the Greeks never, for example, meant *aletheia* in his sense, they never meant anything like a play of concealment and unconcealment. We, therefore, need to turn our attention to what he attempted to show. We have to learn to see the phenomenon which he meant and then speak on our own. That's why you don't find me using Heideggerian language.

QUESTION. Can we return to German history for a moment? The theme of the relation of German historicist historiography and history writing (*historische Schule*) to German national consciousness?

GADAMER. Well, yes. I had already pointed to the significance of Prussia and Protestantism for the development of the writing of history in Germany. But then this isn't unique to Germany during the nineteenth century. It also happened wherever new nation-states were formed, in Italy, Poland, Czechoslovakia. Such history writing was political. But now we face different tasks in a postnationalist age. Now we have to reflect on the world economy in history, we respond to new transnational exigencies. In the past, during my own lifetime, for example, we hardly ever considered social and economic history, while the theme of German unity was pursued. And when we come across remnants of the old attitudes, it strikes me as quite amusing. There was, for example, a conference after the war, a French-German endeavor to construct a more reasonable view of our past conflictual history. Well, it failed miserably, because one couldn't agree on the meaning of the battle of Leipzig (in 1813), when Napoleon was defeated by the Russian and Prussian forces. For the one side this battle meant liberation from the imperialism of Napoleon and, for the French, for the French it was "the betrayal by the Saxons," their desertion of the French/Napoleonic side in order to join the other side.

QUESTION. Doesn't this anachronistic attitude document the persistence of nation-states?

GADAMER. Fortunately, thirty-five or forty years or so have passed since then. Now social and economic history are much more central. As are bigger questions than those of national history. The nation-states of old no longer are central to contemporary history.

QUESTION. You have said that you believe that it is important, to become more aware of the traditions constitutive of one's history. Is this a genuine hermeneutical task to be taken up everywhere? You seem to have an enormous respect for historical realities and what they have become. Many people regard this as a romantic or a conservative view of the past. Do you agree?

GADAMER. I always see limits to change. There is always something which cannot be made over or made at all. Even our democratic election campaigns document this: There is a constant taking into consideration of that which cannot be made the subject of calculation, which cannot be remade. That is why I reject social engineering; realities have to be acknowledged. That is why I criticized Habermas and his program for enlightenment through social science; the implication is social engineering. Now he is also very critical of social engineering. For me a *polis* is always grounded in an ethos. I remain an Aristotelian. We always must acknowledge realities, social realities into which we grow through upbringing and education, and which are simply given, which need not be made.

QUESTION. Would you say then that one needs to be cautious with respect to change?

GADAMER. No, that is not decisive. But from one generation to the next, an 'ethos' is produced, which is the background to change.

QUESTION. You have written an essay entitled: 'Notes on Planning for the Future' (see Chapter 14). It was an address delivered to politicians?

GADAMER. I wanted to warn the politicians. They may not overestimate their capacity to plan. They also need to recognize what is there of its own accord. Someone said to me at the conference in question: Professor Gadamer, you are the person who does not believe that all the changes which have occurred reach down very deeply. I said, yes, exactly.

QUESTION. Are you then opposed to planning?

GADAMER. No. The issue is good planning, planning which takes into account that social planning involves human beings, who are not entirely subject to calculation. The intelligent politician in Germany knows, for example, that what can be said, let us say, in a Bavarian city, may not be said in Duesseldorf.

QUESTION. Do you think that this emphasis upon realism in public life has been underestimated in the reception of your work in North America? By, for example, associating you with Hannah Arendt?

GADAMER. I am much more of a realist than Hannah Arendt. For the rest, you may be in a better position than I to answer this question.

PART 3

Europe and the Humanities

Chapter 12

INTERVIEW: THE 1920s, 1930s, AND THE
PRESENT: NATIONAL SOCIALISM, GERMAN
HISTORY, AND GERMAN CULTURE.

*The two interviews underlying this text both took place in Heidelberg, on July 2
and 4, 1986. Translated by the editors. The quotation at the end comes from the
address entitled 'Von Lehrenden und Lernenden,' delivered on the occasion of
Gadamer's receipt of the Jaspers Prize in 1986. It has been published under this
title in 'Das Erbe Europas,' Frankfurt 1989, Suhrkamp. 158–65. The quoted
and translated passage is from page 158.*

QUESTION. In this last interview, we would like to turn to a different
topic, and a difficult one at that. We would like to raise with you
some questions regarding the nineteen twenties. We might put the
question this way: It is common to see the 1920s treated in the outside world, in North America, for instance, as merely a kind of
preparatory stage to the National Socialist experience of the 1930s.
We are wondering if you would comment on that optic regarding
the 1920s. And secondly, we might ask if you have comments on the
different social currents that might have divided the intellectuals
among each other or separated the intellectuals from the society at
large in the 1920s. Perhaps you would care to comment on either of
those points?

GADAMER. Indeed, you are right to draw attention to the confusions of
this period. And, in essence, the confusion was this: That the mili-
taristic power of Prussia, which had actually built the German
nation, collapsed without warning in 1918, and left us in a situation
for which our social structures gave us no preparation. It is true that
a democratic republic was constituted. It is true that it had a very
well thought out constitution with just one terrible flaw, the Emer-
gency Law that was later used by Hitler. But the confusion was, of
course, also between generations, and it is this confusion which is
expressed in the infamous legend of the "stab in the back." You can
even see that if you think about a figure like the great classical scholar Wilamowitz, the teacher of Werner Jaeger. He was commissioned
to inscribe a memorial to the war dead in Berlin and he composed
the phrase: invictis victi victuri. This means about as much as "To
those who never were defeated—we who have been conquered shall

one day conquer for them." That was the old Prussian and Wilhelminian elite expressing itself. Such a sentence also had a certain attraction to the soldiers and officers that emerged from the war. But the intellectuals—that was a different story. As for myself, for instance, my awakening was actually due to a figure like Theodor Lessing, as I indicated in my autobiography. He adopted a critical relationship to our own culture, and in his book *Europe and Asia* gave me a broader view. I suppose that in some ways Lessing was similar to Spengler, but not primarily nationalistic, and he induced in me and in us severe doubts about the ethos of the older Germany focused on struggle and achievement. So in this way I bade my farewell to the upbringing in my own home. Now another figure important for us in Marburg was a man called Richard Hamann, a student of Simmel, who proclaimed the end of what he called personal culture. His most famous lecture was called "Personal Culture or Objectivity." It is not persons who count, what counts are the material objective circumstances. He was a very left-wing professor who was tremendously important to us students in those days.

QUESTION. Could we perhaps ask a little bit further about that? This seems to be a topic which shows up in different ways and in different circles. The objectivity of the technological age is certainly addressed by Weber in his concept of rationalization, but we also see it in extremists like Jünger, and then this idea also circulates within the Left and shows up again in the period after the Second World War in someone like Marcuse.

GADAMER. Indeed it is true that this is an idea shared between the Left and the Right, and, in fact it is a movement that no one can deny, the switch away from the focus upon great personalities to a focus upon objective and material conditions. The issue was really whether one welcomed this or whether one made it subject to critique. Now a person like Hamann was entirely favorable to this development, but we were much more diffident and uncertain about the matter. And with Heidegger, too, you find that he was exactly as ambiguous on this point as we were. On the one hand, revolutionary over against all of the traditional practices and officials of the university and yet, on the other hand, what became clearer and clearer, disposed to be antitechnological. And even his relation to technology is ambiguous. You know, at the end of his lecture from the fifties, 'Identity and Difference,' it is practically a confession of faith in technology: one must learn to live and cope with technology in a spirit of acceptance. This, of course, was his later period. Now, in the early period, Heidegger in Marburg seemed to have great reservations about this new objectivity and technology. I can remember a lecture in 1924 in

Marburg in which he used the expression "the craze to have everything within reach," a phrase to describe the tempo of the technological age. Everyone had to be first. You had to have the fastest automobile and the fastest airplane. It was a very impressive analysis and critique.

QUESTION. This might be the opportunity to ask you how you yourself experienced the mass culture of the nineteen twenties.

GADAMER. Well you know I was just living in a village, Marburg.

QUESTION. But there was a literature of the big city, Döblin, for example, his novel *Berlin Alexanderplatz*, did this come to your attention?

GADAMER. Of course it did. All of this stuff we read eagerly as it appeared, Döblin above all. *Berlin Alexanderplatz* was a tremendous success, and you know the *Three Penny Opera* was a tremendous success?

QUESTION. You mean you knew the *Three Penny Opera*?

GADAMER. Of course! We students made the *Three Penny Opera* our own music! And of course on the other side there was the formidable influence we all felt from Stefan George.

QUESTION. To take this question of technology a bit further, it is often said, for instance in the United States, that there is a peculiar German schizophrenia about technology, that one is either resigned somehow to just put up with it, or on the other hand, one throws onself into it with wild abandon as we see in a figure like Jünger, with his picture of the worker and total mobilization. So it is often said that there is a typical German schizophrenia over against modernity.

GADAMER. Well, there may be something to that. I can remember that the first lecture that I ever announced was called 'Enlightenment and Romanticism.' I treated the Romantic reaction to the Enlightenment, and in a way that has remained my theme; if you compare *Truth and Method*, you will see that I treat the Enlightenment and the critique of the Romantics of the Enlightenment, the critique in which they think that they have freed themselves from the Enlightenment, and yet were in a certain way just a reaction to it. So this theme has persevered in my work and, in fact, my controversies with Habermas have for the most part been motivated by this question.

QUESTION. But how would you have formulated it back in the 1920s and 1930s and in what way would you have brought this problem to bear upon the events in society that were current at that time? Can you help us a little bit to reconstruct that?

GADAMER. Yes, though when I think again about your question, it seems to me that when the Americans describe this schizophrenia as typically German, they are not quite right. I think that all European countries are exactly the same as Germany in this way. This holds precisely for France. It holds even more for England. This polarity, which can be expressed as the polarity of Romanticism and Enlightenment, was taken up in Germany as a struggle between Left and Right. The German Left said: "Let's at least complete finally the program of the Enlightenment," and the Right said: "That cannot be, because thereby you would destroy the foundations of our national culture."

QUESTION. But is there not a special aggressivity, for example with a figure like Jünger here in Germany, or a certain extreme pessimism in Spengler that would be characteristic of Germany? Are there not, moreover, tendencies in the twenties that specifically characterized the German relation to technology?

GADAMER. No. The special problems of Germany in the 1920s had nothing to do with technology.

QUESTION. What were then the problems peculiar to Germany in the 1920s if not that? Is it the problem of the management of the state? Is it the problem of national survival, the problem of rebuilding the economy, renewing the political life?

GADAMER. You must try to put yourself in the situation which we confronted at that time. We of our generation could not come to terms with the old forms of the German tradition. The old generation were still living in that, and, of course, exercised their influence to retard developments in the country. That is why, for example, in the German student fraternities National Socialism had such a strong following. That certainly did not concern us, the intellectuals. We looked down our noses upon those fellows. But we had a very trying, discouraging situation to confront. You must recall, not only the weaknesses of our own Weimar republic but the hopelessness of the policies being pursued at that time by the French. It was the French, you know, who prevented any reasonable peace settlement. You know that Brüning at that time had good connections with England, and a thorough understanding of English politics and civilization. He worked tirelessly as Chancellor to bring the English together with the Americans, who had always had the view that revenge was completely out of place. The Americans had always held that one must set a limit to the reparation payments, that it is not possible to set an unlimited challenge to an industrial state. An economy cannot function in a way that one is not working for oneself but always for others. But you see, that was the consequence of these policies that were pursued by the French. Germans could not work without realizing that we were not doing it for ourselves.

QUESTION. So it had to do with these enormous sums that were demanded?

GADAMER. No, it had to do with the indefiniteness of the sums. There was no fixed sum. What the Germans, for example, had demanded from the French in 1871 seemed in those times to be a fantastically huge sum, and yet in ten years it was all paid off without great difficulty.

QUESTION. I see, and here there was neither a date nor an amount.

GADAMER. Nothing, nothing. The Davis Agreement and the Young Agreement all failed because of the absolute refusal of the French to limit the reparations. It was altogether a very malodorous policy which the French pursued after the First World War, unknown to us. We did not know that it was always the French who were causing the problem. We just knew that it was the Allies. Now Brüning of course knew, and so did Stresemann, whose policy was to try to prepare the German economy for a time in which we would once again be working for ourselves. And precisely at that point, then, Schleicher fell, exactly at the point when he was about to conclude an agreement for closing down the reparation payments.

QUESTION. And you are suggesting that if that had succeeded a great deal would have been different.

GADAMER. Everything would have been different.

QUESTION. This is tragic; it appears to be another chapter in the tragic history of Germany.

GADAMER. Indeed, that is so. Now it is true that one can reproach Brüning for many things. He was dogmatic and we know meanwhile that he was also a royalist. Now we have his diaries. We know that he wanted to restore the Hohenzollern monarchy. If we had known that, we would never have voted for him.

QUESTION. So you yourself had considerable sympathy for Brüning in those days.

GADAMER. Indeed, yes.

QUESTION. And in view of the choice between what was called democracy in those days and monarchy?

GADAMER. No, no. The choice in those days was between bourgeois society and Soviet-style collectivism, that was the issue.

QUESTION. So it was an intensive conflict of Left and Right.

GADAMER. Of course. The conservatives that Brüning represented, of course, were not the old landed-estate owners, the so-called Junkers. They were to the right of Brüning's Centre Party. In the 1920s they rallied to the National Party.

QUESTION. So you are speaking about the people we call liberal conservatives, those in any case whom Max Weber had always differentiated from the old Prussian establishment. It would seem then that there is a continuity, a liberal continuity, from Weber through to you, to differentiate your tradition from those Junkers in the National Party and also the new radical conservatives like Jünger who were always anti-Republican.

GADAMER. Yes, that's right. Although, I must say I never thought of myself as a conservative.

QUESTION. If you have never seen yourself as a conservative, how would you then describe yourself?

GADAMER. I have always been a liberal from early times to today, and I have always voted for the FDP.

QUESTION. So there is an influence Max Weber exercised upon yourself and your generation that carries through even to today.

GADAMER. Yes, indeed. Max Weber was for us an absolutely central person. Actually, it was through him in a way that we came to the conclusion that we would have to philosophize. We saw that, majestic as that figure was, Max Weber, it would not be possible to be like that. This inner-worldly asceticism of a value-free science which is then perfected by a certain kind of decisionism, we found it majestic but impossible. Heidegger felt that too. So did Jaspers.

QUESTION. Jaspers and Löwith seem to have been the only ones of your group who actually wrote about Max Weber. The generation that lay before the Second World War and before the Nazis stood very close to him, to Weber, but yet you did not write about him.

GADAMER. Yes, you know Max Weber was indeed a curious man, a giant of course, and yet also a quixotic figure. We could see that at this time. He was a quarrelsome person who was always fighting duels, did you know that? No, a very peculiar and very torn man and yet a man marked by a truly staggering and exaggerated heroism.

QUESTION. What we would like to know is what you knew of him in those years in the 1920s. For we realize that you yourself were not working on sociology.

GADAMER. Obviously we all knew the lecture on 'Science as a Vocation' and the lecture on 'Politics as a Vocation,' and some of his methodological writings, but the great works of historical sociology we did not know. One saw him as a symbol of a kind of scientific life with which we could not identify.

QUESTION. And that was...

GADAMER. Value-free science. We could only see that as a fanaticism of objectivity. Karl Löwith, you know, wrote an essay on Max Weber and Marx. It was around 1932, and you have to realize that in those times Marx was present among us as one of the great alternatives.

QUESTION. Of course Marx was an alternative in those days, but was he that for you as well?

GADAMER. Oh yes, for me and for all of us.

QUESTION. That gives us an occasion to ask you a little bit more directly about the Frankfurt school. It is now clear to us that many themes of pessimism and cultural critique were shared between the Left and the Right in those days, and there were many ties between different sectors of the intellectuals. So we are curious about your relation to the Frankfurt school. Did you know them in those years prior to the Third Reich? And what were your impressions and your experiences?

GADAMER. Well, in their midst, you know, we felt rather like the country cousins who'd come to town. We had all of the strengths of the peasantry and all of the weaknesses of the peasantry. These people, Horkheimer, Adorno, appeared to us as amazingly sophisticated intellectuals, and yet we must say not very substantial. And we were used to a much higher degree of competence, not to put too fine a point on it, through the teaching of Heidegger. We did not think that the Frankfurt school were so terribly competent.

QUESTION. You mean not so scrupulous in the interpretation of texts, for example?

GADAMER. Yes, but also in the general manner of work.

QUESTION. But certainly they were very well informed.

GADAMER. That is something else. Being well-informed is not the same as being substantial.

QUESTION. Did you know about Horkheimer's early works, relatively Marxist in character, works like 'Traditional and Critical Theory'? They were thought through very carefully and written very carefully, much different from the kind of work that he later did together with Adorno.

GADAMER. Yes, indeed. We knew that work. I can't say that we studied it closely. But we were aware of it and we did meet with these people quite regularly and we had the impression, yes, they are very clever fellows, we could not ignore that, but, I have to say—and you mustn't take this for anti-Semitism—but there is a kind of a competence that we believed that we possessed as contrasted with the facile form of work that we saw in them. So all I can say is, we felt like country cousins visiting the big city. To hear us talk, you would think we had a superiority complex, and of course hidden behind that, there was an inferiority complex.

QUESTION. And were there not intermediate figures who linked the two circles?

GADAMER. Indeed, especially Kurt Riezler, with whom I formed a very close friendship. He was both a classical scholar and a political figure. You know, he had been the private secretary of Bethman-Hollweg, the Chancellor during the First World War. It was Kurt Riezler's idea to transport Lenin in closed cars across Germany to send him to the Finland Station in Saint Petersburg. He was a young diplomat and a politician whom I admired very, very much. He was a kind of link between our circle and the Frankfurt school. You know that Riezler is one of the persons who actually founded the New School of Social Research in New York City. I last saw him myself in 1938 in Berlin. I visited him and he was telling me that the time had come, he knew now that he had to leave. He told me that he had a daughter and he was worried about her and he left just days or weeks before the 'night of the crystals' (*Reichskristallnacht*), when the attacks on the Jews in Germany were escalating.

QUESTION. You realize that in all these questions we are asking you, what we would really like to understand is the intellectual climate in the years of the 1920s in Germany, and we're asking you as a sort of living witness how you experienced these years.

GADAMER. Well, that's very good, yet you have to realize what a village I was really living in, what a ghetto. Living in Marburg and preoccupied with my academic studies. Of course, in a certain way, people can reproach us about this, that we and others of my generation were not sufficiently alert to the dangers that were posed by Hitler. And they are quite right, in some respects. My belief was that it was absolutely impossible that Hitler could prove to be a figure of significance. This was the general conviction of liberal intellectuals in Germany. Now it is true that there were others, the people that we now call conservatives, but what I have been trying to tell you is the viewpoint of a liberal intellectual youth in the circle to which I belonged. And you must grasp, as I said, the confinements and restrictions of the experience of a young student undertaking academic work under life conditions which were often threatened by hunger. You must grasp that it was only very, very slowly that I began to see the fatal possibility that lay before us. I saw how the student fraternities were becoming more and more nationalistic and like others I just shook my head about it. You have to understand how remote we liberal youth of the intelligensia felt with respect to all these developments.

QUESTION. We are now also interested in your views about the relationship between philosophical studies and social criticism and social study. You know a person like Weber began to develop theories, the account of charisma for instance, which seemed applicable to the Nazi movement in Germany, and other people on the Right began to develop nationalistic and adventurous ideas. Is it not the case that you yourself shared with them a sense of crisis, that you yourself have spoken about the end of liberal consciousness?

GADAMER. Absolutely not. I cannot accept that formulation.

QUESTION. Well then, what formulation would you have used in those days for the state of affairs in the country after 1918?

GADAMER. What I just meant to say is that if you use the word 'liberal' in the modern political sense, I have always spoken of myself as a liberal and have never spoken of the end of liberal consciousness or the liberal era.

QUESTION. What we meant was more 'liberal' in a nineteenth-century cultural sense, such as with liberal theology.

GADAMER. That is absolutely true. There is of course a sense of the word that you have in mind, and you are right, that was gone. We saw that in figures like Karl Barth or also in another sense in Stefan George or in the political romanticism of Carl Schmitt. But when I spoke of myself as a liberal, what I meant for my part was that I and my friends stood against a reactionary, disappointed and resentful movement in wide circles of the German population. We felt utterly distanced from them. It's not that we made common cause with the big liberal newspapers and publications, but what I mean to say is that we just simply felt much more at home with the *Three Penny Opera* than we did, let us say, with a figure of the romantic and nationalist right wing such as Hans Freyer.

QUESTION. He was part of the youth movement, wasn't he?

GADAMER. That's right, the romantic youth movement. But you know, you have been asking me political questions about a time in which I myself was simply not mature. In a dim way and in certain connections, I felt a distance over against these reactionary tendencies of the German youth and of the German bureaucracy. At the same time, I had things in common with them, which undoubtedly influenced me. Yet, influenced as I was, it was always with an inner feeling of discontent, and I fundamentally stuck to the idea there can never be another war. That was absolutely impossible. Our own army of 100,000 soldiers had meanwhile become, in fact, through the progress of technology, a major power again. And I thought that, with weapons such as these that are at the disposal of an army today, surely there is not a politician anywhere who could suppose that he could solve a country's problems by military means. Surely it is unthinkable that a person would seek a military solution merely to gain an advantage for his nation. And I myself, looking at a figure like Hitler, saw in him a monstrous anachronism, amazed that one would think of pursuing a war of revenge, restoring German honor and so on. Even Stefan George seemed to play with ideas like that, but I felt myself quite distanced from the political interpretation of George. Wolters, a close associate of George whom I knew at that time, tried to draw me into it. But I wouldn't do it. I thought to myself, what does this have to do with me, these nationalistic youth groups, what would I have to do with them? I am not saying this to reflect credit upon myself now, far from it. I am simply telling you how I was.

QUESTION. As we said a moment ago, we wanted to understand how the intellectual youth of your time reacted to the currents of action and the currents of thought. Let us recall that a figure like Husserl in his essay 'Philosophy as a Rigorous Science' did envisage the possibility that rigorous science had to respond to the issues of the times, and obviously that means philosophy, and that brings the comparison between psychologism and the *Weltanschauungsphilosophie*. So in this milieu in which people sought to bring philosophy to bear upon reality, we wonder how your own thought and that of Heidegger related itself to the concrete political questions of the time, not the detailed debates, but rather the question of what the fate of the West would be.

GADAMER. Well, I tried earlier to say how we saw a figure like Max Weber. We saw him representing an impossible ideal. Rigorous science, on the one hand, and a type of mystical decisionism, on the other. We urgently desired something different from that. To put it the way Jaspers did, we wanted to grasp in what way reason was incarnate in existence itself. And it is that search which has determined my entire philosophical work. Right to my very last years that impulse is what has held through. What I had known even as a young man is this: I could see the grandeur of the idea of science, but also its weakness over against what we called in those days *das Leben*, life. For me that insight was central as it was for all of our generation, and it was for this reason that Heidegger spoke to us so profoundly, and with the existential pathos that we also saw in Jaspers and also in reading Kierkegaard. Now I have tried to say what it was that we were looking for, but I fear that that does not answer your question directly about the objective currents of society in Germany in that period. It was not a social theory that we elaborated. Instead of that, we were in search of a way to think in which we could see the truth of things, to discover the truth that was there in each thing before us in the world. And this meant that we were utterly distanced from not only the older ethos of German struggle and German fulfillment, but distanced likewise from efforts to control things, to make things, to manage things. So a figure like Stefan George was for me personally the example of an authentic poet and human being who went his way, distanced as he was from mass civilization, following his own star. And this was what we saw in Heidegger, Bultmann, and other teachers in Marburg. Following their star, unswayed by the events of the great world.

QUESTION. And yet in a certain way receptive and aware of them.

GADAMER. Yes, more or less. We all reacted to what was going on. We did not stand outside our society, of course, but our interest did not lie in these events of the political and social order. For this reason I felt quite distant from a man like Gehlen, whom I came to know at that time. We were in utterly different worlds. He was a big city fellow with a certain cynical manner. I, by contrast with Gehlen, was a Romantic.

QUESTION. At this juncture, we, of course, would like to know whether you had any intensive encounter with Nietzsche in this time.

GADAMER. No I did not. And in fact I have never understood the enthusiasm for Nietzsche, neither in those days nor in our own. I have never understood how one has come to see Nietzsche as an epochal figure, or perhaps now I do understand it. Nietzsche is the one, I suppose, who has expressed what it is about modernity that makes life impossible. But the productive use of Nietzsche which so many of my friends and later my students undertook has always been strange to me.

QUESTION. So there was much enthusiasm for Nietzsche at that time?

GADAMER. Yes, relatively great enthusiasm, although, in fact, one cannot compare it to the astonishing enthusiasm for Nietzsche that you find today in France or in the United States. It is true that prior to the First World War there was an enthusiasm for Nietzsche here in Germany, just as there was in England. In fact, all of Europe was inflamed by Nietzscheanism in one fashion or another. We see it in Theodor Lessing, we see it in Thomas Mann, we see it in Gide. His influence was all over the place.

QUESTION. So your distance from Nietzsche is due to your classical studies?

GADAMER. No, it was not really that. I am not sure to what I should attribute it. You know, I grew up in neo-Kantianism. It was epistemology and philosophy of science that concerned me in my studies, and the efforts to constitute a moral philosophy in accord with those movements. Now, I suppose that Leo Strauss was right when he said that my concern was to respond critically to Dilthey, just as it was Heidegger's concern to respond critically to Nietzsche.

QUESTION. So if we might try to summarize the conversation up to this point—we have learned so far, that during the 1920s, before you studied with Heidegger and even after you had begun to study with him, his probing questioning of technology had not yet taken place. And generally nobody was reflecting on it as revealing the potential for destruction built into the modern age.

GADAMER. Exactly. I myself only began to think about this problem toward the end of the 1920s, after reading—among other texts— what Spengler had to say on this topic. Before that, this topic had not yet concerned us. Cultural pessimism and the critique of liberal culture had not yet been connected with this theme. And the most important writings on the question and problem of technology and technique appeared only during the 1930s.

QUESTION. You yourself then never had much sympathy for people like Ernst Jünger?

GADAMER. No. That was a wild romanticism about technology. People like that celebrated its very violence as if it had some magic in it. We were liberals. But people like Jünger never grasped how formative the Enlightenment was for any modern Romanticism.

QUESTION. Maybe you will not mind if we try to broaden our scope now in this conversation. In your recent writings you do take deliberate steps to transcend the limits of German history and its traditions. Having discussed your relation to this history so far, we would like to ask you whether in your recent writings you are now putting forward a different point of view, one which regards the *Geisteswissenschaften* as a product of European or at least of West European history as a whole.

GADAMER. I have always regarded the *Geisteswissenschaften* as an achievement of European history as a whole (but also of North America). When I speak of the European *Geisteswissenschaften*, I refer to a concept of inquiry which arose during the Romantic period, and not only in Germany. There are equivalents to the term in France and Great Britain. This holds, even if there are differences: In Germany one focused on the epistemological problems and opportunities which these inquiries posed, while this never was an issue in Great Britain, or only insofar as one had to contend with the predominance of science, the scientific method. In Germany we stand in the middle, perhaps, between what the French called *les belles lettres* and what was referred to as the 'moral sciences' by John Stuart Mill. But still philosophy remains philosophy and history history. Thus we have the 'philological-historical' sciences in all three cases and perhaps everywhere. One shouldn't just look at the issue of the humanities from the perspective of philosophy. In Germany, of course, this was the prevalent point of view: to think of the *Geisteswissenschaften* in terms of a particular philosophy. With us they acquired a highly specific meaning in *philosophy*. This has not happened elsewhere.

QUESTION. What then, is distinctive of the *Geisteswissenschaften*, 'humanities,' *les belles lettres* outside Germany?

GADAMER. Well, there is a multiplicity of achievements. We merely need to recall the contributions by French scholars to Chinese, Egyptian, and Oriental philology, to the study of languages and linguistics. In Great Britain we have the study of the history of religion, of symbolism, as in the case of Frazer and *The Golden Bough*. There are also important discoveries which have been made by Italians and Scandinavians as well as East Europeans. One merely needs to recall how strongly Poland, Czechoslovakia, Hungary and other Slavic countries were oriented to the West. No, the *Geisteswissenschaften* are not merely a German phenomenon. The situation is somewhat different when one considers Russia. For the tradition of Byzantine and Orthodox Christianity never developed a formal theology as we find it where Catholicism prevailed, nor, therefore, has there arisen an alignment between the teaching of Christian dogmatics and humanism.

QUESTION. Have you changed your views on the *Geisteswissenschaften*, compared to, let us say, the time of *Wahrheit und Methode*? Do you now take a more European view?

GADAMER. No, not at all. The times have changed, world history, not I. There we are in Europe, in this dangerous position of being situated between the two world-power blocs, and certain to be the battleground in case of a nuclear conflagration. Thus we ask ourselves what our role can be (and whether we can play any) in world history. Given the precarious condition of Europe, especially of Western Europe, it is important to consider that we only can choose between two "evils." This is how it always is, in politics and life. The choice is always between two evils, between possibilities which are not the most appealing. Thus a politically thinking person in our part of the world will choose the U.S. side in the global conflict.

QUESTION. Does this not amount to paying a cultural price, even if you gain military protection?

GADAMER. Well, would it not be higher were we to opt for the Soviets? Imagine: a government which knows the truth—that is the Soviet Government. What would happen to research and inquiry under its control? We should not have any illusions here: Soviet foreign policy is geared toward dissolving the bonds which link West Germany to the West.

QUESTION. So how do you see what Heidegger once said, when he spoke of Europe and Germany as caught "in the pincers between Russia and America"?

GADAMER. Certainly, there is some truth to this. What we are talking about here is a choice to be made between two realities of power. It is part of this reality that economic integration has progressed so far. There is a world economy. And Europe controls a small percentage of the capital invested in it, much less than the United States. But then, of course, I have pursued the question of the 'distinctiveness' of Europe in my recent essays for exactly these reasons. The question is: What does Europe, Western Europe, have to offer, given these realities of power? We are reduced to the status of a *Kulturnation*. Our goods are cultural goods, as was the case with Greece under Roman rule. This is what I reflect on, thus learning with the times and taking account of these new realities of Europe.

QUESTION. In an earlier interview, you told us about lectures which you delivered during the early 1930s, on the theme of 'Romanticism and Enlightenment,' obviously a very European theme. Can it be claimed that what you regard as the Enlightenment really amounts to no more than the rationalism of the Enlightenment, its philosophy of science? Doesn't it include a political philosophy?

GADAMER. No, here you are wrong. What I meant actually was the critique of religion during the Enlightenment. That is Enlightenment. And as to its political philosophy, that is another aspect of the whole, the one which came to the fore with the French Revolution and the American Declaration of Independence.

QUESTION. In *Reason in the Age of Science* you argue that Hegel was correct when he said: From now on (his time on) the principle of the freedom of all can no longer be revoked. It is the principle of world history. Richard Bernstein therefore argues that you have become more 'radical' after *Wahrheit und Methode* and that this allusion to Hegel shows this.

GADAMER. No, I have always believed that. I always was a liberal. It is true: I didn't speak about these things during the Third Reich. There was no need to directly report to the executioner for those of us, like myself and my friends, who were part of the opposition. Thus I had begun writing about Greek philosophy, before 1933, in quite a political way, about the Sophists, for example. Now how could I have avoided referring to Carl Schmitt in this context? You know his definition of the 'political' merely in terms of enemies and friends as conceptual opposites (*Gegensatz*). That is very much like the position of a Sophist. But I had to refrain from all this—and so I only published *Plato and the Poets*. And then I turned to physics, the difference between the Aristotelian and Galilean forms of it. And I only published one longer text during the Nazi period, a monograph on Herder. And there was trouble right away, because I objected to the predominance of the Nordic and Germanic races and argued, in terms of the diversity of peoples, cultures, languages; as I do now as well, when I write about Europe. This text is based on a lecture given to French prisoners of war, officers, in 1940 or 1941, after the collapse of France, when I was already Professor in Leipzig. And then I was invited again, in the context of the cultural politics of the Reich. And it is quite true: One accepted this kind of ambiguous assignment. Yes, I knew, the Nazi regime wanted to show there still are those German professors who are not Nazis. That was what one was good for. But then this is what I did: To never speak like a Nazi.

QUESTION. It must have been hard for you to go to France then, while it was occupied.

GADAMER. Well, it was this way: I had friends, French friends, who thought as I did. They were not Nazi sympathizers. But they thought, as I did, that the defeat of France also was a consequence of a very arrogant political attitude maintained by France after the first world war. Without these politics, insisting, e.g., on unlimited reparation payments, Hitler would not have come to power. Similarly, England did not curtail Hitler's expansionist urges. They welcomed the fact, that Germany under Hitler had begun to set limits to French power. They still followed the old 'balance of powers' doctrine.

QUESTION. How then, do you see the present situation? Will Europe unite under the banner of Enlightenment principles, e.g., the principle of the freedom of all? Will old national traditions crumble and disappear?

GADAMER. Well, we still are far from having attained this state of affairs. We haven't overcome nationalism yet. And elsewhere in the world, even less so. In Africa, for example, we are just seeing the birth of new nation-states; while in our case, in the case of the more developed states, we are moving away from that. But as for Europe, you merely have to remember that Mendès-France once blocked the plans for the formation of a combined European military. France prevented the European unification process from including the military. But it could have been done. Imagine what this would mean. But then it would have been likely that Germans should have become the chiefs of staff. German generals would have been in command. How could France have accepted that? They knew the German talent for military organization. And there are also economic obstacles to European unification. France always has to consider its farmers. That isn't so important in Germany. We are like a thoroughfare: We get the raw materials and send them on in an improved state. That's the basis for economic stability here. And when there is inflation, then we pay more for raw materials, but sell them for more as well.

QUESTION. So is it not the case, that the role of traditions has changed in European history, that there are new conditions now, which have to be acknowledged?

GADAMER. Not really. The importance of national traditions, that was over with Hitler. I, the German intellectuals of Weimar, we were republicans. Not so the army and aristocracy, especially these two groups. In 1918 German intellectuals began to think in terms of democracy as a worldwide phenomenon. And I can account for this in my theory. I never defended particular traditions, only that there is a horizon of tradition, which always constitutes the background for change. Thus, what remains in Europe is the specificity or distinctiveness of its history, of a multilingual, geographically small region of the world, a small continent attached to Asia, and with much less population than Asia, which is saturated with history. No, we can no longer strive to be a world power, but a cultural factor. And one notices this when one observes the people coming from abroad to study in Europe. They come to Germany because of philosophy, for philology and the *belles lettres* they go to France, and to England for both, given the language. As Romans would go to Athens or Rhodes in order to study. And to come back to the theme of Europe caught in the "pincers between Russia and America," yes, there is a danger, the general appeal of the American way of life, that is a powerful force. And in that sense the United States may be a danger to peace, because there is a sense of mission which equals that of Soviet Russia. There really are these two antagonistic powers, and Europe caught in the middle, in a threatened position. This is why we have to play the cultural role which I mentioned: as educators, teachers perhaps, as thinkers.

QUESTION. Given the changes which we have discussed, the transformation of Europe and the phenomenon of global integration, is it conceivable that you would rethink some of the themes of *Wahrheit und Methode* in the light of these new 'givens'? Would you take note of the disruption of historical continuities, of traditions, for example?

GADAMER. No, I don't believe there is any need to do so. But I have altered some of the emphasis which I had previously given to the work. I used to think from the perspective of the *Geisteswissenshaften* as the central problem, more so than I do now. Then I took the debate about Dilthey's position as my guide and Heidegger's innovations with respect to it, with respect to the analysis of historical consciousness. Now, when I lecture on hermeneutics, I can raise this entire debate to a more adequate level. I begin from the opposite end, so to speak. I now begin where I ended in *Wahrheit und Methode*. I begin with language, the linguistic structure of experience, with art. In both cases I emphasize their role in the construction of the social, the forming of the social. I hardly mention the human sciences. My argument has not become more political than it was, but it is more direct: I address the phenomena at issue rather than the science or theory of them. This becomes apparent in the long metacritical postscript to *Wahrheit und Methode*, in volume two of my collected works, the new edition of *Wahrheit und Methode*.

QUESTION. It is clear then that you believe that your earlier work, the work of the 1950's (such as *Wahrheit und Methode*), already adequately responded to the changes which had taken place?

GADAMER. Yes, I believe so. That is why I was disappointed when I came to West Germany in 1947. I had, after all, experienced for a period of two years what a Soviet reorganization of German society could look like. And here in the West people wanted to continue on the basis of a Germany prior to 1933. I was shocked, horrified by this failure to take account of the extent of social change which had occurred. Someone of my age at the time, a person of 45 or older, understood that the history of Germany as a nation-state was over. That is why we turned to Europe as a theme. But then this didn't come off fully, this process of European integration. The French were reluctant and then there were new developments abroad; new nation-states were formed in Africa, there was Latin-American nationalism, the nationalism of the Slavic countries despite their satellite status. Much of this took us by surprise, such as—much later—the resurgence of Islam as a world-historical factor. But the history of Europe as a history of the European nation-states, that was over. One can see this in history writing, in the turn to social and economic history, away from mere national history.

QUESTION. Much of what you say now indicates that you have a vision of the future. You speak of democracy as a worldwide phenomenon, the new nation-states, a postnational order, of the changing status of Europe. Do we need a specific vision of the future?

GADAMER. Well, I agree with Ernst Bloch. The principle of hope simply holds true. We need to anticipate what will make human life worthwhile. This can and does have varying contents. But it is there. And as an older man I perhaps have a greater openness to the future, corresponding to a distance from the immediately pressing problems.

QUESTION. Is the philosopher always an older person, spiritually speaking, and in thought?

GADAMER. A prophet who has turned his gaze to the past, yes. Just as a related definition of the historian suggests. But add to this the fact of old age, and then the capacity to envisage larger contexts and relations, i.e., those which transcend the immediately given, is more developed. When I was younger, I couldn't have written about the diversity and distinctiveness of Europe as I do now. It is harder to think abstractly as one ages. But one acquires a capacity to comprehend an infinite wealth of concrete details.

QUESTION. Therefore you do not believe that the philosopher has a special capacity for understanding the future?

GADAMER. People who expect this of us philosophers, they better think for themselves. No, in this sense I agree with Hegel and Heidegger.

QUESTION. With Heidegger? Didn't Heidegger have something like a utopian vision?

GADAMER. No, not really: This idea of the god or gods who are to save us? That is entirely vague. Didn't Heidegger just mean that the planners *cannot* save us? All this is very ambiguous in his case. Quite apart from the fact that his grasp of what was really happening was always very poor, much less developed than mine. But then I don't have his capacity for abstract thought. One can also see this in his interpretations of poetry, of Hölderlin and Trakl. I can see what he means in the case of Hölderlin, Hölderlin appears as Hegel's limit. Yes. But in the case of Trakl, projecting the ontological difference into a poem.... That is most abstract.

QUESTION. But back to you. You often speak of the openness of hermeneutical experience, how we partake in the event of meaning without controlling it. Does this also apply to historical experience?

GADAMER. Certainly. Insofar as hermeneutics is more than a theory of the human sciences, it also has the human situation in the world in its entirety in view. Thus it must be possible to include different cultures and religions, etc., and their relations. What is at issue here is that when something other or different is understood, then we must also concede something, yield—in certain limits—to the truth of the other. That is the essence, the soul of my hermeneutics: To understand someone else is to see the justice, the truth, of their position. And this is what transforms us. And if we then have to become part of a new world civilization, if this is our task, then we shall need a philosophy which is similar to my hermeneutics, a philosophy which teaches us to see the justification for the other's point of view and which thus makes us doubt our own. Therefore one needs to be tolerant in the West toward the Soviet Union. Always insisting on human rights, insisting that they must accept parliamentary democracy in order to industrialize fully, that reveals only our own preoccupations, which do not reflect their history.

QUESTION. Is there something, Professor Gadamer, with which you would like to conclude our long conversations, perhaps something which illustrates your most recent work?

GADAMER. Well, there is a passage from a recent address, my reply to Jaspers. It illustrates the political implications of my work, as I understand them:

The very humanity of our existence depends, finally, upon whether we have learned to see the limits which our own nature has set for us, over against the nature of others. It is this conviction that undergirds the passionate concern that has always filled me, to pass along such knowledge and insight as I have gained. We learn from those who learn from us. Now I do not believe that I have a vocation like that of Karl Jaspers, whom I revere so highly and who has given his name to the prize I am honoured to accept, to articulate positions on the political events of the day. My conviction, rather, is that it is already a sufficient political act to be a thinker and to school others in thought, to practice the free exercise of judgment and to awaken that exercise in others. For my experience has been that my own power of judgment finds its limits, and also its enrichment, whenever I find someone else exercising his own power of judgment. That is the very soul of hermeneutics.

Chapter 13

THE PHILOSOPHY AND RELIGION OF JUDAISM*

In our era, when the lives of human beings on earth are being forged into a unity, we are becoming particularly conscious of the narrowness of the traditions in which we Europeans live. And yet it is the tradition of Western philosophy and science which has modeled the face of this modern unification of human civilization. We are certainly aware of the noble forms of philosophical wisdom which the great Asian cultures have generated by translating their autochthonous religious creations into the medium of thought. Western philosophy and science is, however, solely of Greek origin. Just as the fate of the West was determined in the Persian Wars by the repulsion of the Orient, so too has the intellectual creation of the Greeks, *philosophia*, unambiguously directed the path of humanity up to our time of industry and technology. This path of science which the Greeks took, remained over many centuries very closely connected to the religious thinking of Greek culture. The intellectual clarity of the Olympic religion, which stood out radiant against the dark background of a terrible prehistory, prefigured, as it were, the clear rationality of philosophical and scientific thinking. The marvelous superficiality of the Greeks, their eye for the contours of things, for the permanent essential forms of all natural things, i.e., what preserves constancy and order throughout change, this became the precious inheritance of the young Germanic-Romanic peoples. And from this, modern science eventually grew.

But the unity of Western culture is also determined by a second factor, which, although not born from the Greek spirit, still fused with the Greek inheritance to form a unitary, effective structure. It is Christianity, the religion of the New and Old Testament, the great religion of the West, which owes its ecumenical turn to Christ's missionary commandment and its sovereign spiritual execution by the Apostle Paul. When one asks what the contribution by Judaism was to the effective unity of European culture, then the global answer concerning the Jewish origins of the Christian religion is the answer to a much too narrowly defined question. In truth, it is equally inappropriate to speak of a contribution by Judaism to European culture as, for example, of a contribution by the Greeks. These are the primordial thoughts of the West, which were

---

*Essay published in Stuttgart, 1961.

originally thought in different places. The primordial Greek word for the essence of things is logos and the world which is seen in the light of this logos is called the cosmos. The grand cosmic order, which rules the processes of nature, encompasses also the apparent chaos of human fates and permits, in their ups and downs, the return and stability of the same total order. Another primordial word was spoken originally by the Jewish religion and has come to resound no less deeply in the soul of Western humanity: the word of the personal God, who addresses his own with vengeance and punishment but also with promise. Although the claim to be the chosen people and to stand under the special protection of the Omnipotent is irritatingly and tragically divisive, the Jewish doctrine of being chosen revealed a completely new area beyond the Greek perception of the world, the area of history as a path toward salvation. Logos and the Word of God, the philosopher and the prophet as the interpreters and mediators of these primordial words, cosmos and the history of salvation as the content of their teaching—these are the two great separate roots from which the world tree of our age would grow. Since the time of the Christian Fathers, the history of Greek-Occidental philosophy also gained sustenance from this other root of our being, which reached to the foundation of Jewish prehistory.

The noble unity of the intellectual tradition of Western philosophy, in which we stand and in which the most varied historical forces have melted together, has however, in addition to this, other distinctive moments in its history when the question about the contribution by Judaism to Western philosophy attains a special meaning. In Hellenistic antiquity Philo Judaeus played an important mediating role, as is proven by the continual references by the church fathers to Philo. At the height of the Middle Ages, Moses Maimonides held an equally important mediating role, transmitting Arabian Aristotelianism within the tradition of Judaism to the intellectual creators of medieval Scholasticism. In the end, however, the century of the modern Enlightenment, the eighteenth, is the time of the strongest effects and countereffects between Jewish religious thought and the spirit of modernity. Spinoza and Moses Mendelssohn stood in the front line of the intellectual dispute, which led to the era of liberalism. And again, when the era of optimism concerning progress and of universal reverence for culture perished in the storms of our century, Jewish thinkers, such as Franz Rosenzweig and Martin Buber, played a leading role in the critique of nineteenth-century liberalism, drawing their strength from the religious life of the Jewish community. I wish now to demonstrate how, at these four distinctive moments when great Jewish thinkers raised their voices in the conversation of the centuries, it happened that from the springs of Judaism, philosophical thoughts arose which echoed in everyone's thinking consciousness.

It is easily understandable from their particular intellectual task why the Christian Fathers referred so enthusiastically to Philo Judaeus. Naturally they did not think of him as a Jew or a philosophical interpreter of Jewish religion as such. They saw in him their own, the Christian, truths and greeted him as an important conversation partner who knew how to apply thoughts, using Greek means from within the Greek tradition (which dominated the Hellenistic world), which were close to their own hearts. The Christian proclamation, the teaching of a transcendent God, who as the Savior came into the world and founded the Church, was difficult to express in the terms of classical Greek philosophy. The eternal gods, of whom Homer spoke—Zeus and Athena, Ares, Aphrodite, Persephone—were considered by the Greek philosophers to be basic forms, through which the world presented itself—in government and wisdom, war, love and death—and not as transcendent powers. The multiplicity of this worldly essence of the gods was revealed everywhere in the religious reality of the cult. And when the Greek philosophers began to contemplate the world and being, grasping in thought the order of beings, it was a decidedly worldly religion that they had to translate into the language of concepts.

Now it certainly was already the case with declining Greek culture itself, that the old cosmos of a revealed and natural, although also secret and mysterious order, began to change. Of Poseidonius, the great Stoic of the first century before Christ, Karl Reinhardt could say: "The old cosmos still stands, but one step further and the powers, which it still unites in itself, will become master over it; they no longer lose their secrets in it, it loses itself into their mystery. Thus it becomes intimating, becomes appearance, a symbol, and out of the powers arise ghosts, energies, chains, sources, primordial forms and effluences of the unspeakable, of the primordial mystery of existence." For this development the Jewish religious teaching of a transcendent God could enter into a productive exchange with the direction of Greek thought. Clearly the transcendence of Jehova, his being aniconic, his invisibility, already distinguished him from the heathen god-cults in Jewish prehistory. When philosophical thought, following Plato's speculative advance, finally ruptured the Greek cosmos and thought the One, who is not of this world, then that thought could be supported by Jewish theology and its philosophical interpreter, Philo. Here, the otherworldly transcendence of the Creator had always been thought. Therefore, the thought of creation itself, the great religious thought of Judaism, promised to overcome, in a positive sense, the worldly constraints of the Greek spirit. It is true that while interpreting the Old Testament employing Greek philosophical language, the Jew Philo used extensively the allegorical method, which had already been used by Stoic philosophy in adopting to popular beliefs.

But, what he expressed using this language, was something other than Greek philosophy: the idea of a personal God, the idea of creation and the teaching of the mediation between the otherworldly God and humans through the orders of the angels—Jewish teachings which Catholic Christianity adopted to a great extent, although they must surely have missed in Philo the thought of the incarnation and its mystery.

The genesis of the philosophy of the Middle Ages has been interpreted as the event of the great Hellenization of Christianity. And it is true: the superimposition which the Christian Platonism of the Augustinian type experienced through the reception of genuine Aristotelianism first brought the blossom of Scholasticism to full bloom. The Arabian-Jewish mediation, however, initiated this superimposition. So the Jewish philosophy of the Middle Ages, which reached its greatest perfection in Arabian Spain, was woven into the grand conversation of the times.

Jewish philosophy faced the same thematic as Christian philosophy. They also had to reconcile revelation, which was guaranteed in the sacred texts, with natural reason. Their starting point was the law which Moses received from God on Mount Sinai. This law needed to be demonstrated as being rational. The fundamental form of natural reason appeared to the Jewish thinkers to be that Aristotelian philosophy which had been transmitted to them by the Arabs. Therefore, their thinking was solidly based upon their Jewish inheritance and yet also completely in the sphere of the natural Greek reason. The Greek-influenced philosophy of Judaism therefore received an enduring part from Jewish prophecy. But this philosophy knew how to prove its value and priority using Greek means, especially when it brought Plato's thought into play. Although it was possible for natural reason to understand the world by itself, it was the responsibility of the prophets to grant revelation from the 'world beyond.' So above the traditional form of a Greek wise man, who accomplished a likeness of the divine in the universality of his theoretical life, stood the form of the prophet, to whom God himself spoke and who proclaimed God's will. His word, the authentic source of revelation for Jewish religion, was both insight and act; a warning to and the salvation of a people who had become guilty before God; and a renewal of their reality as God's people and as a political unity.

Such a unity—as an idea—was first formed in Plato's thinking with the demand for the philosopher-kings, who were the only ones able to bring peace to the political corruption of Greek life. Jewish prophetism was understood by Moses Maimonides and his predecessors to be the actual realization of this Platonic utopia: the rule and kingdom of philosophy. Upon this solid basis, the thinking of natural reason could attain the truth of the law. A magnificent thought: the overcoming of the nowhere of the Platonic ideal state by the nowhere of the heavenly

Jerusalem, which lies amidst all lawlessness and suffering, which history has prepared for the children of Israel, and which marks the path of salvation for the chosen people.

The decisive culmination in the reciprocal fertilization of Western philosophy and Jewish thought was attained neither in the classical nor in the medieval enlightenment, but in the modern, the true, the radical Enlightenment. In the seventeenth and eighteenth centuries, with the development of the mathematical natural sciences and their methodological ideal, there occurred a radical questioning of all that had previously been considered valid. It was directed toward the metaphysical tradition of Christianity as well as toward the religious thought of Judaism. Both had to reconcile the old with the new or allow the old to be destroyed by the new. The biblical criticism, which Spinoza was the first to expound with programmatic awareness and in the rationalist spirit of the new understanding of nature, had equally fateful consequences for the religion of the Old Testament as well as the New Testament.

Could the religious traditions of the peoples survive at all while facing the tribunal of the radical belief in reason? Was Spinoza's withdrawal from the Jewish community not symbolic? Was his system of understanding nature and envisioning God a possible mediation and solution? Was it able to prevent his name from becoming the slogan of atheism? And was it not also the free spirits of the epoch in Germany—not to mention France and England of the eighteenth century—did not Lessing and Goethe acknowledge Spinoza in this sense?

On the other hand, continual attempts were made on the Christian as well as on the Jewish side to mediate between the religious tradition and the Enlightenment's radical belief in reason. It is a conversation, based on the Enlightenment, between the devotion to revelation and the belief in reason, which has lasted centuries. It appears to me a tremendous testimony for the importance of Judaism in the last centuries that the Jewish voice can be heard again and again in this conversation. While Lessing—according to Jacobi's report—saw himself as following Spinozism, his educated Jewish friend, Moses Mendelssohn, who lived in Berlin as an employee in a silk company and who interacted with the most important intellectuals of the epoch, held fast to his ancestral religion as the unshaken basis from which he advocated the 'religion of reason.' It is obvious that this could not be accomplished without a reinterpretation and abridgement of the religious tradition. However, in comparison to the Christian, it was easier for the Jew to be enlightened and still devout. The reason lay in his religion. Nathan the wise, as opposed to a Moslem or Christian, was not fortuitously made by Lessing to be the speaker of the religion of tolerance and practical love of one's neighbor. The national limitation, which limited the promise of the Old

Testament to those belonging to the chosen people, contained as well and from the beginning a religious demand for tolerance. Here there was no missionary commandment as in both other world religions competing with Judaism. Inscrutable though the thought of a creator God may be— how much more desperate, in comparison, is the position of the Christian theologian who should be able to comprehend the mystery of the Trinity. No wonder Luther declared the mediation of reason with faith to be impossible and cut the Gordian knot by radically rejecting philosophy. The acceptance of the revealed truths of the Jewish religion was not a comparable imposition opon reason and just because of this, the basis of reason was a moderating medium for all confessional antagonisms into which the Jew was born.

Therefore, Moses Mendelssohn can confront in calm dignity the tactless impositions of Lavater, who wants to force him to convert to the Christian faith, with the avowal of his ancestral belief and respond: "The written and oral laws which constitute our revealed religion are only binding for our nation. All other peoples of the earth, we believe, are directed by God to follow the law of nature and the religion of the patriarchs.... Those who conduct their lives according to these laws will be called 'virtuous men of other nations' by us and are children of eternal bliss. The religion of my fathers does not want to be spread. We should not send missionaries to both Indias or to Greenland in order to preach our religion to these distant peoples.... They follow the law of nature, unfortunately! better than we." It is the truth of natural religion and natural law, which is imposed on all by the Jewish religion alone after it— including the promise—was revealed specifically to the Jews in the Old Testament.

One who hears Mendelssohn argue in this manner will understand that the modern Enlightenment can more easily be reconciled with the religious tradition of Judaism than with the Christian tradition which contains an unsolvable contradiction impossible to hide between reason and revelation. So it is understandable that the 'religion of reason,' the positive result of the Enlightenment, could have been advocated by a large number of Jewish philosophers—from Moses Mendelssohn to Hermann Cohen—to the same degree as by the liberals who had outgrown all religious commitments. Hermann Cohen could even rediscover in Kant's philosophy—in its 'monotheism of ideas' and in its 'primacy of practical reason'—the 'religion of reason from the sources of Judaism.'

And yet, the permeation of Jewish religion and the Enlightenment also could not create a true balance. Spinoza's withdrawal from the Jewish community remained in this respect symbolic. The goal of a rational permeation of the Jewish religious tradition was in itself contradictory. If revelation allows itself to be completely encompassed by thinking reason, then it forfeits its religious binding force. So long as the Jewish law is believed to be the incomprehensible blessing of the Omnipotent, who called the people of Israel at Mount Sinai to be 'His' people, the law is the unsurpassable privilege of the chosen people. If it is recognized as a natural law by natural reason, then it enters into competition with the other truths of reason. Therefore, the teaching of German Idealism, especially Hegel's, was that the standpoint of the law would be correctly overcome by the Christian message of love. For the division of is and ought would always be thought in the law. The true unity and reconciliation would occur in the spirit of love, where all separations would be superseded. This authentic and highest truth of the Christian message, from which the spirit of Judaism is eternally separated, would find its completion in the philosophy of absolute spirit.

Since, however, the meaning of the Christian message must itself evaporate with such a dissolution of the Christian gospel into the truth of philosophical thought, Christianity shared the same fate as the Jewish Enlightenment. The religious history of the nineteenth century became an untenable compromise. Between the synagogue and the religion of liberal education, between the Christian church and the liberal optimism for progress, no permanent balance could succeed.

So it is not surprising that the reaction against the liberal philosophy of culture and theology came from both sides. After the First World War, in whose material battles the cultural consciousness of idealist education was destroyed, the liberal tradition of the nineteenth century was excitedly overrun by 'dialectical' theology and by the so-called existential philosophy—and something similar happened in Jewish thought. At that time, Luther's demand to renounce Aristotle was executed from the Christian-theological side as well as from the philosophical side by especially Karl Barth and Martin Heidegger. And through this, the original Greek thought of the logos came into a radical and critical light. So the Old Testament's primordial thought of the word had to gain a new vitality. Therefore, it was not by accident that Franz Rosenzweig (along with Martin Buber) began a new translation of the Old Testament, like a modern martyr contemplating deeply the faith of his fathers in the face a terrible and incurable disease.

In his great systematic work, *The Star of Redemption*, Franz Rosenzweig, a student of Hermann Cohen and the liberal historian Friedrich Meinecke, developed a novel philosophical justification for the Jewish belief in revelation, in opposition to the Enlightenment and speculative Idealism. Rosenzweig himself later recognized and stated that the starting points and basic thoughts of his work converged with the 'new thinking' which he found represented especially in Martin Heidegger's main work, *Being and Time*. Rosenzweig's book was conceived during the First

World War and appeared in 1921. It is the work of a philosopher who knows himself to be also a theologian and whose conviction is that one cannot philosophize in the present situation without being at the same time a theologian. The reason for this is that the contradiction between the cosmic order, which the Greeks thought, and the destiny of humans, who are conscious of their freedom—and especially their freedom from the mere natural order, within which they nevertheless are still incorporated—, is not solvable from either the perspective of nature or the perspective of human self-consciousness. Greek thinking cannot be restored, but also the titanic attempt of German idealism to deduce, from self-consciousness, nature and spirit and, in this manner, to reconcile the contradictions, fails due to an absolute boundary: purely and simply the factical reality of humans 'who are still there' and philosophize. Idealistic thinking can only think universal essences, that means, however, it has attempted since the Greeks and according to its own essence to think timelessly. With the 'new thinking,' whose time had come, the temporality and historicality of human Dasein was for the first time taken seriously, not incorporated *sub specie aeternitatis* by a philosophy of history into a system of absolute knowledge, as in Hegel, but recognized as an insuperable givenness.

Rosenzweig saw in Heidegger's ontological critique of the concept of consciousness, which founded modern philosophy, something related to his own project, which, after all, was inspired by the religious tradition of Judaism: the already-being [*Schon-Sein*] of humans—in Heidegger formalized as thrownness, the 'in-human' characteristic of Being, which limits the self-positing [*Selbstsetzung*] of transcendental philosophy—is for Rosenzweig the logical warrant for the Old Testament's doctrine of creation. It is the primordiality of the Thou, this primordial thought of Judaism, which proves itself to be fundamental for the understanding of the idea of creation and guarantees the theological solution to the philosophical aporia of facticity. When God addresses Adam, "Where art thou?" humans are revealed their own I and own Here. To this extent God's own Being precedes, in a principle sense, one's own I-Being.

That is the philosophical justification for the teaching concerning the createdness of humans, which Rosenzweig discerns. This is the personal ground, which mediates the opposition of world and human. Inseparable from this is also the mediation which the finitude of the individual experiences through the eternal continuation of the Jewish people in the Old Testament belief. It is based upon the special bond which Jehova forged with his people and climaxes in the promise of eternity. It is realized in the natural blood relationship of the lineage. For the rest of the peoples of the earth, and especially the 'Christian' people of the West, there is no blood relationship established by a promise and standing at the beginning of their history. They understand themselves more readily from the sovereignty of their lands and the cultural community tied to this territory and as being exposed to destruction at some time, shaken by the storms of history. For these reasons, the people of God, specifically because it does not rest on a political but a natural foundation, is certain of its eternity even without state and political power. It stands in its own, its God-given, nature outside world history. The "Star of Redemption" is above them.

Now this distinction of the chosen people—to be certain of their eternity—is, philosophically viewed, itself a historical determination. So this philosophical-theological self-reflection of the Jew despairing over idealism, shares with the 'new thinking' the recognition of the fundamental historicality of human Dasein and Heidegger's critique of transcendental idealism.

Martin Buber later systematically expanded the Jewish contribution to the critique of idealism by emphasizing the fundamental meaning of the 'dialogical principle' and by contrasting the dialogue of humans with God—as it characterizes in the Old Testament the zenith of self-examination and reflection—to the Greek logos philosophy and modern idealism. When Buber, from the perspective of the electedness of the chosen people, interprets in terms of the history of salvation the homelessness of the Jewish people among the differing national cultures—even after the foundation of the state of Israel—including all suffering and persecution which the Jews have ever had to endure, he assigns Jewish thought again a representative responsibility, which leads him again into the vicinity of Heidegger and his teaching of the forgetfulness of Being: to respond to the general homelessness of our epoch, the world's hour of the 'eclipse of God' with the thought of a turning.

The four critical moments in the history of Western thought, which we have examined, are, as demonstrated, moments of a fruitful dialogue with the religious thought of Judaism. One hardly needs to emphasize that one can speak of a contribution by Judaism to European philosophy only in this sense—and not, for example, in the sense of a naturalistic racial concept. Clearly, the intellectual culture of humanity originates from many roots and forces and carries everywhere the signs of its origin. There is an inexplicable determination by nature for all thinking beings, which affects them from birth until death—it encompasses, among others things, the determination of race for the individual and the people. There also is a historical determination of all thinking beings which precedes all freedom and choice of the present generation—it has influenced the Jewish people, as we have seen, perhaps even more than any other historical people. There is, in particular, a formation in the life of the individual starting from childhood and education, which preforms every thinking being, so that one can also infer the forms and directions of thought in philosophers from the school of childhood as from the school of life, for example the school of Jewish 'rationalism' or of Jewish 'mysticism.' So, for example, the Kantian, Salomon Maimon, was able in his autobiography to trace back the absence of system in his thought, which he himself perceived, to the forms of religious education in the synagogue. However, all such psychological, social, and historical explanations and characterizations remain only half-truths and become completely untrue if they conceal the communality of human reason, which rises above all facts of nature and history to the infinite conversation concerning human destiny, which we call philosophy.

Chapter 14

NOTES ON PLANNING FOR THE FUTURE*

It would be no exaggeration to claim that we owe the modern phase of the industrial revolution not so much to the advances in the natural sciences as to the rationalization of their technical and economic application. What appears to me to characterize our epoch is not the surprising control of nature we have achieved, but the development of scientific methods to guide the life of society. Only with this achievement has the victorious course of modern science, beginning in the nineteenth century, become a dominant social factor. The scientific tendencies of thought underlying our civilization have in our time pervaded all aspects of social praxis. Scientific market research, scientific warfare, scientific diplomacy, scientific rearing of the younger generation, scientific leadership of the people—the application of science to all these fields gives expertise a commanding position in the economy and society.

And so the problem of an ordered world assumes primary importance. The old problem of simply understanding the existing order of things is no longer the issue. It has given way to the difficulties of planning and creating an order not yet in being. But, is the question germane: should something that does not yet exist be planned and implemented? It is quite apparent that the kind of world order one would like to see governing international relations does not exist. This, in part, is due to the various ideas about what constitutes the right world order, ideas so incompatible that the overall solution has been suspended in favor of resigned coexistence. But the slogan of coexistence, substantiated by equivalence in nuclear arms, predicates a threat to the problem as posed. Does talk of creating a world order still make sense if, from the start, we are faced with irreconcilable ideas on the constitution of a right order? Can one plan according to a standard of world order if one is ignorant of the end toward which all mediating and possible steps proceed? Does not all planning on a world scale depend on the existence of a definitive mutual concept of the goal? Certainly, there are encouraging advances in such fields as world health, international communication, and possibly even worldwide distribution of food stuffs. But, can we simply proceed along the course of these successes to expand progressively

---

*First published in 1965 in *Daedelus*, the journal of the American Academy of Science.

the scope of uniformly and rationally applied directives, ending up with a universally regulated and rationally ordered world?

The concept of a world order necessarily assumes a substantive differentiation corresponding to the guidelines of the kind of order that is proposed. This is manifest methodologically by taking such a concept and contrasting it with the possible forms of its negation. For it lies in the nature of things that our ideas of right and good are less exact and definite than our notions of wrong and bad. Consequently, the concept of disorder, with whose elimination we are concerned, is always more easily defined; it facilitates the understanding of different meanings of order.

But is it legitimate to transpose those areas of life where disorder dominates and where order should be established on to the whole problem of creating a world order? Let us take the example of economic disorder. The domain of economics allows for an easy conception of rational systematization. Every set of conditions which hinders economic rationality may be termed disorder. In the concept of general well-being there certainly are to be found different interpretations of an economy on a universal scale which cannot be simply reduced to an idea of rationality applicable, perhaps, if the world was a single, large factory. For instance, we have still not resolved whether exceptionally large profits are justified as advancing the standard of living, or whether we should prefer, on the basis of socio-political considerations, a nationalized and correspondingly bureaucratized economy even though it is characterized by a lower degree of performance.

This reflection, however, indicates that it is not possible to separate the economic from the political point of view. Can one define a condition of political disorder whose elimination would make possible a rational consideration of a political order with the same certainty as one speaks of economic disorder and a rational universal economic system? One could claim that the prevention of global self-destruction poses the same unequivocal standard for international politics as does general well-being for a world economic order. But, is this a genuine parallel construction? Can one actually derive from it workable concepts of political systems which would achieve a reasonable amount of unanimity? If one says, for example, that the preservation of peace is the purpose of all politics, then the meaning is severely restricted as long as we are dealing with conventional wars. Taken literally, it means: the *status quo* is the international order to be preserved—a conclusion made possible and meaningful today by the pressures of nuclear equivalence which tend to restrict the latitude for changes in international politics. But, is that a meaningful standard for politics? Politics presupposes the changeability of conditions. Nobody would want to dispute that there are political transformations which are "right" and which could serve the "right" system of universal political order. But according to what criteria is such "correctness" measured? According to a political vision of order? Even when such reasonable political ideals of order are at issue (as, for example, the unification of Europe as suggested by Lord Gladwyn), the standard becomes quite elusive. Would such a Europe be "right," that is, represent a progressive step toward the administration of the world? Would it be "right" even if international business and political concentrations were disturbed, for instance, if the cohesion of the Commonwealth were broken? Would the result be greater order or more disorder?

The problem can be formulated more basically. Is it possible to think of even one vision of political order for the world that would not immediately provoke ideas antagonistic to this vision? Are visions of a global political order conceivable which do not favor one political system detrimental to the other? Should one assert that the existence of contradictions among power interests constitutes disorder? Is not such a condition itself constitutive of the essence of political order?

It is common to consider the existence of underdeveloped nations as a condition making for disorder, and to call the elimination of such a disparity a "politics of development." Here we immediately confront concrete issues amenable to rational solution, for example, the kind of politics dealing with population or with nourishment. In this context it is evident that a population explosion, or, on the other hand, the waste of food stuffs, the nonutilization of natural resources, the destruction of food sources, represents disorder. But all such particular conceptions of order are so enmeshed in international politics and so subject to manifold standards of measurement that it appears impossible to secure agreement. Furthermore, there exists no rational basis for believing that the expansion of those areas in which rational planning and administration is successful would bring a reasonable worldwide political system any closer to realization.

One could with equal justification arrive at the opposite conclusion and admit to the growing danger posed by the application of rational directives to irrational ends, such as is applied in the slogan: "Guns before butter." And one would have to inquire more fundamentally whether it is not precisely the overdependence on science in our business and social life—keeping in mind opinion research and the strategy of opinion shaping—that has increased the uncertainty regarding the intended goals, the content of a world order as it should be, by first subjecting the design of our world to scientifically informed and guided planning, while obfuscating the uncertainty which surrounds the standards. Is the task wrongly posited? Though scientific and rational approaches characterize the advances in innumerable fields of endeavor, can one actually consider the organization of world affairs as a subject of such rational planning and execution?

The question we pose goes completely against the grain of the unquestioned belief in science so characteristic of our age. It has to be asked because it goes further back in time. The problem must be viewed in a more general context, as a broader question posited with the inception of modern science in the seventeenth century and unresolved since then. All reflection about the potential ordering of our world must proceed from the deep tension that exists between the asserted authority of science and the ethics and customs of national forms of life transmitted by religion. We are by now familiar with the tensions which underlie the problems arising from the contact of the ancient cultures of Asia, or those of the so-called underdeveloped nations, with European civilization. But they represent only special aspects of this more general problem. It seems to me less urgent to find ways of reconciling occidental civilization with alien traditions in distant lands and bringing them to fruitful symbiosis, than to evaluate the significance of the civilizing process, made possible by science, in terms of our own cultural heritage and to discover ways of reconciling such progress with our moral and religious traditions. For that in truth is the problem of the world order which occupies us at present, because, by virtue of the civilizing achievements of European science, the problem has been raised to a uniform level of importance throughout the world. One glance at the history of the past few centuries shows clearly that the scientific ideas, which were first implemented in the seventeenth century, and the universal possibilities which they contained, unfolded in a hesitating and gradual manner. With the single exception of nuclear physics, we can assert that the developments exhibited by our contemporary industrial revolution rest on the scientific discoveries of the nineteenth century. This is to say, scientifically speaking, that they were possible even then. But even the liberal nineteenth century hesitated in applying them because of the extent to which ideas were contested by the persisting influences of Christian and moral norms. I refer to the resistance which Darwinism had to overcome. Today these restrictions seem to be diminishing, and the technical possibilities of our scientific discoveries have been correspondingly liberated. The expert makes the possibilities inherent in his field of science available to the public; and popular consciousness, in having to decide on the feasibility of such possibilities, demands nothing less than another science to pass judgment. Here too the exception proves the rule. We need think only of the possibilities of applying genetics to the breeding of the human species, in regard to which man still entertains unresolved elemental fears.

There have been a sufficient number of warning voices that have made themselves heard during the past century in the form of a pessimistic cultural critique, predicting the West's impending collapse. In spite of the reverberations they have enjoyed among social strata threatened with extinction—especially among the nobility, the *haute bourgeoisie*, and the cultured middle class—they carry little conviction, if only because they are themselves immersed in the civilization produced by modern science. I recall the memorable onslaught Max Weber once made upon Stefan George's romantic esotericism. This, however, does not mean that these prophetic voices are not in themselves of documentary value. What they testify, however, is not what they pronounce. They attest to a certain disproportion between a diminishing body of values of disappearing traditions and the continuously self-justifying belief in science. I find it ominous that modern science should revolve only around itself, that it is concerned only with those methods and possibilities which are necessary for the scientific control of things—as if the disparity between the realm of attainable means and possibilities and the norms and goals of life did not exist. But that is precisely the inherent tendency of scientific doctrine: to make superfluous the scrutiny of ends by successfully providing and "controlling" the means at one and the same time.

Thus the question concerning the forms of ordering our contemporary and future world can be posed in scientific terms. What can we accomplish? What must be changed? What must we take into consideration so that the management of our world will become continually frictionless and better? The idea of a perfectly administered world appears to be the ideal to which the outlook and the political convictions of the most advanced nations are committed. Moreover, it seems significant to me that this ideal is presented as one of perfect administration and not as a vision of the future with a predetermined content. It is not like the state of justice in Plato's utopian republic, nor does it endorse the dominance of one people or race over another. Contained in the ideal of administration is a conception of order which does not specify its content. The issue is not which order should rule, but that everything should have its order; this is the express end of all administration. In its essence, the idea of administration—or management—incorporates the ideal of neutrality. It aspires to smooth functioning as a good in itself. That the great powers of our day would prefer to come to terms with each other on the neutral basis of this administrative ideal is not, in all probability, such a utopian hope. From here it is hardly a big step to consider the notion of world administration as the form of order peculiar to the future. In it, the idea of making politics scientifically objective would find its fruition. Is this formal ideal of world administration the fulfillment of the idea of a world order?

It has all taken place once before. The initiate in the Platonic dialogues knows that in the age of Sophist enlightenment the idea of expertise was given a similar universal function. The Greeks knew it as *Techne*, an art, skill, craftsmanship—a science capable of perfectibility. The *idea* of the object to be manufactured constitutes the perspective to which the whole process conforms. The choice of the proper means, the selection of the right materials, the skillful execution of the individual phases of the work—all these allowed themselves to be raised to an ideal perfection, giving credence to Aristotle's dictum: *Techne* loves *tyche* (fortune) and *tyche* loves *techne*. Nevertheless, it is in the essence of *techne* that it does not exist for its own sake or for the perfectibility of the object, as though the latter existed for its own sake. What pertains to the nature and appearance of the perfectible object is wholly dependent on the use for which it is intended. But, regarding the utility of the object, neither the knowledge nor the skill of the craftsman is master. The faculties of the craftsman do not guarantee that the object will be used according to its requirements, or, more decisively, that it will be used for something which is right. It appears that an additional expertise is required to determine its correct utilization, that is, the application of the means to the right ends. And since our whole consumer world is obviously a hierarchical mixture of such means-ends relationships, the idea of a superior *techne* is appealing—a special expertise competent to order all other faculties, a kind of regal expertise: the political *techne*. Is such an idea sensible? The statesman as the expert of all other experts, the art of statecraft as the ultimate expertise? Naturally, what in ancient Greece was called a state was a *polis*, and not the world. But since Greek thought about the *polis* deals solely with the order in the *polis*, and not with what we understand as the great politics of interstate relations, this is merely a question of degree. The perfectly administered world order, in our terms, corresponds precisely with the ideal *polis*.

Meanwhile, the question we face is whether this all-inclusive expertise, which Plato calls political craftsmanship, is anything more than Plato's critical rejoinder against those contemporary politicians whose ignorant diligence ruined his native city. Does the ideal of *techne*, the teachable and learnable expertise, satisfy the demands confronting man's political existence? This is not the place to speak of the range or limits of the idea of *techne* in Platonic philosophy—not to mention the problem of how Platonic philosophy serves distinct political ideas, which could not possibly be ours. But, in recalling Plato, we can help clarify our own problems. He makes us doubt whether the increase in human knowledge could ever encompass and regulate the whole of man's social and civic existence. Perhaps one must say that the Cartesian juxtaposition of *res cogitans* and *res extensa* has correctly appraised all possible modifications of the basically problematic application of the field of "science" to the sphere of "self-consciousness." Only when we start applying science to society, which Descartes with his "notion of morality as provisional" foresaw as a distant possibility, do we confront the full seriousness of the problem. Kant's talk of man as the "citizen of two worlds" adequately expresses this dilemma. That man in his being could become a mere object, susceptible of being reconstructed and manipulated in all his social relationships by another man; moreover, that there would exist an expert other than himself, able to regulate him and all others while being himself managed in his administrative capacity—a suggestion of this kind invites such notorious implications as to render the idea of expertise an ironic caricature, even though it be acclaimed as inspiration and revelation, either by a transcendental divinity of virtue or by what is ultimately good itself.

Even setting aside the question of a position to be occupied by the planner responsible for a reasoned, systematic world order and the rational administrator of that order, it is evident that the complications would prove insoluble if the idea is to apply "science" to the concrete life situation of people and the practical exercise of their commonsense rationality. Here, too, Greek thought seems to be extremely relevant. It is the Aristotelian distinction between *techne* and *phronesis* which clarifies these complications. Practical knowledge which recognizes the feasible in concrete situations in life does not allow for perfection in the same way as does expertise in *techne*. *Techne* is teachable and learnable, and its performance is manifestly independent of the moral and political qualities of human beings. Yet, the practical knowledge and reason which man employs to guide and illuminate life situations are not thus independent. Surely, we recognize here that general knowledge, within certain limits, is applied to concrete cases. When we speak of human nature, of political expertise, of business acumen, we tend to make analogies, inexact, to be sure, to a body of general knowledge and then infer its application. If this were not so, then that philosophy which Aristotle designed for his *ethics* and *politics* would be impossible.

Nevertheless, the logical relations of universals and particulars are not at issue. Neither are the corresponding scientific calculations and predictions of events, the features of modern science. Even if one were to outfit the utopian ideal with a physics of society one could not extricate oneself from the Platonic dilemma which elevates the statesman, the practical political activist, to the rank of supreme specialist. For the knowledge of a supposed physicist of society might make possible a technology of society, but it would not guarantee a wise choice, on the part of the social physicist, from among the technological possibilities open to him. Aristotle devoted much thought to this problem and decided to call it practical knowledge, which concerns itself with concrete situations, a different kind of knowing. This is no hollow irrationalism to which he gives expression.

Rather he identifies the clarity of reason which, in a practical political matter, is always able to discern the feasible in a given situation. Every practical life decision is obviously constituted by a selection of possible alternatives which satisfy our aims. Since Max Weber, the social sciences have justified their scientific legitimacy on the rationality employed in the selection of means. And today they stand on the verge of concretizing and banalizing an increased number of areas which heretofore belonged to the domain of public judgment. But if Max Weber tied the pathos of his value-free sociology to a likewise pathetic adherence to the "God" whom everyone must choose for himself—is it still permissible to abstract, as social science does, from the established ends?

There is no doubt that the prospects of agreement are greater among experts than statesmen. One is always tempted to attribute responsibility to the political directives issued by governments for the breakdown of agreements at international conferences of so-called authorities. But, is this really the case? Undeniably, there are particular concerns in which the rationality of means is unambiguous; on such issues the experts can agree without difficulty. But how seldom are such pure matters of fact really brought up for debate. What an immense amount of self-control a judge must exercise to confine his legal opinion to those aspects of the case for which he, by virtue of his particular expertise, is responsible. The court expert who would be of such extreme scrupulousness would be short of being unfit for the court. The necessity to weigh judgments, which exists for the courts, shows repeatedly that courts deal with assessments whose irrefutability is by no means certain. And it is not only circumstantial evidence that is uncertain. The more the dominant social and political prejudices are brought into play, the more fictitious the pure expert becomes and with him the notion of a scientifically certified rationality. It might hold true for the whole spectrum of the modern social sciences that they are unable to control means-ends relationships, without, at the same time, implying a preference for specific ends. If, in my opinion, one were to trace the inner determinacy of this implication to its logical conclusion, the contradiction between timeless truth, which is sought after by science, and the temporal condition of those who utilize science would be made manifest. For what is feasible is not simply what is possible or, within the realm of the possible, the purely advantageous. Moreover, every advantage and preference is weighed according to a definite standard which one posits, or which has already been established. It is the aggregate of what is socially admissible: the norms, evolved from ethical and political convictions and fortified by training and self-education, which determine this standard.

This should not be misconstrued to mean that there are no ethical or political ideals other than conformity to the established social order and its standards. To do so would be to succumb to another set of inverted abstractions. Meaningful criteria are not simply those posited by society—or those of our ancestors—applied as law to a given case. Rather, every concrete determination by the individual contributes to socially meaningful norms. The problem is similar to that of correct speech. There too we find undisputed agreement on what is admissible, and we subject it to codification. The teaching of languages in schools, for example, makes it necessary that the schoolmaster apply these rules. But language continues to live, and it thrives not according to a strict adherence to rules, but by general innovations in spoken usage, and in the last instance from the contributions of every individual.

Among the philosophers of our century, some of these truths have been represented by the much-maligned school of Existentialism. The concept of "situation" has played a particularly significant role in the rejection of scientific methodology of the Neo-Kantian school of thought. Indeed, according to Karl Jaspers' analysis, the concept of "situation" encompasses a logical structure which transcends the simple relation of universal and particular, of law and case. To find oneself in a "situation" involves an experimental moment which the objective cognition cannot fully grasp. In such a context people are obliged to resort to metaphor. They claim that they must "put themselves in the situation" before they are able to recognize the really expedient and possible from many alternatives. "Situations" do not possess the characteristics of a mere object which one meets face to face; consequently, certainty does not arise from the simple understanding of objectively existing phenomena. Even the adequate knowledge of all objectively given facts, such as are provided by science, cannot fully encompass the perspective as seen from the standpoint of a man involved in a particular situation.

The result of these reflections seems to be that the idea of *making and craftsmanship*, as it has been passed down for ages, represents a false model of cognition. The tension between a formal knowledge available to everyone, as it is associated with the concept of teachable science (for example, *techne*), and the knowledge of what is practical and good for oneself, is, in itself, quite old and familiar. But, it is quite obvious that before the inception of science it has not been raised to a real antinomy. Aristotle, for example, sees no problem in the relation between political science and political sense (*techne* in relation to *phronesis*). The whole corpus of knowledge in which all forms of knowledge participate provides *techne* with a standard as well. *Techne*, in a fundamental sense, is that branch of knowledge which fills the gaps nature left for human skill. That is how things were in the old days. Today, in contrast, the magnificent abstraction with which the methodological ideal of modern science isolates and encloses its subject has ensured a qualitative differentiation between the infinitely expanding knowledge of science, on the one side, and the irretrievable finiteness of actual decisions, on the other. The specialist and the politician are respective embodiments of this rift. A rational model seems unable to define the knowledge necessary for a statesman. Max Weber's exaggerated differentiation between value-free science and ideological decisions makes this failing obvious. Perhaps one could remedy the difficulty by substituting the old *model of piloting*, or steering, for the model of making. This model has the advantage of being able to account for two integral notions: the maintenance of equilibrium, which oscillates in a precisely set amplitude, and guidance, that is, the selection of a direction which is possible within the oscillating equilibrium. That all our planning and execution transpires within an unstable equilibrium, which constitutes the determinations of our life, is quite evident. The idea of equilibrium is not only one of our oldest political concepts of order that limits and defines the degree of active freedom, but it appears to be a structural determinant of life as such, to which all indeterminate, not yet established, possibilities of life are relegated. A man of our technological and scientific civilization can free himself from this restriction no more than can any other living being. Yes, perhaps the actual determinations of man's freedom are to be found here. Only where the forces of equilibrium are maintained can the factors of human volition and desire be of any consequence. To acquire freedom of action presupposes the establishment of an equilibrium. Even in modern natural science we confront something similar. We are increasingly devoting ourselves to discovering the regulative systems of nature. Correspondingly, we are leaving behind the naive belief that the crude means we possess can assist the self-corrective systems of living organisms. And yet, all our research, to the extent to which it provides us with information and understanding, makes—increasingly less crude—interference possible.

And so, the cognitive model of piloting, compared to the idea of planning and making, acquires greater significance. However, this model also cannot hide the kinds of assumptions—knowledge of goals and directions—which are necessary for piloting. Plato also thought that the skill of the pilot illustrated the limits of all skill. He transports all passengers securely to land. But was it good for them that they had arrived? Is it possible that Agamennon's pilot succumbed to doubt after he saw that his master had been murdered?

Perhaps there is no better example to illustrate the present problem than the situation of the doctor. For here the dilemma is experienced in the relationship of science to its practitioner, whose humane function must not be subverted by the merely "scientific." The coexistence of dual faculties in one occupational activity defines the physician's problem. Analogous complications occur whenever a learned profession must strike a balance between practical activity and science, as with lawyers, ministers, and teachers. But the example of medicine epitomizes the conflict. Here modern science, in all its magnitude and promise, collides directly with the historic role of the healer and the assumptions underlying his compassionate activity. We are confronted with a new problem which transcends the questionableness of medicine familiar since ancient times: for in itself, the problem of medicine is old: How much is "science," a practical science, to be sure, a *techne*, and, consequently, an art? While every other creatively pragmatic knowledge verifies its "knowledge" in the results it achieves, the task of medicine remains irreducibly ambiguous. In each case of its intercession it is debatable whether the measures taken by a doctor resulted in a cure, or whether nature came to its own assistance. Therefore, the whole art of healing—quite in contrast to other branches of *technai*—has, since antiquity, required a special apologia.

This is doubtless due to the vagueness of the concept we call health. It is a norm defying clear definition. We might better call it a condition, which, since time immemorial, has been characterized by the concept of balance, or equipoise. Balance, however, has the attribute of a certain set of oscillations which equalize each other to keep the whole in equilibrium. When the bounds are exceeded the balance is offset completely and, if at all possible, must be corrected by a new expenditure of effort. Consequently, the reestablishment of equipoise is nothing more than the reintroduction of an oscillating equilibrium. This attributes to "interference" a special set of limitations. Or, to express it in more general terms, a fundamental tension exists in the connection of "knowing" to "doing." Particular relations can be studied in terms of a causal analysis proper to the natural sciences. However, the organism as a whole can be understood, as Kant has shown, only from a teleological point of view. In this respect, modern medicine shares the general difficulties being investigated by contemporary scientific biology. The tremendous advances achieved in this sphere, especially by what is called information theory and cybernetics, have reduced to feasibility what appeared utopian to Kant: the aspiration to become the "Newton of a blade of grass." Nothing said here affects the validity of morphological methods, and there seems to be no reason that a morphological approach should not be compatible with causal analysis. The behavioral sciences, for example, apply certain preliminary morphological assumptions in interpreting the behavior under observation as being not merely the result of a mechanical cause-effect relationship—although there would be nothing inconsistent in considering the existence of such a relationship. Should it eventually become possible to create living organisms in a test tube, it would not be senseless to study the *behavior* of such constructed organisms. The idea of science justifies the use of both methods and directs them to the same end: to explore a realm of experience scientifically and to open it up for useful purposes. To make something available does not mean simply to reconstruct it. It also entails the ability to predict the course of spontaneous development which, for instance, a living organism might undergo under specific circumstances.

But precisely here the specific difficulties of medicine prove informative. And, I believe, the medical dilemma is closely analogous to the one we face in discussing the theme of world order. The tremendous advances made by modern medicine in dealing with really critical illnesses lay bare problematic complications which the subscribers of the Hippocratic oath will have to take into account. Obviously, the practical demands of helping and healing do not alone bear the burden of responsibility for the fact that the purely technical use of science is too restricted and inadequate a model. Certainly, it is also the level of our knowledge and, consequently, its limitations which necessitate in the end that the doctor trust his intuition and instinct, and, when these do not suffice, that he will revert to simple methods of trial and error. But there appears to be no contradiction in contemplating a perfect biology, which would also raise medicine to a scientific perfection of a scope we cannot yet imagine. But precisely then, I should think, those complications we are beginning to perceive at the present early stage would become explicit. Take, for example, the prolongation of life which contemporary medical technology is attempting to realize. The identity of the person, who as patient confronts the doctor, has no place in such a scheme of things. Similar difficulties posed by the possibilities of genetic control have already been mentioned. It seems that the circumscribed and finite nature of life makes the conflict that exists between the glorious promises of natural science and man's understanding of himself unavoidable.

Let us apply these reflections to the state of affairs in the modern world and to the tasks we face. Here we will not make suggestions toward a scientific mastering of the problems of global order. In this respect, we should stress that science still has a tremendous future, even though it is far from certain that occidental civilization will proceed without resistance eventually to displace and suffocate all other human forms of order. But that is precisely the problem. The creation of a technically uniform civilized man, who acquires the use of a correspondingly uniform language—and English is far advanced in filling that role— would certainly simplify the ideal of a scientific administration. But the relevant question is precisely whether such an ideal is desirable. Perhaps developments in linguistics can provide us with an insight into how the leveling process will work itself out in our civilization. The system of sign notation, which both requires the services of a technical apparatus and makes it possible, develops a dialectic all its own. It ceases to be simply a means for the attainment of ends, since it excludes the ends which the apparatus does not identify or transmit. The perfect functioning of an international language for the transmission of information derives from the restricted content which can be expressed in it.

The attempt to perfect a logical and perfect universal language of theoretical cognition for use in science, as the advocates of the "Unity of Science" movement are to do, will meet the same fate. Were it perfected, it might successfully eliminate all imprecision and ambiguity in interhuman understanding. We would not even have to wait for the invention of a future world language. It would suffice to incorporate all living national languages into a system of transliterated equations so that an ideal translating machine could guarantee a uniform intelligibility. This is all possible and perhaps quite near. But here again it might be unavoidable that the universal means would become universal ends. Therefore, we would not have acquired a means to say and communicate everything imaginable; we would, however, have obtained a means—and we are on the way to achieving it—which would ensure that only the data assimilated in the programming would be communicated, or even thought. The forbidding possibility of speech control, which has evolved with the growth of modern mass media, expresses clearly how the dialectic of such means and ends operates. In our own day this dilemma is reflected in the confrontation of the Cold War antagonists: What in one part of the world is called democracy and freedom appears only as speech control in the other part of the world. There it is interpreted as a device for mass manipulation and domestication. But that demonstrates only the incompleteness of the system. The manipulation of language has permeated everything and has become an end in itself. In the process it has concealed itself and passes unnoticed.

One should keep such extreme possibilities in mind in order not to lose sight of certain features which are characteristic of all elemental life experiences and our experience of the world in general. To say that the language in which we become immersed as we grow up is more than just a set of symbols serving the needs of a civilizing apparatus should not be misinterpreted as a romantic idolization of a mother tongue. It is indisputable that every language has a tendency toward schematization. As a language is learned, it creates a view of the world which conforms to the character of the speech conventions that have been established in the language. A thing is defined by the words one uses. The brilliant inventiveness of two- or three-year-old children and their use of language is brought to a halt by the demands of communication made by the environment. Nevertheless, it seems to me that in contrast to every artificially devised system of signs, the living aspect of language perfects and develops itself in association with the living traditions that encompass historical humanity. This secures for the life of every language an inner infinity. This boundlessness is preserved still more when man, while learning a foreign language, steps into an alien system of meanings and, by comparison, experiences the wealth and poverty of his own speech. Man's irreducible finitude is displayed here too. Everyone must learn to speak for himself and in the process establish his own history. And, should even the most farfetched mechanization of society be successful, man will not lose this uniqueness. The age of *posthistory* into which we are now proceeding will find its limits in this distinctiveness of man.

In conclusion we must inquire what significance this type of rumination can have in the face of the overwhelming trend toward a scientific form of civilization. That the popular critiques of technology share the insincerity of all other forms of culture criticism has been mentioned earlier. One should certainly not expect that, by becoming cognizant of the factors which set limits to the technological dream of the present, we could or should be able to influence the measured advance of progress. All the more reason for asking what the awakening of consciousness is to achieve.

The answer to it will not be the same in all situations. The possibilities of conquering nature will have a different significance and a higher esteem where nature is still largely uncontrolled, and where people continually struggle with physical deprivation, poverty, and sickness. The elites of countries characterized by such backwardness will fully endorse and support scientifically programmed planning. They will also be sensitive to the retarding effects of religious influence on social norms. If the execution of the plan requires a high level of morale and strict discipline, then it will be seen to that political qualifications and a consciously worked out ideology are brought into play to secure the success of the plan. In the highly developed nations it is unlikely that we will oppose the imaginative planner who promises to increase human well-being. Here too, one will have to fight the obstacles which are embodied in property relations and profit incentives. But, the more we liberate ourselves from external needs and excessive labor, and, if it ever becomes possible, the more we modify the life tempo of our modern industrial society, all the less we will expect salvation only from scientific planning of the future.

Different levels of economic development are not crucial here. Differences between cultures and traditions now also become important for our comprehension of an ever more integrated world. Consequently, the task of developing our awareness of extant differences between peoples and nations assumes a priority in a world where planning and progress seem to guarantee the attainment of everything. Such an "awakening of consciousness," however, is now hardly ever brought about by science. It is more readily a result of a critique of science. Its greatest effect is education to tolerance. Confirmed ideas of orderly public life, as, for example, the ideal of democracy (either in the Western or Eastern sense), will develop an inner consciousness of their own requirements, while economic progress, though equally desired in all parts of the world, will not have the same meaning throughout.

With justified anxiety one may ask what our growing awareness of these problems, as long as it remains confined to small intellectual circles, is to accomplish. To demand more than the sharpening of our understanding of these problems, to expect that the solution of these inclusive difficulties of international politics will be provided by some kind of brain trust, would be ridiculous. Meanwhile, contact among nations increases and leads them in greater measure to an awareness of what it is that separates them or unites them. The problem of intellectuals is a problem of its own. But, what is mirrored in their understanding—their naive superiority notwithstanding—can become the conscious property of everyone.

In conclusion it might be permissible to inquire into the role philosophy plays in solving the dilemma we have described. Does it still possess a relevant function in a scientific culture attaining to perfection? First, we must reject certain widespread assumptions about philosophy in addition to views which philosophy itself entertains. To require that philosophy be some kind of superscience, able to provide an all-encompassing framework for the specialized sciences, is scientific dilettantism. This is no longer practicable: it is an obligation philosophy set for itself in classical times when it indeed constituted a comprehensive science. Furthermore, to expect philosophy to be the source of foundational doctrines of logic and methodology is no less frivolous. The various specialized scientific disciplines would gain nothing from this, for they have long since borrowed methods and systems of notation from each other, assimilating to their own needs what seemed appropriate. The philosophy of science is certainly a legitimate task of philosophy, but it is not needed by the sciences. As to the question, whether philosophy can still function as the universal agent for the development of consciousness, this question cannot be answered by the theory of science. On the contrary, it assumes to answer before it has fully understood the question. To develop our awareness of what *is*, necessarily also requires understanding what science is. But it equally includes preserving the openness of mind and recognition of the fact that not everything that *is*, is or could become the object of science.

In contemporary philosophical discourse we can find essentially two answers which further the development of conscious awareness. In the first instance, philosophical discourse can sharpen and radicalize the understanding of what really exists. To this task belongs the destruction of all romantic illusions regarding the good old days and the snug security provided by a Christian cosmos. It must also heighten the awareness that God has been obscured for us and that we live in the age of the eclipse of God (Martin Buber), and that the question of being has fallen into forgetfulness, as our metaphysical tradition is absorbed into the realm of science (Martin Heidegger). Philosophy would then recognize itself as a kind of secularized eschatology, establishing a kind of expectancy of a possible reversal. It cannot say what it expects. But it becomes filled with the need for a reversal, a turning, as it radically anticipates the consequences of the present age. But he who in this way simply subordinates himself to that which *is*, refuses to deal with the ensuing consequences and accepts that the future will pursue its course without direction.

Nevertheless, there is another possible answer concerning the purpose of developing our consciousness, which appears to me to be in full accord with our own desire to know. It could be that the technological dream entertained by our time is really just a dream, a series of changes and transformation in our world, which, when compared to the actual and enduring realities of our life, has a phantomlike and arbitrary character. To become conscious of what is could also mean precisely to become aware of how little things change, even where everything appears to be changing. What is involved is not a plea for the preservation of the existing order (or disorder). The concern is simply with a readjustment of our consciousness. Conservatives and revolutionaries alike seem to me to require a similar rectification of their understanding. Unchanging and enduring realities—birth and death, youth and age, native and foreign land, commitment and freedom—demand the same recognition from all of us. These realities have measured out what human beings can plan and what they can achieve. Continents and empires, revolutions in power and in thought, the planning and organization of life on our planet and outside it, will not be able to exceed a measure which perhaps no one knows and to which, nevertheless, we are all subject.

Chapter 15

THE LIMITATIONS OF THE EXPERT*

In order to discover something about the limitations of the expert, it is necessary to draw a few conceptual distinctions. Philosophy is not, as one often hears, the professional art of splitting hairs, the search for artificially precise definitions—one who attempts to philosophize must first of all have an attentive ear for the language in which the thinking experience of many generations has been sedimented, long before we begin to attempt our own thinking. So, in this case as well, it is not superficial when I first ask whom we call experts and why we do this. One realizes immediately that this is a relatively new word, at least as a foreign word in the German language. And one asks oneself why this is such a new word.

Now with the great stream of experiences and images that flow in upon humanity it is precisely when something begins to stand out from the stream with a particular profile that we give it a name. So it is in this case as well. Evidently there was occasion to distinguish the role of the expert by the expression *expertus*. This surely does not only mean someone who is experienced. That is the Latin sense of the word *expertus*. It is not a profession to gain experience and to have gained experience, i.e., to be experienced. However, there is now a profession of mediating between the scientific culture of modernity and its social manifestations in practical life.

Therefore, the expert has an intermediate position. He is not the embodiment of the scientist or the researcher or the teacher. The expert stands between science, in which he must be competent and social and political praxis. Thereby it is already clear that he is not the authority for final decisions. The German word that we use for experts, is generally *Gutachter*. *Gutachten* is a good old German word and has been used since the sixteenth century, if I remember correctly. One must, however, listen to the word. *Gutachten* means, and in *Gutachten* resounds, something of what we mean in *achten* [honor] and *erachten* [deem]. 'Meines Erachtens' [in my opinion], one says and means: I do not know this so absolutely — perhaps one should ask another about it; but if I were asked, I would give this or that answer. In addition the *Gutachter* or the expert is subordinate to the actual decision makers in social and political life. This has actually

---

*Essay published in Darmstadt, 1967.

been established, for example, in the legal system. A court is not forced to accept the testimony of the expert witness as decisive for the judgment or verdict. The *Gutachter*, the expert, is one who is listened to. He does not—or should we better say, he should not—take the place of the actual decision maker.

With this I believe the critical background of the theme is clear. For one cannot but be concerned at the major role now taken on by the scientific expert in our social and political life. One could consider what occurs in the important cases in the judicial system, i.e., where it really concerns great and important things—for example, in legal cases between large oil companies or steel industries, or in the case of major scandals, or something similar. We have experienced all of this. So today, it is important to get the most respected experts on one's side. Previously the lawyer, or as he was called in France, *le Maître*. was the real master, that is to say the person whom it was important to have at one's side, whether one was defendant or prosecutor. Today the expert has become, in many cases, the most sought-after person and is often, it appears to me, the decisive one.

Now it is clear that the position occupied by the expert between science and research on the one hand and decision making in law and social policy, on the other hand, is somewhat insecure and ambivalent. The increasing importance of the role which the expert plays in our society is rather a serious symptom for the increasing ignorance of the decision makers. This is not their fault: it is due to the degree of complexity of our whole administrative and social, industrial, commercial, and private life. The old perspicuity—which the reasonable man acquired through his life experiences and upon which a broad discretion in arriving at a verdict has been granted to the judge in certain legal systems, as in England, until today—fails, in the meantime, all too often. It is no accident that given today's social and legal system we listen more and more to the expert and force the decision on him. The initial starting point for our reflection is, therefore, that we note a certain predominance of experts in social and political life and so have to ask ourselves whether the reasons, which have led to the category, "the expert," are of such an indubitable legitimacy that this may be accepted.

The explanatory power of science is tremendous. Facing the continuing increase in knowledge resulting from research and, corresponding to this, the higher recognition of science and research, one cannot do otherwise than to also acknowledge the expert. Nevertheless, especially given this state of affairs, we may all ask whether too much is demanded of science and whether it can play the principal role in so many questions of public life requiring decision. There is a catalogue of questions which follow from this. For example, it causes difficulties for the researcher, as well as for the expert, that they have to respond to society's high expectations. They are coerced to have, so to speak, the final word, although a researcher, in truth, never accepts something like a final word. Therefore, experts disagree more often than not. In any case, it is a highly oppressive situation to be in such high demand.

I am the son of a chemist who became an authority due to his research on alkaloids. Because of this, he was occasionally called for as an expert in complicated poisoning trials. I am convinced that the courts were never very pleased with his expert testimony. He was a true researcher and always emphasized all that we do not know. That, however, is not what a court wishes to hear. The court wishes to know what was possible. But it is unavoidable in certain cases that some possibilities must always remain open. Naturally there are clear cases where one can say that what the accused or his defence claims cannot be so. Nevertheless, there are many unknown factors, for example in poisoning trials, which in some circumstances could have produced the same symptoms and results as the presumed poison in the indictment. The case which I have considered is, in a sense, an extreme case, and yet it is instructive in two ways. On the one hand, it shows what one can clearly characterize as being known. On the other hand, it shows what possibilities one cannot eliminate. Science is seldom in the position to make so clear a distinction. So it often happens that the limitations of a scientific statement do not satisfy society's desire for direction and information. One need only consider the situation after the horrible nuclear accident in the Ukraine. The long term consequences of events such as this surpass the competence of science. Here we know nothing. Nevertheless, the experts are required to comment under pressure from the public and in the face of the public's legitimate desire for information. The people want to know how large the uncertainty factor really is in all nuclear reactors of this type, and similar things. So we encounter the conflict of the experts in this area. Almost every day in the first week after the accident, one could read or hear some new expert evaluation concerning this problem. And in most cases what was stated, were merely extrapolations from an insufficient scientific basis. The responsible researcher will express this fact to some degree. But he does not control how his statement will be presented to the public.

From the side of the politicians, there is another political factor. They must attempt to avoid unnecessary hysteria. But they must also withstand the commercial and industrial interests, which pressure for the concealment of the true dangers as far as possible. So we find the expert in a field of distortions caused by interests, in opposition to which he must express himself as his scientific conscience demands. And yet in such a situation he must also express himself in such a manner as his conscience as a citizen and his function as an expert demand.

Everything which I have stated up to this point has not actually been a statement about the limitations of science or a statement about the responsibility of science. This is a new theme, concerning which I cannot be completely silent here, because it does touch upon the position of the experts in our society. Both questions are evidently affected by very similar conditions. The researcher and the expert are both under pressure from society. The questions which we wish to ask science today are so essential that we are forced, so to speak, to make experts out of every scientist. That is, to make him into someone who can give us true directions for acting because of his superior knowledge and the superiority of his experience. Therefore, a more encompassing deliberation is required in order to determine the really legitimate function of the expert in society. Evidently there exists in the subject matter itself a certain tension between knowing and acting in general, and the practicability and correctness of the application of this knowledge and ability. This is not a peculiarity of the scientific culture of modernity. It should have its parallel in all civilizations, as does the principle of the division of labor, at least in a raw and coarse form. Specialization is such a self-evident developmental tendency of commercial and social life that this it requires no particular cultural conditions, as soon as the stage of sedentariness has been attained. Certainly there need not always be a conflict between those with specialized abilities on the one hand and the nonspecialist decision makers concerned with practical application on the other hand. But it is likely that conflicts will arise here. With reference to the specialist's knowledge and ability, it is not at first significant whether the specialist is a scientist in the modern sense, or—as in the original sense—a skilled and experienced shepherd, hunter, craftsman. In both cases, it concerns the ability to produce or the mastery of a subject matter. But in both cases this knowledge and ability is of another type than that knowledge which must choose the proper application for the good. Without a doubt, there is a close relationship here.

When Aristotle described this rational element in all decision making in human action, he evidently considered both aspects in their indivisible unity in the concept of phronesis. One is that rationality which is used in discovering the correct means for a given end. The other is used in discovering the end, becoming conscious of it and retaining it, in other words, the rationality in the choice of ends and not only in the choice of means. Here the expression, choice of ends, is very dubious. For, although it is correct that in facing various possibilities to achieve an end, one weighs the various means and finally chooses among them, it is not equally evident that the end, to which the means should correspond, is chosen. Of course, a certain totality of normative orientations is transmitted to human beings in the course of their up-bringing. It determines to a large extent the structure of our social life. In the end, this conditions one to such an extent that one only finds one thing and not something else to be natural and correct. Certainly this preconditioning through education, custom and social adjustment does not mean a complete sacrifice of rational justification, and to that extent there remains preserved an element of choice in every case of determining an end. What is right for life and its goodness will be seen as an end and so chosen. The rationality of practical reason rules our actions as well as the adequacy of the means used in acting.

This final inseparability of practical prudence from moral reasonableness may appear to be completely evident. But practical action, in the sense of discovering the suitable means for a given end, always already appears in all societies in a dual form: One, I will characterize as learnable knowledge, called techne by the Greeks. Its mastery is demonstrated by acquiring a particular specialized ability. The other form concerns the choice of the practical means for a given end. Here this choice is left to the responsibility of the individual's own power to judge and deliberate, without there being a specialist at one's disposal. It is important to keep this distinction mind. Only then can one understand why the expert continually falls into that unpleasant situation of being in conflict with the decision makers. This conflict evidently belongs to the basic structure of social life. It is well-known to us as the unrelenting question concerning the good, through which Socrates made himself hated by his fellow citizens. Neither the politicians nor the writers, as we would call them—that is the poets— nor the craftsmen could answer the question concerning the good. That surpassed their competence as specialists. This relationship is problematic even in a simple economy of craft production. As Plato expressed this: the one who needs something produced has the directing function, while the one who produces it remains bound by this direction. The subordination of economic reason under social reason appears incontestable. But it is just as incontestable that this subordination is disputed and that continually the competence of one attempts to prevail over the other. The ideal of a pure welfare state society [*Versorgungsgesellschaft*] is not only utopian, it also designates an inherently unstable situation. In human community life one is always concerned with domination and subordination, therefore with power. Even in Plato's ideal city-state, one begins from this presupposition: no justification is required for assuming that human needs will never limit themselves of their own accord. From this standpoint, one understands that in modern industrial society, the relationship between production and demand has virtually been reversed: it is advantageous for the economy and it prospers when a producer succeeds in awakening a demand, i.e., implants needs in human desire. That is modern economic life. Even if it is constitutive of human nature and human society that needs are continually increasing and demand satisfaction, it still does make a difference whether a whole economic system is based upon the satisfaction of needs or upon the continual awakening of new needs. In the latter case, the pressure increases on the producer, as does the demand for technical knowledge and the pressure on those who control the process of production. Correspondingly, the role of the expert in modern society is conditioned by pressures and a situation which requires that the voice of science assert itself in opposition to the interests and needs of society. The language of facts is another motif which belongs in this context. It does not concern the limitations of science as such, but its social effectiveness. To be concerned with the facts is the well-known claim of, especially, natural scientific research. It is accustomed to pride itself in this, avoiding the vague and uncertain statements of the other so-called sciences. Yet, everyone knows that, in truth, the concept of fact, appealed to here, always implies a context of arguments, which itself is not simply a fact, but dependent upon expectations and interests. It is also well-known how persuasive and useful for propaganda the quantitative treatment of facts and their relationships can be. Statistics is one of the most powerful means of propaganda—not for instructing but for subtly suggesting particular reactions. Therefore, the critique of the concept "fact" is an integral part of all critical science itself. And the true difference between the natural sciences and the humanities does not lie here either. Certainly, it becomes particularly visible in the humanities, for example in history, that not mere facts but facts in a particular meaningful relationship actually fulfill the claim to be facts. When Napoleon caught a cold in the battle of Wagram, this may have actual weight as a historical fact which explains his defeat. Clearly this cold was a fact, and yet not every cold in this sense is a meaningful fact to which one may refer. The same is also true, mutatis mutandis, for facts which, for example, have been proven through an experiment—as if the experiment was not itself arranged to respond to a specific question thus yielding its answer. And it is this situation which first gives weight to the fact which is measurable and ascertainable. These considerations do not at all challenge the idea that striving for objectivity and the elimination of all subjective factors is the serious researcher's concern and that exactly this virtue of his, to be self-critical, earns the greatest admiration.

But it must also be recognized that the researcher's unconditional concern with critical self-control often is not sufficient to meet the demand for knowledge. One cannot just speak as a researcher and scientist when practical consequences, following from one's judgment, need to be considered.

However, we are now placing, so to speak, a fundamentally unacceptable restriction on the back of the scholar or the expert. It is one thing to take responsibility for the consequences of knowledge, but unquestionably something quite different to practice all the self-discipline and sacrifice which lead to the acquisition of knowledge and ability. To hold science responsible, just because there is the threat of a misuse of its findings, appears to me to be unfair. Furthermore, when there is a controversy regarding this, still another expert will be called upon to tell us whether misuse threatens in this case or whether we can safely use this capacity which science has given us. This produces an infinite regress, which finally forces us to understand that the expert cannot take such a responsibility. Rather each person who belongs to human society shares this responsibility. This is not at all new, despite the fact that modern society is more complex than Western civilization in its beginnings. It is the responsibility which we have always known to be addressed by the Socratic question: that in the end we ourselves are examined and must answer. A passage from a Platonic dialogue [*Charmides* 173a] may speak to this. It states:

"I wish to relate a dream. Whether it came through the gate of the true and good or through the gate of the false and bad dreams, this question I will leave aside. If science became completely decisive among us, then everything would happen strictly according to science. No pilot would exist who did not know his job, no doctor, no general and absolutely no one, who did not really have a command of his work. The result would be that we would be far healthier than today; we would safely survive all the risks of driving and making war; our machines, our clothes and shoes, in short everything which we need would be perfectly made, and much more besides, because we would always let ourselves be guided by only true experts. And beyond this, we would wish to acknowledge prognostics as the science of the future. Concerning this, science must take pains to scare off all charlatans and to establish the actual experts among the prognosticators as the planners of the future. If all of this could be made to came to pass, then it would certainly follow that humans would scientifically act and scientifically live. Science would watch carefully and prevent every attempt at dilettantism. However, if we did everything in this scientific manner, we can nevertheless still not quite convince ourselves whether we would have done well and would be happy.

"But can one at all have another ideal for doing something well other than the one of science?"

"Perhaps not, but I would still like to know a small detail: Which science do you mean?"

This is a literal translation, which strikes us as embarrassingly modern, because the Greek concept *episteme* is rendered, correctly, as "science." The Greek word means just as much "knowledge" as "science." But can science be substituted for knowledge everywhere? Also for the knowledge of the good? Could there be a science of the good? The differentiation of meaning which occurs between knowledge [*Wissen*] and science [*Wissenschaft*] in the German language—by the way, not until the nineteenth century—exactly mirrors, on the semantic level, the temptation, which also lies in the Greek argument: instead of knowing and deciding for oneself, to rely on the knowledge of another. In truth, we must always choose for ourselves, and whether we actually attain the good or just the better remains, in general, uncertain. To that extent, the famous "knowing that one does not know," that was so characteristic of Socrates is not so unique, or rather: not knowing as such is nothing unique. But to admit this to oneself is not so easy. Furthermore, it appears to be a universal human trait to claim to know what is better and thus to make the correct choice. This is reflected also in the Greek expression which Aristotle introduced: *prohairesis*, generally translated as *Vorzugswahl* [the preferred choice]—naturally a horribly artificial expression for something which equally encompasses preferring as well as choosing by anticipating the consequences. This is a sort of semantic background to the development of science. The more an institutionalized form of competence is constructed, which proffers the expert, the specialist, as an escape from our own not knowing, the more one covers up the limitations of such information and the necessity of making one's own decisions. Therefore, the Socratic argument, which we discussed, indicates a fundamental tendency of humans, which has attained a critical climax in our increasingly bureaucratized civilization. Self-responsibility is to be replaced by science and its responsibility.

The actual problem is not that this, as such, is wrong. Where there is science, one should use its knowledge. Our nature as social beings is such that we never are in the position to provide for ourselves in all life situations merely by using our own knowledge and ability. The development of the modern institution of science implies just this, that in all practical decision-making situations, we must utilize all possibilities for information and learning. That is an aspect of human reality and not just one of a bureaucratized society. As social beings we must be able to have recourse to the knowledge and ability of others. One trusts the other, because one credits him with correct knowledge. This is the root of the true concept of authority. It demonstrates the indispensability of authority for the structure of society, in this case the authority of knowledge. Therefore the authority which the anonymous institution of science correctly represents for the layperson, certainly belongs to modern civilization. Our society is not deformed just because experts are consulted and recognized for the superiority of their knowledge. Quite the opposite. It is almost a duty for human beings to incorporate as much knowledge as is possible in any of their decisions. Max Weber 's famous expression "purposive rationality" [*Zweckrationalität*] applies here. For Weber demonstrated that there was a great danger implicit in those decisions which are determined by emotion or interest: In them the will to be rational is absent which would tie the attainability of the end to the rational determination of means. Max Weber saw a weakness in modern individualism because it permitted the subordination of the duty to know to the indeterminate authority of a good will, of a good intention, or of a pure conscience. The distinction between an ethics of conviction and an ethics of responsibility signifies exactly this point.

That does not at all mean that all decisions must depend on those who know as the final authority. The delusion of the rationalistically oriented Enlightenment of the eighteenth as well as the twentieth century is that there are experts for all decisions. Basically we should follow Kant who specifically distinguished between the conditional imperative of prudence, where in fact purposive rationality alone rules, and the unconditional imperative of the morally commanded. This unconditional categorical imperative states that there is something which I can never discharge to the knowledge of another. That exactly defines the concept of responsibility and, in a certain sense, also the concept of conscience. One who could have known better or could have acquired a better understanding knows himself to be responsible for the results of his decisions. Without a doubt, this is contained in the concept of practical reason which the Greeks developed. However, one does Kant an injustice, when one holds, and has held, that his distinction between the hypothetical imperatives of prudence and the categorical imperative of morality implies the separability of both imperatives. Reason is indivisible. In my view, one of Kant's greatest merits is that he taught in his pedagogy that one always underestimates the child when one believes that one cannot appeal to his reason. This thing is evidently true also for the sense of justice, which requires early training and care. It can even be observed with pets. In any case, to share with others, to be able to lose in a game and similar things are extremely important in the education of preschool children. When this type of early moulding has not occurred, this often leads to the most serious consequences in later life. In my view, Kant, following Rousseau, has the incontestable merit of having given definite limits to the utilitarian optimism of the ruling class of the eighteenth century; he thus rejected their Enlightenment pride in politics and social policy. His teaching concerning the categorical imperative means nothing other than that there are certain unconditional limitations in the pursuit of our own goals and ends. Thus one of the illustrations which he gave for his categorical imperative is completely convincing to us: one should recognize each person as an end in himself and never treat a person only as a means. Naturally, that does not mean that one does not frequently use the other as a means for one's own ends. But it does mean that the other cannot be made to perform or not perform a service against his will or without his free consent. What 'free' means here is very much in question given the existing dependencies which everyone has. In a certain sense we are all servants to the totality of our social being. But because we are politically equal, as citizens, we are servants through a free choice and bound to accept the corresponding responsibilities. Only when we respect the other as an end in himself can we have respect for ourselves. That is an inheritance of the eighteenth century and therefore a fruit of Western Christian culture, which today is shared by humanity: there may not be slavery; there is to be equality before the law. The whole problematic of human rights follows from this. For the secularized ideals of Christian culture, self-evident as they were to a person living at the end of the eighteenth century, now pose numerous difficulties and are contested in many ways, with the conditions for human life having become much more complex. And so one dreams of a legal order binding for all of humanity, an order which has been achieved to a large extent in certain areas, e.g., in the international conventions governing warfare. Even if right and law have their most evident foundations in essential human nature, there remains much room for disagreement: especially regarding the validity of existing orders of law, custom and society and regarding the application of the law under these concrete conditions. The idea of an expert also poses difficulties for me, for example in the form of the legal expert, even though there are such experts in limited areas, e.g., in international law. Here a fundamental barrier for all legal systems appears, which is always present in all thinking about them. And it is quite in order to consider legal and lawful measures wherever shared fundamental convictions can be presupposed. But even then one will have to take into account that legal regulations always provoke their own circumvention. Even in the question of gene technology and its misuse, one cannot really eliminate this consideration. Basically there must be another presupposition by means of which that, which is abhorred and rejected by all, is effectively prevented. Certainly it is the task of politicians to regulate the human communal life by means of legislation. And the separation of legislative from executive authority in modern states has the advantage that the freely chosen representatives of the people are entrusted with the responsibility to make the laws. And certainly the specialist, the expert, necessarily plays his role in this political process of controlling and making laws. There is room here for purposive rationality as has become apparent, for example, in the well-known discussions about the introduction of the death penalty or its abolition. The discussion instantiates a purposive rational consideration—namely, that deterrence will by no means be more effective due to capital punishment—

converging with a completely different one: the principle of respect for life which is grounded in religion. Therefore, a certain amount of such convergence between the human sense of solidarity and the legal regulations, which are imposed upon and required by people, is surely an indispensable condition for the efficiency of a constitutional state. Aristotle had already clearly recognized that justice can never be realized in legal systems in such a manner as would be desirable—and adequate to the always unforseen particular case. But this mere approximating function of a legal order to justice, remains itself dependent upon a politically expressed consent by those who live under these laws. This is the essential presupposition for the functioning of a legal system.

Certain considerations follow from this for the question of responsibility. Clearly each person who freely chooses is responsible for their decisions. This is also true for the researcher and scientist. Our discussion has shown that especially the expert, who officially advises the decision makers, has a very delicate dual responsibility: a responsibility for the anticipated results of a scientifically acceptable insight and, on the other hand, the responsibility to hold to what science has actually learned and asserts, uninfluenced by the pressure of interests and the expectations of the public. To this degree the expert stands in the center of the problem. Here one must, I believe, carefully distinguish between the responsibility which properly belongs to science and the responsibility of the scientist. Here, in fact, a specific ethos of responsibility will be required of anyone who speaks in the name of science. This ethos differs from that of the expert who recognizes himself to be conjoined to the political decision-making process through his official function. Fundamentally, the expert surely shares this latter responsibility with all of us, since we are all political citizens and must also partake in the responsibility for what occurs. We need to ask ourselves whether the balance between these two responsibilities and, therefore, the meaning of the responsibility which each citizen has for the common good, have been sufficiently cared for. During three centuries of an ever-increasing frenzy of making and being able to make, we have been less concerned than we should have been to keep alive the consciousness of our own responsibility as citizens and members of society. Now we are surrounded by a preponderance of dangerous arts and abilities. Consider the example of medicine. We know from our own life experience how medicine has made exceptional progress through fantastic achievements, not only in surgery but in many other areas. The weapons, which medicine controls, are now so precisely targeted that there are just a few who can use them without ever making mistakes. That is unavoidable. But it is not unavoidable that the common social welfare system, which the modern state has created, leads one (even in this area) to regard the physician and his means as something technologically available. Thus the doctor is burdened with society's own task of caring for its health and preventing illness. Again it appears to me that the actual problematic of the expert, who is the physician in this case, does not so much lie with the responsibility of the expert but with our own responsibility for ourselves. Therefore, I believe that the large area of actual heath care, which today is called preventative medicine, has been neglected—in the mistaken reliance upon the competence of modern medical science. I wish to illustrate this with an example: When, about ten years ago at the so-called Ciba-colloquium in London, the possibility of manipulating human genes became generally known, a wave of solidarity appeared, uniting people. For such a manipulation of human genes provoked disgust and protest. And then one is tempted to construct barriers by legal means. But it is also evident that we cannot renounce the possibilities that gene-technology offers, whether in its direct application to human beings or to farming, animal husbandry or other domains. Here as well there is, therefore, no possibility of chaining down science as such. There exists only the possibility of a responsible application of its results, something for which society as a whole and its political organization must take responsibility.

I am convinced that even in a highly bureaucratized, thoroughly organized and thoroughly specialized society, it is possible to strengthen existing solidarities. Our public life appears to me to be defective in so far as there is too much emphasis upon the different and disputed, upon that which is contested or in doubt. What we truly have in common and what unites us thus remains, so to speak, without a voice. Probably we are harvesting the fruits of a long training in the perception of differences and in the sensibility demanded by it. Our historical education aims in this direction, our political habits permit confrontations and the bellicose attitude to become commonplace. In my view we could only gain by contemplating the deep solidarities underlying all norms of human life. And in the face of the loss of the unifying power of religion and of the churches, we must retrieve what has become a social task for us in the last centuries: to become aware of what unites us. One may, I believe, also direct this appeal to today's politicians: to not always present us with the drama of their internal conflicts and of focusing on the next successful election, but also to present those common elements which unite us in being responsible for our future and the future of our children and children's children. The actual consequence of the limitations of the expert is, it appears to me, that we recognize these limitations as our own. We need to acknowledge as our responsibility all that which is entailed by our decisions. This is a responsibility which cannot be shifted to the expert's shoulders.

Chapter 16

THE FUTURE OF THE
EUROPEAN HUMANITIES*

What one calls *Geisteswissenschaften* in Germany does not have an exact equivalent in the other European languages. In France one speaks of *lettres*, in the English-speaking countries of the moral sciences or humanities, etc. But even if a correct linguistic equivalent is missing, one may nevertheless state that the humanities play altogether and everywhere within the diversity of Europe a very special role which is to the highest degree a common one. This communality consists primarily in the fact that Europe is a multilingual whole constituted by various national linguistic cultures. Every view concerning the future of the world and the role which European culture through its humanities may play for the future, has to take into consideration that Europe is a multilingual system. One can surely predict a standard language for the natural sciences in the future. But for the humanities it will probably be different. Indications for this are visible today. The essential discoveries in the natural sciences, at least when they come from multilingual Europe, usually are reported in English, the standard language. This may not yet be completely true for Eastern Europe. However, there are unavoidable reasons—such as the internal interdependencies and total communality of research interests in natural science—which, in the end, simply necessitate such an operational language of science.

In the humanities, however, things look different. One may frankly say that the multiplicity of European national languages is intimately related to the humanities and their function within human cultural life. One cannot even imagine that this cultural world, practical though it might be, could come to an agreement concerning an international operational language for the humanities, as has been occurring in the natural sciences for some time. Why is this the case? To contemplate this already means to say something about what the humanities are today and what they could mean for the future of Europe.

Let us first inquire how these so-called humanities were developed in the first place. The prediction of the future is to a great extent denied to humans. Inasmuch as we are at all able to have some anticipations, we must always take into account the mystery of human freedom, which

---

*Essay, published in Graz, Austria in 1983.

through the actualization of its potential always and again presents surprises. Inasmuch as predictions and thinking ahead are sensibly and seriously founded and are not simply a thoughtless dreaming of the scientific exploration of the so-called future—and such dreaming will not be made more ingenious by calling itself futurology—, it will always only be able to develop all its thinking ahead by thinking back. That is an understandable scientific necessity. Therefore, what Europe can be in the future, and more, what Europe is today, can only be discussed when one asks how Europe has become what it is today.

To discuss the role of science for the future of Europe, one must begin from an initial fundamental statement whose evidence appears to me undeniable. This statement declares that the shape of science itself almost defines Europe. Science has determined Europe in its historical being and becoming; it has almost determined when something is called European. That certainly does not mean that other cultures, on their part, have not developed their own productive achievements and continuing traditions in certain areas of the scientific knowledge of the world. One need only remember what the Near East and Egypt bequeathed the developing European science in Greece. However, what one can say without reservation is that only in Europe did the pattern of science crystallize into an autonomous and ruling cultural structure. Especially modern world history has been determined in its cultural and civilizing organization through science in an obvious manner. Since the course of the technical and industrial revolution has overtaken the whole earth with increasing intensity, the leading position of science in culture has not been limited to Europe. However, since modern science and research, education and higher education everywhere follow the European model—or its American reproduction—this is all still a result of European science. This proposition is completely independent from how one may judge the future prospects of a humanity ruled in this manner by science and its technical application. Therefore, we will initiate our deliberations with the fundamental statement that the development of science shaped Europe.

In order to make this clear, the uniqueness of this event must be more carefully described. Certainly there was never a cultural world or cultural sphere where a "science" gained from experience has not been administered and transmitted. Equally, there has never been a cultural sphere among the variety of human cultures created which has been so extensively dominated by science. So it is most indicative that such a profound differentiation and articulation of human knowledge and the human desire to know, emerge only in Europe, as can be seen in the concepts of religion, philosophy, art, and science. To this differentiation there is no original counterpart in other cultures, not even in high cultures. These four concepts represent a thoroughly European mode of thinking. It would be futile, to search for such categories, which are self-evident for us, within other traditions and to burden, for example, the wise sayings of the great Chinese thinkers or the epic tradition of India with such differentiations. The same is true for the extinct cultures, such as the great high cultures of the Near East and Egypt. Of course, one can approach all these cultures using our separating and differentiating concepts of today. One may even include the contributions of all these cultures to our scientific knowledge. One will proceed in the same manner even in a religious dialogue or in an encompassing overview of the artistic accomplishments of humanity. However, in doing this, one will have adopted prejudgments without wanting to and will have certainly missed the self-understanding of these cultures. Slowly, just this insight dawns on us, not only in our historical consciousness but also in our experience while actually approaching foreign peoples and cultures through our research interests. One begins to doubt the questionnaire of naive field research in sciences such as ethnology, anthropology, and ethology. We record as a first result: One of the fundamental characteristics of Europe is the differentiation of philosophy, religion, art, and science. It originated in Greek culture and shaped the Greek-Christian cultural unity of the Occident.

This is certainly not the only differentiation which characterizes Europe. There are other distinctions which have taken part in the further differentiation of European culture. If we look at the Greek-Christian cultural tradition, a fundamental internal difference within this tradition will immediately appear: the difference between East and West. It is clear that this difference has the fall of the Roman Empire, with the political split of the Roman Empire into the Eastern and Western Empire, as its background. Connected with this is the schism within Christianity which permitted the development of two separate Christian churches: the so-called Greek Orthodox Church and the Roman Catholic Church. This separation, however, appears to me finally to nearly define European cultural unity. In any case, in the area of church politics, the suffering due to this separation and the attempt to reunite the churches have been well known facts for centuries, which have found expression in the ecumenical movement.

This also affects the area of the humanities. Here the separating is perhaps stronger than the uniting. One may say without exaggeration that Eastern Europe, at least in as much as it belongs to the Orthodox Church—the present political division between East and West is clearly not ecclesiastical—has not attained in our humanities an equal intellectual presence as the manifold Western cultures of Europe have. The eastern cultures are not as alive in our historical consciousness as the Western cultures. One does not need to be a prophet in order to predict that in the future Europe will certainly have to work on this imbalance and that especially the humanities will have to contribute to its reduction. The plain fact of the political and military power of Eastern Europe will see to it that the historical-philological study of East-European cultures will be fostered in West-European science. Why such a balance has been missing for so long has its reason in the history of the Western cultural world of Europe, but naturally also in the increasing significance of world trade across the oceans. When one looks at the globe, Western Europe appears in relation to the expansive land mass of Eastern Europe as one large harbor landscape, as if it were almost created for the expeditions to the new worlds.

Within these conditions the cultural unity of the Western world formed itself through a series of attempts to revive its classical inheritance. After the most violent storms of the period of migrations had passed and the Roman Church had established itself as the solid reigning power, renaissances within the German-Roman nationalities, who had assumed the inheritance of the Roman Empire, continually accompanied the history of the Western world since the Carolingian Renaissance. Only slowly does it begin to penetrate our historical consciousness that a similar tradition building activity originated with Byzantium for the eastern half of Europe and that a deeper appropriation of this tradition had occurred in similar reminiscences. But without a doubt, the tradition of the Western cultural world has been formed by an especially contentious history.

For one thing, the differentiation of languages reached a much higher degree than in general occurred for the Slavic languages of Eastern Europe.

The antagonism between church and state, which dominated the history of the Middle Ages in the West, is equally underrepresented in the Byzantine realm: there, there was neither so strict a centralism in the regime of the church nor was there such a unified idea of empire and imperial power. Added to this is finally the schism within Western Christianity since the Reformation. The conflict and competition between the Roman Catholics and the Protestants have themselves played an important role in the deepening of the differentiation process in Western Europe. This is especially apparent if one inspects the final stage of this rich tradition of European culture, which is exhibited to us in the marvelous succession of artistic styles which ended with the historical and reductionist experimental phase of the nineteenth and twentieth centuries. It is like a break in tradition, which one can almost touch and which certainly began with the French Revolution and its conscious denial of the past. Of course, the emancipation of the Third Estate, which the French Revolution accomplished, was not only a break in tradition. In a certain sense, it was rather the maturation of a slow development concerning municipal and class structures of economic life. But even the conscious break with tradition, which led to the bloody confrontation between the superannuated dynastic absolutism and the upward mobile powers of society, did not mean only a break, but at the same time the creation of a new consciousness of continuity in the reaction to this break.

With this we approach the development constituting our theme and upon which the tension between natural sciences and humanities in our European culture is based. After the break with tradition caused by the French Revolution came the reaction of Romanticism. Romanticism glorified the Christian Middle Ages and the epic prehistory of the European peoples. It represented, therefore, a last glorification of the cultural and religious unity of Christianity in Europe, which was intensified, for example, by Novalis to eschatological expectations: "When numbers and figures no longer...." The elaboration of speculative idealism from Fichte to Hegel is just the philosophical counterpart to this and presents an equally ingenious as a presumptuous attempt to supersede tradition and revolution, antiquity and modernity, the oldest metaphysics and the newest science in a final synthesis. Something like this could not last long. The enduring effect of this Romantic reaction, which deeply conditions the European consciousness, was something else: the rise of historical consciousness.

In the light of historical thinking, connecting lines across all breaks and revolutions of world history become again apparent. Historical thinking did not in truth first begin with the Romantic reaction to the French Revolution. It has always been a sustaining element in all traditional orientations. Contemplating one's origins and an interest in the history of one's home, land, church, or dynasty, have for a long time played their role in the historical life of humanity. Every tradition is as such not an organic event but depends on the conscious effort to preserve what has passed.

The historical consciousness which came to prevail in the nineteenth century is however something else. The intensification of the historical sense brings about the fundamental conviction that for humans there is not a valid and binding understanding of the whole of reality and that no first philosophy or metaphysics has a solid foundation besides the natural sciences based on mathematics.

I therefore formulate the second fundamental proposition of my deliberations: The role of the humanities for the future of Europe is based upon historical consciousness. It will no longer permit universally valid truths in the sense of metaphysics, which may be recognized as the *philosophia perennis* behind all changes in thinking. But now one must

question whether this fruit of the Romantic reaction to the abstract constructions of the radical political Enlightenment and to the speculative
presumptuousness of Idealism is truly a new beginning or whether it is
itself not a result—as in all historical events the new is also always what
has been long in preparation.

Indeed we will be required to go back further—to the seventeenth
century. The great fact of natural sciences based on mathematics was a
true revolution in science—but in the end clearly the only one which
truly deserves this name. What developed with the new mechanics of
Galileo and with the diffusion of the mathematical foundation of all
empirical sciences, was the actual beginning of modernity. It did not
begin on a certain date—this game of the historian has been played
enough—but with the methodological ideal of modern science. The
unity of the traditional, comprehensive science, which carried the general
name "philosophia," divided itself into an irreconcilable dualism of two
worlds, a cosmos of the empirical sciences and a cosmos of the world-orientation based upon linguistic traditions. The well-known philosophical
expression for this division is the distinction which Descartes drew
between the *res cogitans* and the *res extensa*. With this, a wedge was driven
into the comprehensive science of tradition which resulted in the duality
of the natural sciences and humanities within science.

In the beginning it was still a development within the framework of
traditional metaphysics. It is distinctive for the continuity of European
thought that the tradition of metaphysics was able to assert itself even in
the time of the Enlightenment and the emergence of the modern empirical sciences; it even had its effect in the time of Romanticism. Exactly
this is conspicuous in the presumptuous synthesis which post-Kantian
German Idealism dared.

Ernst Troeltsch may have been correct when he regarded this late
fruit of metaphysics as just an episode in the total enlightenment process
of modernity. But he may have been incorrect when he held the future of
metaphysics had already been sealed in the nineteenth century. The natural propensity for metaphysics in humans is not so easily suppressed—
even if the form of metaphysics as the "first science" may not be capable
of a lasting revival. In truth it was just the humanities which more or less
consciously assumed this great inheritance of human questioning concerning the final things and which has given philosophy since then a historical orientation.

We have made clear that the pace of humanistic research in Germany has been determined by the spirit of Romanticism and therefore
found its scientific expression especially in the "historical school." Certainly historical-critical research, this new way of thinking in science,
radiated over the whole European cultural world, but to different

degrees. The development of the humanities and their cultural function in other civilized European countries, to which Russia at that time certainly belonged, was not exactly the same as in Germany, where Romanticism originated. In Germany another powerful force was influential: the Protestant tradition of the daring and critical insistence upon the freedom of each Christian. This accelerated the success of the humanities and especially historical science in nineteenth-century Germany. In other countries, where other social conditions prevailed and where the religious schism was not effective in the same manner, things were different. This is reflected, for example, in England's early democratic tradition, which introduced something of the spirit of the Roman Republic, its will to dominate and its ideal of humanity, even into the name, moral sciences. It is also reflected in France where a grand moral and literary tradition dominated public life and still dominates today; therefore what is represented under the collective concept of *lettres* is what we call the Geisteswissenschaften.

It is clearly a drama of a special type which we observe when we study the relationship of the humanities to the specific foundations of the traditions of the European peoples. What emerges in the various names for the "humanities" points to a deeper relation connecting the new historical consciousness to the modern territories and nations. This becomes particularly clear in the founding of new sovereign nations, as has occurred in recent history. The historical sciences, especially, acquire a great importance for the new political unities; using the historical sciences they try to justify their own identity from their past. Therefore, Herder's teaching concerning the national-folk spirit had a tremendous effect on the Slavic East. In a similar manner the results of the Second World War, for example, the reconstitution of Poland, but also the reconstitution of Germany in the East, have received important social impulses from historical research and writing.

But these are only the European examples closest to us. In truth this concerns a global process, which began with the end of colonial times and the emancipation of the members of the British Empire. Everyone faced the same problem of more deeply justifying their own identity and their independent development to a national state; and that includes, in addition to all the economic and political aspects, those for which the humanities are important. Thus the humanities which developed in Europe cannot avoid the task, which they have already accepted by their mere existence.

This brings us to our central theme. It concerns the future of Europe and the role of the humanities for this future of Europe in the world. Today, it concerns not only Europe, but the new unity of civilizations which is brought forth by worldwide communication and a world economy. And it concerns the new civilizational multiplicity to which human culture on our planet is beginning to unfold. This is a history full of questions. It does not only concern so-called foreign aid and its plight nor just that, with the development of an investment politics in underdeveloped countries, the deeper and more intellectual presuppositions of the famous know-how are not being developed at the same time. It does concern a much deeper problematic, namely how the experiences of thought which modern Europe has lived through can acquire some relevance on a planetary scale. According to the criterion of economic-technological progress, the concept of development may have a specific economic and social-political meaning. But that this is not all, is beginning to be felt the most in the contemporary world by exactly the most developed countries.

The results of the modern scientific Enlightenment are visible not only in the economic growth of the highly developed countries, but also in the growing imbalance between economic and social-human progress. The concept of development and the question about the goal of development, according to which development is measured, have lost their unequivocal meaning. Of course, economic prosperity will carry within itself its own teleology and be able to justify itself immanently. We are just beginning to discover this as a specific difficulty: how one, as a member of a highly developed country, can remain credible in the exchange with politicians and intellectuals who are working on technological development in underdeveloped countries, when one begins to address the problematic that our progress poses.

Exactly at this point the insights of the humanities, it appears to me, achieve a new relevance. Many countries in this world are in search of a form of civilization which would accomplish the trick of uniting their own traditions and the deeply rooted values of their forms of life with ideas of economic progress derived from Europe. The greater part of humanity is facing this question. It addresses us as well. Are our schools and educational programs actually employed in the right way, when we export them to the third world? Or are they in the end only grafted, causing more alienation of the elite from their ancestral traditions, rather than contributing to the future of these countries? The tragedy of the "black Orpheus" is well known. We only stand admiring the artistic talents of Africa or Asia. Our sculptors, our painters, our musicians and our poets marvel and learn.

However, is what we have to offer, what we control, scientific-technological perfection, really always a gift? One can doubt this even if we enhance our economic aid with the export of know-how.

Sooner or later the disparity between their own being and that of the Europeans will arise in the consciousness of the people of the Third

World; and then, all new efforts which we are presently pursuing could prove to be just subtle forms of colonization and likewise fail. Signs for this are present today. Sometimes it is already no longer the adaptation of the European Enlightenment and its form of civilization which engages the perceptive minds in other countries but rather the question of how people and society will be able to achieve a true development from the basis of their own tradition. Herder will then become prominent again and not only as the interpreter of the "voice of the people in songs" and not only as the critic of a one-sided Enlightenment and as the prophetic reviver of the "national spirits." The imperishable mark effective in all the humanities is the element of tradition and evolved being, which the humanities represent and can best be expressed in the concept of "culture," which corresponds to that nature developed by cultivation. This element will then suddenly communicate.

Certainly the humanities have also been rigorously disciplined by the methodological ideal of modernity and to that extent follow the natural scientific ideal of science. One who is not blind will even recognize that the technological progressiveness of our era has also a new and increased influence on the humanities. The methods and forms of expression in the humanities testify to this. One must almost ask oneself whether a shift within the so-called humanities is in preparation in the second half of our century which may extend a lot further and one day could make the name "humanities" completely obsolete. I am referring to the increasing participation of the mathematical and statistical methods. They are beginning to give the social sciences in particular a new character. Because of these new tendencies we are having more and more difficulties when we try in some cases—e.g., in the organization of academies of science—to characterize the present-day humanities as the historical-philological sciences, by which one previously could have almost completely characterized the whole of the humanities. It appears as if modern mass society and the social-scientific, organizational and economic problems it produces, opens the way for a conception of science which differs only slightly in its methodological understanding from the natural sciences. Applying the strict requirements of natural scientific research, one may say of these social sciences that their experiential scope and their experiential basis are insufficient as a foundation. But this is only a relative critique. This could change. Just as extended weather forecasts are becoming increasingly more reliable. The new computer era, which is approaching, permits such a tremendous increase in the quantitative-statistical collection and storage of information, that one may ask oneself whether the life of society is not becoming more and more calculable by the organizational ingenuity of an administered world—thus possibly meeting expectations derived from natural science in the authentic sense.

Would social science then not be a full partner with natural science, if it were able to accomplish the investigation of the nature of society with the goal of controlling this nature?

It is quite another question whether there are any limits to such a development or whether such a development is desirable at all. This question, however, could coincide with the question whether it is at all possible. One can indeed imagine the future human of mass society as a true genius of accommodation and in the exact obedience to rules. But it still remains an open question whether such a social training offers a promising future if our freedom is not awakened and protected. Here as well the cultural content of the humanities could make an indispensable contribution to life in the future.

One may ask, for example, to what extent the new methods of information storage could disclose new future possibilities in the classical sciences themselves, in the philological-historical humanities. One should consider the far-reaching effects of the age of reproducibility which today are already apparent to everyone and which everyone uses. Who would reject this? And yet: is this a frivolous achievement? New mechanical means of communication of the most varied kinds have separated the appearance of the modern researcher from the old image which the homo literatus once presented when he sat with his ink bottle and his feather in front of blank paper or when he studied with difficulty old printed or written folios. One who can no longer write without a typewriter, one who can no longer calculate without a calculator, one who can no longer live without an exact schedule of the flow of information flooding him, for him the discovery of his own identity—and this is at the same time the discovery of an expression for himself—has been moved to substantially remote limits. Where is his own handwriting or intellectual script? The data bank of the future will extend these limits by giant steps. Vast quantities of information will become easily accessed. Will criticism of them and the winning of insights, which lie dormant in them, become equally accessible?

Should we draw the conclusion that the humanities' special role for the social life of humanity in the visible future has been exhausted? Or do we have reason to assign the technical advances, which the humanities also will certainly use in the future, a subordinate, a merely technical, meaning? Or must we consider even a negative evaluation of such a development? One could also formulate the question thus and thereby draw a universal conclusion for this perspective: will the continuation of the industrial revolution lead to the leveling of the cultural articulation of Europe and the spreading of a standardized world civilization, in which the history of the planet almost stands still in the ideal status of a rational world bureaucracy—or, to the contrary, will history remain history with all its catastrophes, tensions, and its manifold differentiations, as has been the essential characteristic of humanity since the building of the Tower of Babel?

However, before we turn our attention to this question, we will first be required to examine again the whole question of the opposition between the natural sciences and the humanities. Because today, exactly from the side of the natural sciences, it is being proposed that the old dualism of the two groups of sciences has been overcome. One likes to trace this dualism back to a one-sided philosophical view of the contemporary natural sciences. It is true that the epistemological problematic of the nineteenth century and its consequences for the philosophy of science had to conclude with the distinction between the concepts of nature and freedom. Underlying this is the fundamental Kantian distinction between the appearance and the thing in itself and the limitation of the validity claim of the categories of our understanding to the domain of appearances. The fact, upon which the epistemology of the nineteenth century based this distinction and limitation, was the one of the mathematical natural sciences and their completion in the physical system of Newton, the discoverer of the mechanics and dynamics of the universe.

But there were on the other hand the concepts of freedom, which, since Fichte, the post-Kantian philosophers used in order to defend scientifically and epistemologically the Kantian separation of freedom as a fact of reason from the domain of appearance. But Kant's discussion of a double causality, a natural causality and a causality from freedom, was misleading. For one understood this to mean the intelligible cooperation of two codetermining factors for bringing about real events in the world. But that was clearly not Kant's opinion, who insisted rather on the most stringent separation of the noumenal character of human beings from their empirical appearance and from empirical appearances in general. Under the opposing pair of determinism and indeterminism, this Kantian point of departure has undergone many variations and interpretations, and it haunts the nineteenth century. How noumenal factors could be thought to affect empirical events, remained fundamentally undecided. It could not be clarified by Kantian means. For the Kantian enlightenment especially insisted upon the acceptance of the primacy of practical reason and human freedom, as postulates of reason. The latter were not to be subject to explanatory requirements.

When, within the natural sciences themselves, the problem of indeterminism was renewed in this century in the microscopic world of nuclear physics, impatient theoreticians used this problem in order to establish the missing link between the world of appearances and the world of freedom. This quickly proved itself, of course, to be inconsistent. Human consciousness of freedom presents itself not so much in the freedom of choice as in responsibility and the reasonableness of all our actions, and therefore as the autonomy of moral reason. It sounds peculiar when freedom is defined as the ability to initiate on one's own a chain of causes. Freedom itself cannot be thought of as a causality in the world of appearances.

In the meantime, one has become aware, from the root of the question itself, of the dubious nature of Kant's critical epistemological problematic. Kant wanted to prove the validity of the categories for the world of appearances and thereby to completely void the famous scandal of philosophy, about which he had complained: namely, that the reality of the external world was still an unproven assertion. But can there at all be a consciousness which is totally aware of its perceptions and certain of the reference to reality of its perceptions? Do not human beings belong, from the beginning on, to the great evolution of the universe, so that this Being-in-the-world represents, even scientifically, their true original condition? The system of concepts, which we employ in thinking through our experience, does not require any justification, because it is itself the product of natural evolution within which the accommodation of the living entity to its environment has always and already been justified as its primary condition for existence. Even if the history of the earth or even the universe may have to be thought of according to a scale which exceeds all human powers of imagination, and even if, on the other hand, the history of humans on this earth and especially their historical traditions in which their history has been preserved appear by that scale as purely insignificant—nevertheless, by means of this new perspective, the order of nature would be methodologically transformed back into a process, into a history, within which human history would, in the end, also have its well-recognized place. With this then, the old dualism of nature and freedom would in principle have been overcome. This reasoning is confirmed from the other side by what has been stated above concerning the change in the style of the humanities and the preponderance of the social sciences. And explanatory models have also been established in other cultural sciences, e.g., under the slogan of structuralism. They promise to clarify such inaccessible areas as the mythical tradition of a people, the secret of the structure of language or the mechanisms of the unconscious. Are we really about to enter into the era of posthistory, in which stable structures are becoming crystallized, even if based on evolution? One can understand this thus: in all the cultural accomplishments of humanity the tremendous process of accommodation of living beings to this world has, so to speak, reached its final state. To demonstrate this, consider an example: Behind the multiplicity of existing languages, Chomsky attempted to establish the true universals of language, which should underlie the particular structural laws of every actual language.

One counters today that in this he was too greatly influenced by his own language, English. He cannot claim universal validity for his results. Therefore, the diversity of languages remains, as well as similarities and total differences between them. The predicative structure of the Indo-Germanic sentence appears from this position as a historical novelty; different linguistic worlds, in which we attempt to think, promise different insights. So language may not be a universal in the sense of a unitary principle of construction for all possible languages. But it certainly is to be accepted for all of humanity in our late stage of evolution as one of its most important provisions. It is not self-evident that the thinking of modern science with its method of measuring and objectifying can at all comprehend what elsewhere is experienced as everywhere present. Cultures in which the ever-presence of smell is always in the foreground of consciousness will certainly have to express themselves differently in the realm of language.

Or let us take another example. Slowly our knowledge of the history of the earth and the events on this earth's surface approaches the time when the traces of humanity become denser and the historical relationships appear reconstructible. It is not unreasonable to suppose in the future of research an ever narrower concentration and an ever greater density of our picture of the past of humanity. Already today, in some cases the relationship between prehistory and historical tradition discloses itself as a corroborated result. Does this finally mean that we are approaching an era where there will be a true unified science? It may have to avoid the one-sidedness of so-called physicalism and yet be able to construct intelligible relationships between results of enormously different scales and be able to relate the evolution of the universe to the short time of the known history of humanity. Now I ask: Would this or will this lead to the disappearance of the individuality of the humanities in their uniqueness? Will they be absorbed into a new methodological and unitary structure?

Can we infer something from the experiences of our century for this question concerning our future? I think we can. The tendency toward the unification of our world-picture and our relation to the world, which corresponds to the leveling tendency and the growing mobility of today's human society, is countered by a tendency toward differentiation and toward a new articulation of previously hidden distinctions. Just as Romanticism awakened the spirit of the people and opposed the constructive ideal of Rationalism, so today counter movements arise in politics opposed to the increasing centralization and the formation of extraterritorial spheres of influence. The sovereign nation-states of the past, which were founded upon actual power and the sovereignty of self-defence, are disappearing more and more under the pressure of the superpowers. However, at the same time we notice everywhere a striving for cultural autonomy, which oddly contrasts with the reality of the power relationships. Even in Europe we observe this to some extent in the dissociation of Ireland from the United Kingdom, in the feud between the Flemish and Walloon languages, and in the secession attempts, which today, for example, cause tensions between Castile and Catalonia and which probably everywhere will lead to regional cultural autonomism, as is already used by the Soviet Union as a cleverly cultivated safety-valve for the pressure of the centralized Russian planned economy and single party system.

But it is especially on the global scale that such tendencies can be predicted for the future and will constitute the end of the colonial period and its confusion. Now, so many old countries follow new paths and new countries search for the old paths. Thus Europe appears to acquire a new relevance. It has the richest historical experience. For it contains in the smallest space the largest polymorphism and a pluralism of linguistic, political, religious, and ethnic traditions, which it has had to cope with for many centuries. Today's tendency toward unification and the leveling of all differences should not lead to the mistaken thought that the deeply rooted pluralism of the cultures, languages and historical fates can actually be suppressed or even should be suppressed. The task could lie in the opposite direction: to develop within a civilization of ever increasing uniformity the authentic life of the regions, the human groups and their forms of life. The homelessness with which the modern industrial world threatens humans drives one to search for home. What follows from this?

With such ideas of the coexistence of differences, one must take care not to introduce a false claim for tolerance or better a false concept of tolerance. It is a widespread mistake to take tolerance to be a virtue which abandons insisting on one's own position and represents the other one as equally valid. We may examine our own European tradition concerning this. Here we see, for example, the bloody and destructive religious wars which resulting from the Reformation devastated Central Europe in the beginning of modern times; or we see how in the seventeenth century the pressure of Islam finally encountered an insurmountable resistance before the gates of Vienna. We encounter, up to the present, how intolerance and the forceful suppression of the other is determining the struggle for world dominance. One asks oneself where the ideals of enlightened humanity and tolerance still have authority. However, one may still say this: Only where strength is, is there tolerance. The acceptance of the other certainly does not mean that one would not be completely conscious of one's own inalienable Being. It is rather one's own strength, especially the strength of one's own existential certainty, which permits one to be tolerant. Practice in such tolerance, as has been accomplished in a painful manner in Christian Europe, appears to me to be a good preparation for the greater tasks which await the world.

In the same manner as tolerance so must scientific objectivity, which is presupposed in the humanities, be based upon an inner strength. Here, as well, it does not concern abandoning and extinguishing the self for the sake of universal acceptance, but rather the risking of one's own for the understanding and recognition of the other. The authentic task of the human future which has truly gained global significance lies in the area of human coexistence. I would not venture to say that this is the task of the humanities. I would rather venture that the tasks, as they will be awakened to an increasing degree in such a pluralistically interwoven state of humanity, are the ones which will present the humanities with ever new challenges; they will involve research in history, in the history of language, the history of literature, in art history, legal history, economic history, and in the history of religion—all which directly influence actual realities. I wish to illustrate with a particular problem what I have to draw as the general conclusion. It concerns the role which the history of religion can and will necessarily play in the era of atheism. The oldest traces which we know for the phenomenon of religion clearly lie in burial rites. There the signature of being human can first be recognized. And it appears to me very significant that these symbolisms have proven influential even in the atheistic social systems of the present and certainly will continue to be for the near future. Burial rituals, monumental tombs, graveyards, mourning rituals, forms of lamentation—all of these are articulated in the most varied forms within humanity and point well beyond the boundaries set by the religious customs administered by churches. Yet every religion itself, due to its essence, will necessarily insist that it knows itself to be the true path to salvation. But this does not affect the universality of religious or secularized forms of living and dying which accompany humanity. These are unalterable realities of the human experience of being which no power in the world can suppress. Now I ask myself whether the power of perseverance of lived customs, beliefs, and values may not be noticed even more in an era of equalization and the coming world civilization. It appears to me that just this recognition of the forces of continuity in human cultural life will constitute the inner limit for the expansion of the world civilization of today. And I propose that the productivity of the so-called humanities consists in their being able to sharpen our awareness of the forces of continuity in life. They thereby insist upon an acknowledgment of experienced realities for the tasks of the future.

Certainly there will be not only differentiations, but also the constitution of new and extended geographical areas, within which new solidarities must grow and be transmitted into the living experience of everyone. This is a task which Europe also has to face for its own future. The present reflections, which we are attempting here together, are themselves already an illustration for this question. What can Europe still be in a changed world where Europe, not only politically but also perhaps in many other respects as well, will be reduced to a very modest role in the shaping of the world? Before any possible political formation of a unified Europe, the intellectual unity of Europe appears to me to be a reality—and a task which finds its deepest foundation in the consciousness of the diversity of this our Europe. That Europe consciously preserves the essential particularity of lived traditions in the competition and exchange of cultures appears to me to be like a most visible sign of life and like the deepest spiritual breath, through which Europe becomes conscious of itself. To participate in this appears to me to be the continuing contribution which the humanities must perform not only for the future of Europe but for the future of humanity.

Chapter 17

CITIZENS OF TWO WORLDS*

Where science is concerned, one needs to consider Europe, the unity of Europe, and its role in the world conversation which we are entering. No matter how one will describe science more accurately and whatever the specific character of the human sciences may be, it is undeniable that the science which developed in Greece represents the differentiating characteristic of the world culture emanating from Europe. Certainly one must admit—and we recognize this more and more—that the Greeks also were able to learn from other cultures and that, for example, the Babylonians had accomplished important results in the areas of mathematics and astronomy, and similarly the Egyptians, as the Greeks were especially cognizant. The grand high cultures of antiquity influenced Greek thinking even more through the theoretical form of the most diverse religious traditions. Nevertheless, it is still true that the form of science—in the widest possible sense of the word—received its actual character in Greece and this in a sense which does not yet incorporate the specific meaning of the modern empirical sciences, by means of which Europe is changing the world today. We must realize this in its total magnitude. Through the scientific impulse, which entered the intellectual growth of Europe, a differentiation in the forms of expression and thought arose which had never occurred anywhere else in the cultural life of humanity. I am referring to the fact that science and philosophy formed an independent form of spirit, which separated itself from religion and poetry. It even divorced religion from poetry and assigned art its own, even if very precarious, form of truth. This fact as such is universally known. We find ourselves completely helpless when we try to categorize, for example, the wisdom of the Far East into our classifying concepts of philosophy, science, religion, art, and poetry. It is undeniable: in Greece, the world spirit first made the turn which led to these distinctions. In a very broad sense, we can call what happened there and what structured the history of the West "enlightenment," enlightenment through science.

What does science mean here? Perhaps it will prove to be true that the awakening of science in Greece, on the one hand, and the development of the scientific culture of modernity, on the other hand, despite all

---

*Address delivered in Castelgandolfo, 1983.

the continuity in Western history, will exhibit so great a difference that the unity of meaning in the concept of enlightenment will also be affected. This question introduces an open and controversial theme today in our own self-understanding. If I am not mistaken this also affects the philosophical implications which Levinas developed from the concept of *savoir*. When Levinas contrasts *savoir* to the transcendence of the other, he makes thematic a completely different mode of demarcation than had arisen in the history of science in the West. It even appears to me as if especially in the forming and reforming of science, which occurred in Western history, the transcendence of the other played a determining role and did not just represent a "beyond" of all "science" and its "immanence." The "completely Other" of God, the otherness of the others, neighbors, that other of nature enclosed in itself—they all do not surrender to our "savoir." This announces itself already in the fact that the concept of philosophy and its relationship to the concept of science have had their own history. Originally the concept of philosophy certainly did not coincide with meaning which we associate with the concept today. Clearly the Greek word *philosophia* meant the essence of all theoretical passions, all devotion to pure cognition without concern for the use or profit which could result form it. Plato first gave the word a new accent. Philosophia meant for him not "knowledge" but the desire for knowledge, the striving for *sophia*, wisdom, the possession of truth reserved only for the gods. In the contrast between human and divine knowledge, there exists a motif which arose to a new determining meaning in the modern history of science. This points to the problem of philosophy as a science. In the use of language in antiquity and its continuation, Plato's characterization that philosophia is merely the striving for truth did not actually prevail. Only with the development of the modern empirical sciences, did this Platonic characterization come alive in the meaning of the word. Admittedly a shift in meaning occurred at the same time. It became just as difficult and just as necessary to define the right of philosophy in opposition to the modern sciences as it had been necessary to define it in opposition to the claim of the Greek "sophistic." The reciprocal relations between philosophy and science have since then been a problem for philosophy itself requiring continual reconsideration.

From these etymological observations we can already conclude that language and its articulation of world experience will play a central role for our question concerning the unity and difference of "science." For the Greeks language is primarily what is said in it, *logos* as *ta legomena*. According to this view, language is not that system of signs which our linguists study or which our philosophy of language discusses as its problem area. The concept of logos means rather the quintessence [*Inbegriff*] of those insights of humanity which have been deposited in language and passed on in linguistic form. And it is this concept of logos which fundamentally determined the Greek concept of science. To be able to be answerable for, to be able to be accountable for, to justify and to prove—all of these are implied in the "logic" and "dialectic" of the Greeks. In addition, the central expression for the sciences used by the Greeks was, *ta mathemata*: what one can teach and learn, and that means that experience would thereby be neither helpful nor even indispensable. In this sense mathematics is the model form of "science" for the Greeks. Thus mathematics had a sense which was essentially different from the role which it plays for the concept of science in the modern investigation of nature. The exemplary role of mathematics for Greek knowledge ultimately indicates the ideal of linguistic transmission and therefore that teaching and learning are inseparably connected to cognition.

With such an observation concerning language we approach the question which interests us. It is a fascinating history which the cognition of nature has had in our culture and clearly language has thereby had a fundamental importance for our whole history of thought. It was in connection with the particular structure of the Indo-European languages that a concept of "substance" developed in Greek thinking on the long path of enlightenment and related to it a concept of all that is attributable to substance. The predicative structure of a judgement describes evidently not only the logical form of the sentence, but also the conceptual articulation of reality. This is not self-evident. To begin the essence of language consists in the puzzling wonder of naming and the meaning of the name. Obviously, this precedes all particular structures of languages and language families. And it represents even now an element of our linguistic self-understanding. Word and object appear at first to be inseparably united with one another. For every speaker foreign languages, where the same thing is named and pronounced differently, are disturbing and at first quite unbelievable. A language family like ours, whose grammar is so dependent upon the relation between the verb and the noun, the predicate and the subject, was predisposed at the same time to the dissolution of the unity of word and object—and therefore to "science." That *onoma* is only the name that one "gives" to an object or person, is a revolutionary insight, which we find first in Parmenides: "Therefore everything will be just a name, that the mortals have established in their language, convinced it is true," (according to Diels/Kranz, *Fragmente der Vorsokratiker*, 8.38). That an entity may have changing names, that the same object may experience different predications, implies an understanding of being, which the Greeks themselves interpreted as their great accomplishment in cognition. The emphasis of this concept of the subject as the stable basis of changing predications and assertions is what characterized the concept of science in Greek thought. This characterization includes in opposition to changing experience a claim to truth which excludes experience from being actual knowledge. Only of that which is always as it is and which one can therefore know without seeing and experiencing anew, can there be science in its actual sense. The mere regularities which one can discover in the changes within experience are only in a weaker sense cognizable and the nonrecurring concrete can never be "known" as mathematical or logical truths can. Therefore Plato expressed the contingency of reality only in mythical form and Aristotle worked out the transformation of this metaphor into "physics" only as a doctrine of the forms of reality. His "physics" is a morphology.

When one considers this, the emergence of the modern empirical sciences in the seventeenth century is an event through which the complete concept of knowledge is newly determined. And thereby the position of philosophy and its claim to be all encompassing are made more questionable. The new ideal of method and the objectivity of cognition guaranteed by this method have forced knowledge, as it were, out of the context of teaching and living and driven it out of knowledge shared in language and society. They have introduced a new tension into what is meant by human knowledge and human experience. From now on mathematics is not so much the model for the sciences, as it was for the Greeks. Rather it becomes the central and true content of our knowledge of the experienceable world itself. For the Greeks it is self-evident that "experience" is not "knowledge"—although experience is always the basis upon which the *logoi* and *doxai* build which prove themselves as knowledge, and although experience is necessary for the practical application of knowledge. On the other hand, for modern thought it is self-evident that knowledge and science must prove themselves on the facts of experience. Cognition which is truly "knowledge" can only be acquired through the application of mathematics to experience and must protect itself from the images, the *idola fori*, suggested by linguistic conventions. And yet there is a rich tradition of human knowledge, which comes to us from our historical past and speaks to us and is valid for us as what has proven itself, has been believed, and hoped for throughout history—as it were, the other half of the truth.

So I am able to see the unity of our culture only from the perspective that the emergence of the modern empirical sciences in the seventeenth century is the event in which the previous form of the totality of knowledge, of philosophy or philosophia in the broadest sense of the word, began to disintegrate. Philosophy itself became a problematic enterprise. What sort of philosophy is still possible alongside the sciences, after the development of modern natural science and its encyclopedic treatment in the seventeenth and eighteenth centuries, is the question all modern philosophy faces. I have repeatedly indicated in my work how the concept of "system" has invaded the language of philosophy due to this precarious situation. This word is naturally older, and it is good Greek. It means every type of structure in the sense of the coexistence of differences. However as a concept, this word escalates into the formulation of the task to bring into a unity of thought the incompatible, the mutually incompatible. In this manner, the astronomical concept of the world systems developed after ancient astronomy was faced with the Platonic requirement to explain the irregularity of the planetary orbits from the presupposition of the circular motions of the heavens. In modernity, to continue the analogy, it is the planetary system of the modern empirical sciences which must become related in ever new approximations to the main center, to the inherited totality of knowledge, which is called philosophia. So the word "system" entered philosophy in the late seventeenth century to mark the mediation of the new science with the older metaphysics. The last important attempt of such a mediation, which is to be taken seriously, was the attempt of German Idealism to integrate the empirical sciences into the tradition of metaphysics from the new perspective of transcendental philosophy—a final but only temporarily valid project considering the insoluble task.

If that is so then the forming of European civilization by science implies not only a distinction, but brings with it a profound tension into the modern world. On the one hand, the tradition of our culture, which formed us, determines our self-understanding by means of its linguistic-conceptual structure which originated in the Greek dialectic and metaphysics. On the other hand, the modern empirical sciences have transformed our world and our whole understanding of the world. The two stand side by side.

That Kant justified both constitutes, in fact, his epoch-making significance. He recognized the boundaries of pure reason, proved their limitation to possible experience, and at the same time he justified the autonomy of practical reason. The limitation of the use of the categories and especially of causality to the appearances given in experience meant, on the one hand, the total justification of the scientific investigation of appearances—even when it concerned life or the social-historical world. On the other hand, however, the limitation of causality to experience is at the same time the justification of practical reason, in so far as its "causality from freedom" did not contradict theoretical reason. Kant's accomplishment of having justified the priority of practical reason, was then developed by German Idealism to such an extent that this priority conferred its status upon the concept of spirit and all its objectifications in economy and society, law and state. These objectifications are not only appearances and therefore the "object" of science, but also always intelligible facts of freedom, and that means that their truth can only be obtained in another manner.

Although this agrees with the tradition of the difference between theoretical and practical philosophy, which goes back to Aristotle, it nevertheless receives another character due to the development of modern science. The Kantian distinction between theoretical and practical reason led to the scientific and theoretical consequence of differentiating "concepts of nature" and "concepts of freedom." Within the German-speaking realm they became known as the dualism of the natural sciences and the humanities. In other countries there was no precisely corresponding distinction since concepts such as "lettres" or "literary criticism" did not even subsume certain parts of the humanities under the concept of science. It was the epistemological turn of Neo-Kantianism in Germany which, following Hegel's concept of spirit but not his speculative apriorism, expanded the concept of experience and the sciences of experience to include the historical-philological sciences. This culminated, for example, in the value theory of Southwest-German Neo-Kantianism, which then also served as the basis for the social sciences. In such an expansion to the "cultural sciences," the fact of science remained decisive: the "object of cognition" found its complete and single determination in it.

In our century philosophy has now begun to question the fact of science and its epistemological justification. This step was taken in Germany by the phenomenological movement. With its turn "to the things themselves," which Husserl introduced, it was no longer just the cognition of science whose a priori presuppositions philosophy had to prove; rather one became concerned with the phenomena of the "life world." The later Husserl used this term for the prescientific dimension of experience. His descriptive phenomenological investigation of essences began with it. Husserl later became more profoundly aware of the problematic of the "life world" and then he recognized a multiplicity of life worlds, whose underlying structures determine all our forms of apprehending reality. But clearly his own interest remained the Neo-Kantian epistemological one of justifying an incontestable, ultimate foundation to counter the charge of the relativity of these life worlds. The final foundation consists in the fact that the transcendental ego, this null-point of subjectivity, must justify all "objective" validity—therefore also the life world's relativity, which inheres in the "eidos" life world itself.

However, the paradox of the relativity of the life world is that one can become conscious of it, thus acknowledging the boundaries of one's own life world; but this does not enable us to transcend them. These are the irretrievable preconditions of possible cognition which determine our historicality. They are given before all "objectivity" in cognition and behavior—and that implies that any discussion of a pure subject loses any meaning, including the I-pole of the transcendental ego. Therefore, the relativity of the life world does not actually mean the limit of what is objectifiable, but rather means a positive condition for the type of objectivity achievable within the horizon of the life world.

One of the open problems Husserl left to phenomenological research is whether and how the claim of philosophy to be rigorous science permits a justification in so far as the "eidos" life world, the a priori horizon, presents the eidetic dimension; and whether its function can therefore be grounded through the apodictic evidence of the transcendental ego. Heidegger's radical questioning concerning the meaning of Being, which he sought in the horizon of time, began here. And continuing from Heidegger, I have attempted to clarify a bit further the fundamental hermeneutic constitution of the "life world." That the interpreter belongs to the context of meaning which he seeks to understand, necessitates, I believe, another meaning of objectivity than is the case in the natural sciences.

So it makes no sense to me to see a correspondence to physics here. That the nuclear physics of our century has reached limitations since it became apparent that the idea of an "absolute observer" is untenable, because the act of measurement in the atomic realm always implies a disturbing influence on the system, certainly modified the fundamental concepts of classical physics. However, this does not at all touch the sense of objective cognition and science. Science knows how to state *this* belongingness of the observer to the observed in the mathematical exactness of equations. Considering this, the modern physics of our century appears to me to be the consistent continuation of Galileo's physics which was based on mathematics and worked out with mathematical measurements. The recognized limits of objectification are in truth new objective discoveries, which the efforts of modern research have been able to accomplish. That thereby certain presuppositions of classical physics must have been discarded as questionable borrowings from the "life world," e.g., the "perceptibility" and the determinism of all "resulting states" by means of previous states, does not at all change the fact that it is the same mathematical physics.

The situation appears to be to be similar concerning the consequences which will be drawn today from the theory of evolution for epistemology and philosophy of science. There can be nothing surprising for the philosophical question itself that science and its development will also retain their place in the great perspective in which the general theory of evolution describes the "history" of our universe. The belongingness of humans to their world can be understood from both sides as the result of evolution: a new edition of the doctrine of "innate ideas," agreeing with the latest cosmological knowledge. "Their objective reality," which was the subject of the Kantian question, is in a sense, already solved. In the meantime, phenomenological research had also overcome, especially in the teaching of the intentionality of consciousness, the artificiality of the dual-substance-teaching of Cartesianism. Beginning here, Scheler had already identified the priority of self-consciousness and the separation of subject and object as a metaphysical, residual problem. Heidegger had shown this to be the burden resulting from the Greek ontology of the "present-at-hand," whose concepts determine the philosophical self-understanding of modern science. Therefore the theory of evolution is something like a new "physical" proof for idealism, admittedly an empirically better founded one than the one offered by Schelling's philosophy of nature.

In principle, however, the attempt using the theory of evolution, like all "reconciliation" attempts between the natural sciences and the "moral sciences," remains a deeply questionable matter, which appears to me no less problematic than at its time the speculative physics of German idealism. Neither the expansion of the Kantian apriorism beyond the boundaries of "pure natural science" by the Neo-Kantians nor such a reinterpretation by the modern empirical sciences could supersede Kant's fundamental notion: we are citizens of two worlds. We live not only in the sensible, we also live from the "supersensible standpoint" of freedom—even if these concepts of the Platonic tradition only characterize the problematic and could not lead to the solution of the problem presented by the priority of practical reason. While one must consider the fact of freedom with Kant as a fact of reason, the theory of evolution belongs in the area of "theoretical" reason and the empirical sciences. Freedom, however, is not an object of experience, but a presupposition of practical reason. Now one may counter that the plurality and relativity of the life worlds, which as such are an object of experience and also reflect the fact that human beings are capable of reason, would have to evoke the "ghost of relativism." But we cannot escape the lifeworld as a fundamental condition. Our task remains to integrate and subordinate the theoretical knowledge and the technical possibilities of human beings to their "praxis." It by no means consists in the transformation of the actual life world, which is just the world of praxis, into a theoretically justified technical construct. Therefore one must ask whether we do not have to learn something especially from the Greek heritage of our thought, which indeed has left us "science," but a science which remains integrated in the conditions of the human life world and in the guiding concept of its thinking, *physis*.

Here it appears to me that Plato's dialectic achieves a new exemplary status. Plato had understood the task of philosophy to be the awakening in our thought of what in truth already lies in our life world experience and its sedimentation in language, and therefore he termed all cognition recollection. Recollection is precisely not a mere repeating of cognition, but "experience" [*Erfahrung*] in the truest sense of the word, a journey

[*Fahrt*] whose goal unites what is known with new knowledge into a permanent knowledge. In order to judge the significance of this, we must return to the idea of practical philosophy and the concept of praxis as they were developed before they became dependent upon theoretical knowledge and its application, which we know today as applied science. Therefore, we must ask: What is praxis, what does praxis mean? Here we can learn from Aristotle: he formed the concept of praxis not in opposition to "theoria" but in opposition to the craft and art of production; he developed the difference between techne, the knowledge which directs making, and phronesis, the knowledge which directs praxis. The differentiation does not mean a separation but an ordering, namely, the integrating and subordinating of techne and its ability under phronesis and its praxis. So it appears to me clearly dangerous when one restricts practical philosophy in the modern manner to a theory of action. Certainly an action is an activity which is initiated by a moral decision, a prohairesis, an element of praxis. But at least concerning action one should consider the plurality of agents, and that means a whole intricate system of action and reaction, of acting and suffering. Only then can one avoid the prejudices of modern subjectivism and not be caught by the certainly ingenious synthesis through which Hegel developed an escape out of the philosophy of self-consciousness and subjectivity. So the doctrine of objective spirit and absolute spirit still represent an important step beyond the narrow Kantian foundation for moral philosophy in the concepts of duty and obligation. But does this doctrine accomplish the return which is actually required, the return to the Greek question concerning the Good and that practical philosophy which is based on the experience of human praxis and its *aretai*, its "excellences"?

Practical philosophy is not the application of theory to praxis, as we naturally use it in the area of practical activity, but arises itself from the experience of praxis due to the reason and reasonableness inherent in it. Praxis does not merely mean acting according to rules and is not merely the application of knowledge, but means the whole original situatedness of humans in their natural and social environment. In Greece one ends a letter with the closing, *eu prattein*, which could be translated with "wishing you well" [*laß es dir gutgehen*]. In some regions of Germany one also says "take care" [mach's gut]. However, this doing [*Machen*] is not a doing of something, but refers to the whole living situation of the one to whom this friendly wish is addressed. In such a view of praxis there lies the primary belongingness of all who live together.

What does this recollection of the broad sense of praxis as it was developed in Greek thought mean for us? No one doubts that the immediacy of one's interactions, which was the basis of everyone's political activity in the Greek city-state, exists in the present world-civilization in very different quantities and forms, especially considering that now all communication occurs by technical means. And therefore it contains new tasks and problems. Nevertheless, what one is being offered by Greek thought does not appear to me to be a romantic return to the past, but is rather a remembering of something constant. For the relationship between what one can do and that it would be good to do it, is not merely a problem in the new global technological society. The Greek world faced exactly the same problem and the Socratic question aimed at exactly this situation. It legitimates expert knowledge within its limits and exposes at the same time its incompetence in relation to what is truly the Good. One should not say that those were other times and that on the other hand in the modern, scientifically based, technical civilization the automatism of means has finally come to rule over human freedom and the ability to decide on what is good and that therefore everything depends on scientifically grounded ability. This is based on a false presupposition. As if it has ever been an easy task to yield to the goals set by politics and political reason in relation to all the calculated possibilities of acting. And in just the same way, it was not an easy task in the classical world to stem the abuse of power, toward which the politically powerful were driven, by means of reasonable public institutions. Concerning this, Plato's utopian republic could instruct us, just as the experience of our modern mass democracy could, which at least has recognized and practices the principle of the separation of powers as the most effective form of controlling power. The "nature" of humans does not change. Abuse of power is the original problem of human coexistence and the complete prevention of this abuse is possible only in a utopia.

Plato certainly knew this and therefore opposed his "city of education" to the city of politics. The final communality of humans with one another, which makes possible state and city life, appears here in a utopian structure where all individuality has been surrendered.

It is obvious that the modern state only poorly corresponds to the ancient city-state and its forms of life. And yet both are based on the same unchanging fundamental presupposition. I would like to call it the presupposition of solidarity. I mean that self-evident communality which alone allows for the common establishment of decisions which each considers to be correct in the areas of moral, social, and political life. For the Greeks this insight was in an undiscussed manner self-evident and even was reflected in their use of language. The Greek concept of the friend articulated the complete life of society. Among friends everything was held in common, that was the old Pythagorean tradition in Greek thought. Here in the extreme form of the ideal, the tacit presupposition is expressed under which it is at all possible to have something like the peaceful regulation of human communal life, a legal order. As could be demonstrated, the efficiency of the modern legal system still depends upon the same presupposition. No one wants to assert that the romantic image of friendship and a general love of one's neighbor are the supporting basis for either the ancient polis or the modern technocratic metropolis. However, it appears to me that the important presuppositions for solving the modern world's problems are none other than the ones formulated in the Greek experience of thought. In any case the progress of science and its rational application to social life will not create so totally different a situation that "friendship" would not be required, that is a sustaining solidarity which alone makes possible the organized structure of human coexistence. It would certainly be a misunderstanding, if one believed that in a changed world a past thinking as such could be renewed. What is important is rather to use it as a corrective and to recognize the bottleneck of modern subjectivism and modern voluntarism. These are errors caused not so much by human beings as such, and not by science, and not through science, but by the superstitious faith in science held in modern society. In this sense I believe that the grand monologue, which the sciences in their ideal completion could be, must always remain embedded in the communicative communality, where we are as humans. Therefore, it appears to me to be true that a science of humans must accept the modern concept of science in all its methodological strictness. But we must also learn and understand its limits. We must learn to restrict our scientific capacities to a responsible knowledge, which is nourished by the cultural inheritance of humanity. One should always keep exactly this in mind especially when promoting a science of humans.

A type of self-encounter can also occur with another and in relation to what is different. However, the task of learning to recognize the common in another and in something different, is more pressing than ever. In our ever smaller world, cultures, religions, customs, and values of the most different variety are encountered. It would be an illusion to think that only a rational system of utilities, so to say, a religion of world economy, could regulate human coexistence on this constantly smaller planet. The science of humans knows that more and more political virtue will be required, just as science has always demanded human virtue. The same is true considering the diversity of languages. There as well, in the reflective performance of our existence, we are confronted with a diversity of other languages. And we should not believe it to be our task or prerogative to force on others the questions which have arisen from our own life experience and have been sedimented in our own language. Also here and up to the point of conceptual thinking, we will have to take the conversation between languages into our care as well as the possibilities of communication, which they offer. The science of humans in their complete diversity becomes a moral and philosophical task for us all.

Chapter 18

THE DIVERSITY OF EUROPE:
INHERITANCE AND FUTURE*

Being eighty-five, I am an oldest child of the century which is being reviewed in this lecture series. I have lived through this stormy epoch from my childhood until today and may therefore qualify as a witness. Not a witness who presumes to speak as an expert about political and social events, but as one who may recall what has happened in order to raise the question what philosophy, the area about which I do have something to say, has to do with our situation, with our fears, our hopes, and our expectations.

Everyone should be aware that a theoretical person, who has devoted his life to pure knowledge, also depends upon the social situation and political praxis. Society itself first provides for that distance which is required of us as our professional task. It would be insane to believe that the life devoted to theory would ever be independent of the political and social life and its constraints. The myth of the ivory tower where theoretical people live is an unreal fantasy. We all stand in the middle of the social system.

Those of us who have lived through two world wars and their interludes and results, can truly not be tempted to believe ourselves to be in an ivory tower. However, what have we learned from this? We should ask with Hofmannsthal: "What is the use of having seen a lot?" Perhaps it nevertheless means something when I relate, for example, how I, as a young student in 1913, received for the first time on the occasion of an exhibition, pastries baked in vegetable oil, coconut oil. That was a completely fantastic novelty in Silesia which overflowed with butter and where I grew up—this was, by the way, an aspect of the German colonial politics of 1913. It may also mean something when I recall how the first Zeppelin filled us with wonder, this cigar floating in the sky. It was the case that one began even as a child to feel something of the time, of its self-consciousness, its beliefs, also its hopes, and certainly also its fears. As is the way with children, it was mainly the occasional subtle earnestness in the words of my father that led me to feel that not everything was at its best in the world. So I will not forget the moment of the outbreak of the war in 1914, when I enthusiastically cried out with the frivolity of

---

*Essay published in Stuttgart, 1985.

221

a curious child: "Oh that's fine" and my father with a furrowed brow replied: "You don't know what you're saying."

But I will not continue to support my credibility through such references to my age and my memories. My task is to ask how today's Europe, where we live, appears from such a distance as the years have lent me, and how all the things of today have become what they are. In Homer there is a beautiful phrase which describes the seer, the man who sees the future. It is a verse which says of the seer Calchas that he recognizes what is, what will be and what has been. The phrase means that there is no cognition of reality and also no prophesying into the future which is not able to unite the past, what has been, with what is present and with what we must be aware of. Therefore, I will look back in order to look forward, not from the basis of a special competence, but as a thinking person, as all people are, and ask myself how what exists today came to be.

The epoch of the two world wars and the intervening time began when I was a youth. With one blow the optimistic view of the future and the belief in progress came to an end. Of course, with the outbreak of the First World War the whole populace was carried away during the first weeks in patriotic intoxication and general enthusiasm. It was the same in all nations of Europe. The Second World War was not at all comparable. I experienced the outbreak of the Second World War in Leipzig—a funeral atmosphere lay everywhere. In 1914 a nationalist tidal wave flooded everything so that in all nations even the international workers movement collapsed into nationalist factions and sustained, supported, and suffered through the terrible world event of the First World War. One who still has a dim memory of the time before the First World War will remember a statement which comes from Talleyrand. He said that anyone who did not know the world before the French Revolution had not known the sweetness of life.

It is far from my purpose to idealize the events which preceded the time of catastrophes of the two world wars. Nevertheless, it precipitated such a tremendous change and in the end affected the position of Europe in the world, and therefore also the expectations of the youth which then as now, sought its difficult paths in an uncertain world. The epoch of both world wars enlarged all things to a global scale. Politics is no longer concerned with the balance of powers in Europe: this fundamental principle of foreign policy which everyone understood. Since then, it concerns a global balance, a question of the coexistence of frightening concentrations of power. Even the word "national economy," which we still use in economics, sounds peculiarly outdated. What are nations, what is "national economy" in the time of multinationals, in the age of world economy, in an age which receives its actual shape from the industrial revolution? Clearly this is all a result of the enormous technical developments, which were driven by the destructive rage of the two world wars. The industrial revolution increased again its intensity at the end of this epoch, in the second half of our century, in the time of reconstruction. It has flooded over us and sweeps us along. There is an inviolable law in this process, an iron necessity: not to remain behind. And only in this way can one even create the chances for life and the survival of everyone—yet suddenly just this law has become at the same time a threat to the life and everyone's survival.

This is the new situation in which Europe—and not only Europe—finds itself after the developments of the last decades. We are no longer alone in our small, fragmented, rich, and multifarious portion of the earth. We have become involved in an event and are threatened by an event, which is not limited to our narrow homeland. I must strictly emphasize the fundamental aspect of this: I mean the inner consistency of these events, which have led us to this critical boundary. For the first time an arsenal of weapons has been created, whose use does not guarantee victory, but would rather result only in the collective suicide of human civilization. And perhaps even more serious—for as far as I know, no one knows how to master this crisis—the ecological crisis, the exhaustion, destruction, and desolation of the natural basis of our home, the earth. These two threats resulted quite logically from the population explosion and at the same time the enormous increase in the standard of living in the developed countries. And today they threaten the human conditions for life in general.

I say this in all seriousness, there is no alternative. This word, alternative, has such a strange connotation in our political daily events, because everyone, who can think and is sincere, knows that there is no alternative. Only a directing and guiding of the processes which are already occurring can perhaps allow for the survival of everyone. And this will require of us all still different efforts than those in economics or foreign affairs. That is the conclusion from which we must proceed. Europe is inseparably tied to the world crisis, and this crisis has no patent solution. Rather everyone involved in the political or economic process is very conscious of the fact that we are slowly approaching, in the West and the East, the border zone of life and survival. And we must see that the avoidance of a crossing of the border is in everyone's interest.

When I, as a scholar, describe this picture known to us all, it reminds me of something similar which I know very well from my studies of Greek philosophy. I mean the experience which Plato had at the beginning of his own philosophical life in his home city of Athens. Concerning this we have a rare document, the so-called seventh letter of Plato, a political circular in which he (or someone well-informed whom he asked to write it) briefly tells the story of his decision to pursue philosophy. He relates there how a number of hard and stormy events occurred in his youth—the Peloponnesian War, the defeat of Athens, the installing of a presumptuous and tyrannical aristocratic group by the victorious Spartans, the so-called Thirty Tyrants—and how this group, which was associated with him through his family, was then overthrown and replaced by a restored democracy. But exactly this democracy, which was greeted as a liberator, sentenced the man Plato most honored and admired, Socrates, in an impiety trial to death by drinking poison. That was the fateful experience which pointed Plato toward the path of philosophy. In the end he had to recognize that not only his own city was badly governed but that, as far as he could see around him, all cities were badly governed in the same way, and therefore that nothing beneficial could be expected from public life. So he followed the path of philosophy. Naturally the word "philosophy" had then a much broader sense than signified in my modest professorship. Philosophy means following theoretical interests, means a life which poses the questions concerning the truth and the good in such a manner that neither one's own profit nor public utility is considered. In this broader sense, it appears to me that Plato's experience can certainly be applied to our situation. Not that I wish to claim that all our nations are badly governed. However, I do believe that one must say that the commercial and economic foundations of our whole political life are in a situation which appears similar in having no solution and at least requiring further deliberation. This situation is comparable to the one which Greece faced in the time of its political degeneration as Plato sensed it.

Let us first ask what philosophy has to offer in such a situation. For this we first need to clarify what philosophy actually is and how this fact that there is philosophy in our sense is intimately connected to our European civilization. For us as well philosophy retains a very broad sense. The word philosophy, in its general meaning of *theoria*, was for a long time the collective term for all sciences. Even Newton's famous *Foundations of Natural Science*, through which he became the founder of modern physics, is entitled *Philosophiae naturalis principia mathematica*, the elements and foundations of the knowledge of nature. It is a fact that philosophy has been associated with the appearance of science since the beginning of our Western culture. This is the novelty which brought Europe together into a unity and which today, from the scientific culture created in Europe, contributes to the dangerous situation of world civilization through its dispersion everywhere.

Clearly at that time the path of thinking and the desire to know were not limited to the small corner of the world, Europe. We know of the great accomplishments of the high cultures of the Near East, we know of Latin America, of South Asia, and East Asia. Therefore, we know that culture does not necessarily—and elsewhere it did not—take the path of science and its potency. It was just Europe which took this path. Only in Europe did such a differentiation in our intellectual activities occur as we know them from the distinction of science, art, and religion from philosophy. Who could even say whether Chuang-tse, or another of the Chinese wise men, was more a theologian, more a knower, more a thinker or more a poet? In Europe, our intellectual fate has achieved its structure through the confrontation of the highest tensions among these forms of intellectual creativity. Especially the relationship between philosophy and science has become of decisive importance for the present situation of Europe. Everyone knows how much, for example, the language of art, and even the religious tone in the language of art of distant cultures, can appear to us as almost a direct self-encounter. Who would dare claim a priority for Europe in this? But the form of science, and the form of the concept which supports the philosophical mastery of the knowledge of the world, these are obviously particularities, advantages and also tasks which alone have given European civilization its character, and later the world its character, after Christianity had adopted and modified them.

It was just in Greece that both developed, science and philosophy. The Greeks created mathematics, certainly referring to the previous work of especially the Babylonians and Egyptians, as we know better today than before. But it was the Greeks who created Euclidian geometry, which is still taught in an almost unchanged form in the beginning levels of our secondary schools. They acquired, collected and passed on scientific knowledge in many other areas: medicine, astronomy, and music. They absorbed a wide range of experience—Dante termed the great concluding wise man and thinker of Greek philosophy, Aristotle, the master of those who know.

And yet what we call science *today* is a modern creation. We have even adopted an expression for this which causes, so to speak, an inner convulsion for every humanist. We call them the sciences of experience [*Erfahrungswissenschaften*]. For a humanist that is an oxymoron, because, for the Greeks, experience was not required for science. One knows that two plus two is four with such certainty that it would be absurd to relate this to experience and to busily count things. Where one still requires experience, one has not reached the highest form of knowledge, the insight into the rational order of reality. That is how a Greek thinks. Within certain restrictions the whole Christian Middle Ages thought in the same manner, since they accepted the inheritance of the Greek and Roman civilizations and therefore the collective title philosophy still united the totality of their knowledge.

However, in the seventeenth century, and I cannot overemphasize this, the decisive change occurred, by means of which the relation between philosophy and science has become a continual problem for our intellectual culture. The whole rich treasure of culturally inherited knowledge—which had developed in religion and art and literature and in any number of other arts, and the abilities in medicine, astronomy, philology, and rhetoric—found itself confronted in the seventeenth century with a new concept of knowledge. That was like a new beginning. The decisive breakthrough occurred with Galileo. Here was a man, who explicitly stated of himself and his new science of mechanics, *mente concipio*, I conceive in mind, and meant with this the pure conditions for the appearances of motion in nature. He discovered, for example, the laws for free fall in this manner, since he began from something which he, in fact, could only conceive in his mind: falling in a vacuum. At that time it was not possible to construct an experiment where one could observe a body falling without resistance. I can still remember today, although I have remained a pure novice on the path of modern natural science, how impressed I was upon observing in a physics class that in a vacuum chamber a down feather and piece of lead actually fell with exactly the same speed. The power of abstraction, which was necessary to have this thought, and the power of imaginative construction, which was required to isolate the conditioning factors, to measure them quantitatively, to symbolize and relate them to one another—these were in fact new things, which would cause the fateful change in the relationship of humans to the world. Until that time, the human power of invention was used more in those areas which nature had left open. Then the time announced itself in which human efficiency learned to reform nature into artificial products and our world was transformed into a single great factory of industrial work: a unique advancement which is slowly leading us into the neighborhood of a new danger zone.

With the creation of the modern empirical sciences, "philosophy," the joyful pursuit of theory, faced an enormous challenge. How did it meet this challenge? How did human thinking deal with this new idea of science? I will not retell the history of modern philosophy. But if one is to understand what the thoughtful solution of our problems today requires of us, which is our task, then we must think back for a moment on what the advent of modern science meant for human thinking and the position of humans in the world.

The knowledge of tradition, which until now had been inherited under the collective name philosophy, was founded upon what was called metaphysics. This name signifies several things: it signifies what is behind physics and forms its foundation. Physics here does not mean what we call physics, but means that humanistic physics of Aristotle, where fire moves upwards because it is at home there with the shining stars and where a stone falls because that is where all other stones are and it belongs there. This may appear comical to us, but it was an understandable whole which appeared to the senses as the order of events in nature, and it completely corresponded to the way humans acted, the way they structured their lives as a society, created laws and institutions, and cared for their general well-being through purposeful work. A large homogeneous structure of determined order and goals existed in this world-image, which had its final justification in metaphysics.

Today it is different. Under the signature of modern science there exists, to give it a name, an arrow-straight will, which thinks up possibilities, constructively investigates them, and in the end evokes them into being, constructs them, and realizes them—daring and precise at the same time. An unbounded field of investigation and production has unfolded which everywhere advances into the unknown. On the other hand, human society has found itself embedded for thousands of years in a world, a complex totality of institutions, morals, and customs, with which it has been familiar and at home. So philosophy faces the new task of mediating between these extremes of the investigating advent into the unknown and the preservation of a trusted and understandable knowledge of life.

With this began the era of the philosophical systems. This word did not exist previously in the philosophical vocabulary. It appeared first in the seventeenth and eighteenth centuries, because a new task appeared with the new sciences. The expression "system" is, of course, a generally known conceptual word. We know it especially from Greek number theory and music theory, and from there it was transferred to the structure of the world system and cosmos. So we speak of the Ptolemaic system where the earth stands in the center and the sun, moon, and stars rotate around it, and then of the Copernican system which ushered in a new understanding of the universe. It is significant enough that philosophy availed itself of the word "system." In the Ptolemaic, geocentric system, the other heavenly bodies which we call planets, were so termed because they were wandering stars. They were a problem. How can one incorporate this into the wonderful regularity and order of the daily movements of the heavens, the fixed positions of the fixed stars, the periodic events of sunrise and sunset, the change of day and night, the seasons? How can it be that the morning star and the evening star are the same star, instead of rotating around the earth as they ought to? In fact, the original meaning of the word "system" means to join together into a unity and harmony what is falling apart. In Plato's time the paths of the planets presented this task to the astronomers and forced them to adopt highly complicated explanations for the apparent movements of the wandering stars. The heliocentric system put these problems to rest. So when philosophy adopted this same expression, it understood the situation in the same manner, as bringing together what was falling apart, and sought to discover its unity and harmony. So the sciences became analogous to the planets, our wandering bodies of knowledge, which did not fit into the goal-oriented framework of our conscious action, free choice, and ordering, but rather brought things into a new availability, which permitted one to begin to do what one wished. That is the meaning of "to produce."

But should one really say: what one wishes? Perhaps it would be a wiser characterization if one said: what one ought to wish. In any case, we have arrived at the critical point in the development, which then in the seventeenth century, introduced the great new tension in our world view. A long learning process led from the Galilean beginnings to, finally, modern science. First in the nineteenth century the tremendous development of the sciences led to the encompassing technical applications of our new knowledge and abilities, so that one began to call it the "industrial revolution," which since then has rolled over us in ever new waves. If one begins with this experience, that the new foundations for our knowledge were laid in the seventeenth century, then one understands why the mediating task of philosophy must have become ever more hopeless in relation to the progress of modern scientific research. How could there be a mediation between the old, harmonious-sensuous world view, which then was based upon a teleological physics and metaphysics, and the advent of a new knowledge and ability aiming toward unlimited goals? It is understandable that philosophy must finally withdraw ever further in its continually new attempts to mediate between metaphysics and empirical science. That led to the circumstance that, in the nineteenth century, the actual project of academic philosophy in the university became epistemology, that means the theory of scientific cognition. Therefore, the still unsatisfied and abiding desire for "metaphysics," for an answer to the question about the meaning of the whole, fell into the hands of outsiders, who advanced the so-called worldviews—for example in the style of Schopenhauer at the end of the nineteenth century or of Marx or Nietzsche in our century. The inner desire of the human soul for a meaningful interrelatedness of the whole, which should also ground the meaning of one's own life and desires in agreement with "nature," was not to be satisfied by science and its theoretical justification. That was the situation in the nineteenth century, from which we come, and so I now ask: what has become of philosophy in our time and how can it, being what it is, perhaps contribute to the critical problems in our time?

With this formulation of the question I wish to indicate that I will not speak of the so-called philosophy of science or the theory of science. This is certainly a respectable, logical continuation of nineteenth-century epistemology, which has improved upon the latter by cleansing itself of many untenable theses which at that time still determined thinking and which I would call metaphysical residues. What is of burning interest today is, however, clearly a more radical question than just one about the justification of the epistemological value of science. We are concerned about the defense of the totality of our cultural treasure, perhaps to protect it from threats, and to prepare us all for the task of humanity which is approaching us. We do not know whether there will be catastrophes or a growing poverty or the arduous work of limiting and guiding the one-dimensional will, which pushes forward, as if driven by its own law, heading toward self-destruction. Let us ask ourselves what philosophy has done for this task of our century. At the same time, I will communicate my own paths of thought, which I have followed as a learning beginner and later as one who continues what has been initiated.

It is often good to begin, especially for novices, with an explanation of a word. The word I am thinking of is a new creation and also a very simple word. It is "lifeworld" [Lebenswelt]. The word certainly sounds as German as could be. Nevertheless, it is an artificially created concept, for which we thank the great researcher and founder of the phenomenological school, Edmund Husserl, who especially in his time at Freiburg, but also already in Göttingen, raised questions beyond the previous boundaries of epistemological investigations. Epistemology had always been a theory of scientific knowledge. Scientific knowledge was the only knowledge that counted for the nineteenth century, by whose philosophical representatives I was myself raised—I come from the Marburg school. Husserl investigated for the first time what structured the life-world. He did not attempt to make the processes of perception understandable as psychological facts on the basis of some sort of mechanical association and disassociation or on the basis of the organization of the elements of representation, as was typical at that time. He rather demonstrated how in even the simplest and most natural experiences of our everyday life completely different rules apply, which we are able to discover. I will illustrate this with a simple case: here is this glass. I see it in front of me. I see it from my position. I cannot see it at the same time and in the same way as the audience sees it. Every perception sees always only that side presented to it and screens out the other side. In a certain sense, this is trivial. However, one can present this as a general and evident law of perception. One can seek and find in the other senses similar modifications, and one can advance from there to important descriptions of our cognizing. That was phenomenology, the account of knowledge as it appears. It does not promise to explain cognition where one begins with the stimuli and then connects them together, as in a machine, to constitute a representation. It proceeds by simply describing and recognizes the lawfulness in the world of perception. What comes to be conceptually described in this manner must not always be so elementary and trivial as this "pure perception." Or is this actually not so trivial? What does pure perception mean? Is it a pure perception (in case I did not want to demonstrate with my example a "pure perception") when I take this glass in my hand? It is certainly not that. I rather play with the idea of taking a sip from it—as I just did. Therefore, I take it as what can here offer my throat some refreshment. I do not simply see something that is there and measurable and determinable by the means of natural science, but rather I take it as what it should be. So I perceive it [nehme es wahr, take it truly] and that means I understand it as it is in truth and not, for example, as a thing in space and time or as a decorative piece, into which some loving soul will place roses, but as what is there for the speaker at the lectern. To take something as something means interpreting. And in actual lived life, there is much more there than the so-called pure determination of what is the case. Science forces one to heroic and ascetic abstractions, to permit only certified facts and to found one's knowledge upon this. It is far from me to deny that this is a lofty moral accomplishment, which science achieves and which it requires of the researcher. Every moment he must be critical enough not to allow hasty hypotheses and expectations or favored ideas to go unexamined, but must critically examine these and then expose them to scientific criticism. The community of researchers constitutes especially in the natural sciences, in the normal case, an incorruptible corrective.

Nevertheless, something of higher significance occurs in philosophy's turn to the experience of the lifeworld. This was very clearly seen by not only Husserl and other members of the phenomenological school, but especially by Heidegger, and at the same time by American pragmatism. Here, there evidently occurred a deeper questioning than was used by modern science in its task of causal explanation and the thereby achievable control of the processes in nature—and perhaps even in society. Now we have reached what we call praxis. Praxis is not to be understood here in that theoretical sense where it means nothing more than the application of theory. It concerns praxis in an original sense, in that Greek sense, in which praxis had an—I might almost say—inactive sense. A Greek letter closed with the expression *eu prattein*, which one translates: *"Laß es dir gutgehen"* [wishing you well]. How life is treating one [*wie es einem geht*], is what praxis means. Whether well, whether badly, in any case that one is in some state, that we are therefore not masters and rulers of our life situation, but that one will be affected by this or that, hindered in much, disappointed by lots of things, and often also happy over a success that went beyond what one had only dreamed. In such praxis lies clearly a new proximity to the totality of our position in the world as humans. Temporality, finitude, planning and projecting, remembering, forgetting, and being forgotten are immediately associated with this.

Therefore, we are concerned here with everything which falls under the concept, historicity, in the twentieth century and which has become a major theme in our philosophical work. Considering this, we first think of one of the great achievements of the nineteenth century, the development of the historical sense, the refining of our faculty for apprehending the past, so that we no longer usurp it in a naive manner, as for example the great painter, Altdorfer, did when he painted Alexander in battle using the military uniforms from the Renaissance. We have instead become sensitive to the otherness of the past. That is certainly a dangerous innovation. It was Nietzsche who presented his warning thesis concerning the advantage and disadvantage of history for life. And it is certainly true that historical consciousness constitutes a type of critical reserve which warns against any dogmatism and, at the same time, against all possibilities of certain knowledge in the area of historical events.

How can we then at all still speak of truth and knowledge with a clear conscience? Are they not all conditioned cognitions and, as a radical consequence, to speak with Nietzsche, only conditions of the will to power, conditions of our interests, to which we, consciously or unconsciously, subordinate our convictions? It may be a destructive radicalism which thinks thus. However, let us remember what became so beautifully clear in the word praxis, namely that at first and usually we do not have the distance we require for objective determinations in the sense of knowledge. We can attempt to attain such a distance. That is the exemplary ability of the researcher. We can force ourselves to be as objective as possible. That is the exemplary ability of the impartial thinker. However, we may not forget that we, as living beings, are by nature ensnared in many ways, and that means that we are totally and completely embedded within praxis. We are always already completely encompassed by our expectations and hopes, our prejudices and our fears, even when we just take something as something—as when I take this glass of water in order to take a sip from it. It is always an exceptional situation when a researcher harvests objective knowledge. And he, more than anyone, knows that they are exceptional situations, when he considers the enormous effort needed to design the experimental situation and even when he considers the tremendous responsibility which such an increase in human power and human ability gives to the one who applies this knowledge for practical purposes. That however is praxis, where everyone shares in the responsibility for his society, for his nation and finally for humanity. In his role as a citizen or as a world citizen, the researcher does not simply have the proud, bold and rare independence which makes him a true researcher. Since living in the practical world, he has to decide and choose just as others do, and that means that he also does not have the guarantee of critically secured results for his decisions. Once I had the opportunity in a discussion of this problem to quote a passage from a Platonic dialogue (*Charmides* 173a ff.) without saying who I quoted. It was the following passage:

I wish to relate a dream. Whether it came through the gate of the true and good or through the gate of the false and bad dreams, this question I will leave aside. If science became completely decisive among us, then everything would happen strictly according to science. No pilot would exist who did not know his job, no doctor, no general and absolutely no one, who did not really have a command of his work. The result would be that we would be far healthier than today; we would safely survive all the risks of driving and making war; our machines, our clothes and shoes, in short everything, which we need, would be perfectly made, and much more besides, because we would always let ourselves be guided by only true experts. And beyond this, we would wish to acknowledge prognostics as the science of the future. Concerning this, science must take pains to scare off all charlatans and to establish the actual experts among the prognosticators as the planners of the future. If all of this could be made to came to pass, then it would certainly follow that humans would scientifically act and scientifically live. Science would watch carefully and prevent every attempt of dilettantism. However, if we did everything in this scientific manner, we can nevertheless still not quite convince ourselves whether we would have done well and would be happy.

"But can one at all have another ideal for doing something well other than the one of science?"

"Perhaps not, but I would still like to know a small detail: Which science do you mean?"

One recognizes the famous question of Socrates, which he posed to all experts of the world once and for all—although they may be quite knowledgeable about their own affairs, is it, however, good to transpose into praxis what they know and can do? This, neither the scientific researcher as such can claim to answer, nor can one simply accept what he, perhaps in enthusiasm for his own accomplishment, thinks and promises concerning this question.

It is evidently still the same problem which we face today, only that given modern science and its range of technical applicability, it carries an increased responsibility for us. Because now it concerns the whole existence of humans in nature, and it concerns the task of controlling the development of our abilities and our mastery over natural powers in such a manner that nature will not be destroyed and laid waste by us, but preserved together with our existence on this earth. Nature can no longer be viewed as a mere object for exploitation, it must be experienced as a partner in all its appearances; but that means it must be understood as the other with whom we live together.

Philosophy in our century has begun to ponder what this means. I do not wish to name names here. I note only that hermeneutics, which follows Dilthey and Heidegger and to which I have dedicated my own work, has contributed to this. Hermeneutics is a word which most people do not know and do not need to know. But they are nevertheless affected by the hermeneutic experience and not exempted. They too try to take something as something and finally to understand everything around them and to act accordingly. And on top of this, that something is mostly somebody who has his own demands to press. Such hermeneutic behavior seems to have its essential character in the fact that the other first appears as an other. The other is not my dominion and I am not sovereign—not in the way that many explained natural appearances in the area of natural science have been made subservient. We find this manner of speaking of control especially with doctors. They have adopted this somewhat pretentious expression because, in the battle against the powerful forces of nature in their area, there is really only a little that they truly control. It may be sensible to say that one controls certain diseases. But it is certainly not sensible to say that one controls health. This is another relation to nature which I do not know how to describe. The secret of health, "in" which we are, is exactly not an object for us. Is nature an other for us when we feel well? Is it not rather inseparable from us, the other of our self, as we have been taught by the classical languages, where they do not say "the one and the other" but rather "the other and the other"? And finally, is not also the totally other—the famous definition of the divinity proposed by Rudolf Otto, with all the emphasis on its being totally other—not just the other of our self? And does that not extend to the nearest other, to You and everything that is Yours? Does there exist at all something other which is not the other of our self? Certainly not in the case where the other is also a human.

It is truly a tremendous task which faces every human every moment. His prejudices—his being saturated with wishes, drives, hopes, and interests—must be held under control to such an extent that the other is not made invisible or does not remain invisible. It is not easy to acknowledge that the other could be right, that oneself and one's own interests could be wrong. There is a beautiful religious essay by Kierkegaard *The Edification Implied in the Thought that as Against God We Are Always in the Wrong*. This solace, which is encountered here in a religious form, is in truth a basic constant that shapes our whole human experience. We must learn to respect others and otherness. This implies that we must learn that we could be wrong. We must learn how to lose the game—that begins with the age of two or maybe even earlier. He, who has not learned this early, will not be able to completely handle the greater tasks of adult life.

The theoretical and practical implications of this are far-reaching. In conclusion, I wish to clarify this using an example which at the same time describes one of our essential tasks.

To live with an other, to live as the other of the other, this basic task of human being applies in the smallest and in larger contexts. How we learn to live as an individual with the other while we are growing up and entering life, as one says, is evidently also applicable to larger human groups, for peoples and nations. In this, Europe may have a privileged position because it, more than other groups of nations, could and needed to learn to live with others, even when the others were different.

First, there is the diversity of languages in Europe. Here the other in his otherness is placed very near. This neighborhood of the other is at the same time conveyed to us in spite of all the differences between us. The otherness of the neighbor is not only the otherness to be shyly avoided. It is also the inviting otherness which contributes to the encountering of one's own self. We are all others and we are all our selves. This appears to me to be the application possible in our situation. We have had a long time to learn, not only because of the tremendous factual knowledge, which research into nature has made possible for us and which, as a world civilization, cannot deny its European roots. Also the coexistence of different cultures and languages, religions, and confessions, supports us. We all, as humans and as peoples and nations, break the laws of such coexistence infinitely often, and yet in actual life, with the good will of partners, something common is always rebuilt. In general this appears to me to be the same task everywhere. And it appears to me that here, the diversity of languages, this neighborhood of the other in a narrow space, and the equality of the other in an even narrower space, are a true training ground. This does not just mean, for example, the unity of Europe in the sense of a political alliance. I mean that we have to learn together what our European task means to us and we have to do this for the future of humanity as a whole.

For this reason I completely disagree with the desired goal of a single language either for Europe or for humanity. This may be practical and is already practiced today in some special areas such as in international communication. Language, however, is primarily what the natural linguistic community speaks and only the natural linguistic communities will be able to build with one another what unites them and what they recognize in others. If in the future a declaration of love will only be answered by the partner saying okay, then that is evidently not the same as the type of community which is initiated when a boy or girl in love attempts to express him- or herself in a bashful stammering or in a poor love poem. This is true in general. It even has direct significance for the philosophy of science. If one sees nothing else in language except a practical system of signs, then, from the perspective of the "unity of science" (as it was formulated by the Vienna Circle), one may well expect correct communication from a unified language. And this may be correct for the investigation and control of nature. Faced with the diversity of the various sciences, which live from the traditions and treasures found in the cultural languages and in the linguistic cultures of all peoples, it is exactly the otherness, the recognition of our self, the re-encountering of the other, in language, art, religion, law, and history, which is able to guide us toward a true communality. We call these sciences, which are based upon this diversity of linguistic and linguistically transmitted traditions, the human sciences [Geisteswissenschaften]. They stand close to the living cultures, to their historically developed being and to the otherness which demands not only cognition but also recognition. So they are much closer than the wonderfully clear constructions which support the research process in the natural sciences. Everyone certainly recognizes and values how difficult it is in the investigation of nature, and not only there, to avoid biases caused by the continual interference of language. Thomas Kuhn once made a fitting observation, which was naturally nothing new for the experts. He noted that in the beginning Max Planck termed the so-called quantum (which he had just baptized) an element, as if it were an elementary particle which one could combine with others and so complete the construction of the whole. In today's physics we know that although they still speak of atoms, they have had to abandon the image that there are corpuscular, final, elementary particles; following the exigencies of their scientific activities, they have changed to the completely different images of symmetry and symmetrical equivalences. But even more there occurs a continual critique of language in the human sciences. The natural language, the naturally spoken language, is always at the same time a source for biases, which must be permitted to be corrected by experience. However, it is not only this. It is, on the other hand, also an offering to recognize oneself and to make recognizable for us again all knowledge established in language, which exists in poetry, philosophy, historical narrative, religion, law, and customs, i.e., in all that constitutes a culture. It will always remain a task of scientific self-discipline to not allow prejudices and biases to go uncriticized. Where one is not concerned with learning how to control something, we will always and again learn through experiencing our own biases, the otherness of the other in its other-being. To participate with the other and to be a part of the other is the most and the best that we can strive for and accomplish.

So it may not be unjustified to conclude from our discussion a final political consequence. We may perhaps survive as humanity if we would be able to learn that we may not simply exploit our means of power and effective possibilities, but must learn to stop and respect the other as an other, whether it is nature or the grown cultures of peoples and nations; and if we would be able to learn to experience the other and the others, as the other of our self, in order to participate with one another.

SOURCES

First locations for all the essays and addresses included are given, as well as references to later publications, with the exception of references to the published and projected volumes of Hans-Georg Gadamer: Gesammelte Werke, J. C. B. Mohr (Paul Siebeck) Tübingen.

1. "The Primordiality of Science": Rectoral Address. "Über die Ursprünglichkeit der Wissenschaft." Rektoratsrede. Johann Ambrosius Barth-Leipzig 1947. *Leipziger Universitätsreden Heft 14*.

2. "The University of Leipzig: 1409–1959. A Former Rector Commemorates the 550th Anniversary of its Founding." "Rede auf die Universität Leipzig." *Ruperto-Carola* (Journal of the University of Heidelberg) 12, Heft 27, 1960, 203–13.

3. "The University of Heidelberg and the Birth of Modern Science." Die Universität Heidelberg und die Geburt der modernen Wissenschaft. *Sonderpublikation des Springer Verlags*. Berlin/Heidelberg, 1987, Sonderdruck, 1–21.

4. "The Idea of the University: Yesterday, Today, Tomorrow." "Die Idee der Universität, Gestern, Heute, Morgen" (Public address delivered in 1986 on the occasion of the celebration of the 600th anniversary of the University of Heidelberg. Heidelberg, Municipal Theater). Published in: *Die Idee der Universität. Versuch einer Standortbestimmung*. Berlin/Heidelberg: Springer Verlag, 1988, 2–22.

5. "Are the Poets Falling Silent?" "Verstummen die Dichter?" In: Zeitwende/Die neue Furche. 41. Jg. Heft 5, September 1970: 344–52. And in: *Poetica. Ausgewählte Essays*. Frankfurt: Insel Verlag, 1977, 103–18.

6. "The Verse and the Whole." "Der Vers und das Ganze," in P. Lutz, P. L. Lehmann, R. Wolff (eds.) *Das Stefan George Seminar 1978 in Bingen*. Bingen, 1979, 33–39.

7. "Hölderlin and George." First published as "Hölderlin und George." In *Hölderlin-Jahrbuch*, Jg. 15, 1967/68. Tübingen 1969, 79–91. A partial translation of this appeared in the Southern Journal of Philosophy. A revised text appeared as: "Hölderlin und George." In: Heftrich u.a. (eds.) *Stefan George Kolloquium*. Köln 1971, 118–32. A second revised

version appeared in *Poetica. Ausgewählte Essays.* Frankfurt: Insel Verlag, 1977, 39–67.

8. "Under the Shadow of Nihilism," "Im Schatten des Nihilismus," in H. Dethier and E. Williams (eds.): *Cultural Hermeneutics of Modern Art. In Honor of Jan Aler.* Amsterdam: Rodopi, 1988.

9. "The Philosophy and Religion of Judaism." First published as: "Die Philosophie und Religion des Judentums," in: L. Reinisch (ed.): *Die Juden und die Kultur.* Vortragsreihe des Bayerischen Rundfunks, Stuttgart: Kohlhammer, 1961, 78–90. Reprinted in: Hans-Georg Gadamer. *Kleine Schriften Band I.* Tübingen: J. C. B. Mohr (Paul Siebeck), 1967, 201–10

10. "Notes on Planning for the Future," Colloquium of the Rockefeller Foundation 1965, in *Daedalus, Journal of the American Academy of Science,* 95, 1966: 572–89. Slightly revised version also published in German in: Hans-Georg Gadamer, *Kleine Schriften. Band I.* Tübingen: J. C. B. Mohr (Paul Siebeck), 1967, 161–78.

11. "The Limitations of the Expert." "Die Grenzen des Experten." An initial version was published as: "Die Grenzen des Expertentums." K. Schlechta (ed.), *Neuntes Darmstädter Gespräch, Der Mensch und seine Zukunft.* Darmstadt. 1967, 160–68. The new and completely revised version of the text translated was published in: Hans-Georg Gadamer, *Das Erbe Europas.* Frankfurt: Suhrkamp, 1989, 136–57.

12. "The Future of the European Humanities." "Die Zukunft der europäischen Geisteswissenschaften." F. König and K. Rahner (eds.), *Europa-Horizonte der Hoffnung.* Graz: Styr Verlag, 1983, 243–61. Reprinted in: Hans-Georg Gadamer, *Das Erbe Europas,* as cited, 35–62.

13. "Citizens of Two Worlds." "Bürger Zweier Welten." Castelgandolfo. Gespräche, 1983. *Der Mensch in den modernen Wissenschaften.* Stuttgart: Klett-Cotta, 1985, 185–99.

14. "The Diversity of Europe: Inheritance and Future." "Die Vielfalt Europas, Erbe und Zukunft." Stuttgart: Sonderdruck. Robert Bosch Stiftung, 1983. Reprinted in: Hans-Georg Gadamer, *Das Erbe Europas,* as cited, 7–34.

Made in United States
Troutdale, OR
04/29/2024

19525009R00163